SAILING for
BEGINNERS

SAILING *for* BEGINNERS

Revised and Updated

by MOULTON H. FARNHAM

EDITOR-AT-LARGE, **Boating** MAGAZINE

COLLIER BOOKS
A Division of Macmillan Publishing Co., Inc.
New York
COLLIER MACMILLAN PUBLISHERS
London

Copyright © 1967, 1981 by Moulton H. Farnham

Macmillan Publishing Co., Inc.
866 Third Avenue, New York, N.Y. 10022
Collier Macmillan Canada, Ltd.

Library of Congress Cataloging in Publication Data

Farnham, Moulton H.
    Sailing for beginners.

    Includes index.
    1. Sailing.   I. Title.
GV811.F3   1981   797.1′24   80-27077
ISBN 0-02-537140-1

First Revised Edition 1981

Printed in the United States of America

To the memory of

MARION

"... I know, where'er I go

That there hath passed away a glory from the earth."

Acknowledgments

No BOOK is written single-handed, really. And this book is not an exception; it could never have been born without the help of many people.

I would list first the multitudinous members, young and old, of many sailing, seamanship, and piloting classes who, over the years, as captive audiences, have endured my experiments in communicating various aspects of sea lore.

Next I would pay tribute to three of the skippers with whom I have had the privilege of sailing, cruising, and racing and on whose boats my own sea skills were vastly expanded:

The late CARLETON S. COOKE—lawyer; longtime member of the Cruising Club of America; co-founder of the amateur sailing group, The Corinthians; and co-owner, with his brother Tom, of the 56′ Roué-designed ketch *Seven Bells*.

The late WILLIAM SNAITH—architect, musician, author, and artist, whose 47′ ocean racing yawl, *Figaro III,* I had the honor to navigate when we won a transatlantic race from Bermuda to Sweden.

SUMNER A. (HUEY) LONG—engineer, shipowner, and world sailor, on whose first *Ondine,* a 53′ wooden yawl, I was introduced to the pleasures of cruising and racing in European waters, including the Scandinavian.

Most of the sailing photographs in this book are the result of repeated sessions—many of them frustratingly windless—on that fickle body of water, Long Island Sound, by the most dedicated crew an author could ever hope for: Nina Wemyss and her son Wally Wemyss, Jr., both survivors of my sailing classes at the Lloyd Neck (New York) Bath Club, and James H. Ripple, builder-owner and successful racing skipper of Blue Jay No. 3410 *Vixen*.

Illustrator Ernest C. Schroeder—sculptor, painter, sailor, boat designer and builder—not only supplied the excellent drawings and sketches to illuminate the text, but also contributed much useful information on the construction and maintenance of both wooden and fiberglass boats.

To Irving Jakobson, of Jakobson Shipyard, Oyster Bay, New York, I am grateful for assistance on the technical aspects of aluminum hulls and spars. Lawrence Kean, Technical Director of BOATING, and the Blue Jay Association's Chief Measurer, was most helpful in reviewing the entire text and in making valuable suggestions for clarifying the doctrine. He also helped substantially with the photography.

Finally, I would acknowledge the indispensable service performed by my late wife Marion who, as my first student so many years ago, suffered in almost saintly silence the fulminations of a neophyte instructor who was himself still struggling with many of the fundamentals of sailing.

M. H. F.

Easton, Md.
June, 1978

Contents

CONTENTS

Foreword

You're walking down a dock toward a small sailboat tied up at the end. There's a pleasant breeze blowing—a perfect sailing day. As you reach the dock's end, a friendly stranger steps forward and, with a smile, motions toward the boat.

"Wouldn't you like to sail it awhile?" he asks.

Of course you would—else you wouldn't be reading this book. But where do you start? How do you go about it? What do you do first?

This book tells you the answers.

It is written for the beginning sailor. You don't have to know anything about a boat to understand it.

But if you read the text carefully, and study the pictures, you will soon have a grasp of the basic skills you need to master the art of sailing.

The rest you will learn on the water. Though a book can speed your understanding, competence in handling a boat comes only from actual practice.

A word of caution before you start: Always respect the water. For the real thrill of sailing comes from realizing that you are playing with two powerful and potentially dangerous elements—*wind* and *water.*

Oddly, this remote danger contributes to the deep pleasure of sitting at the helm of a sailboat and by your own skill controlling the power of the wind to take you where you want to go. Always, in the back of your mind, you are aware of the forces with which you are playing.

But, inevitably, if you spend enough time on the water, the day will come when a sudden squall will overtake you, and you will be face to face with the hidden power of wind and water. When that day comes, your skill as a sailor will have its initiation.

If you find this a sobering thought, let it underscore the need to learn your lessons well. There is no way to enjoy the thrill of sailing without the possible danger.

But you needn't be frightened. Small sailboats, properly handled, are amazingly safe. Every year long ocean passages are made in them without incident. The sloop *Spray,* which Capt. Joshua Slocum sailed single-handed in the first small-boat circumnavigation of the globe, was only 36' 9" long on deck, and many even smaller boats have duplicated this epic feat. The emphasis is on skillful handling and confidence in your own ability.

These come from practice, and more practice. They are the entrance requirements to this thrilling world of sailing.

Meanwhile, you have an absorbing assignment at hand—to become so familiar with the facts and terms of sailing, that your progress toward skill under sail will be swift and certain once you get out on the water.

A fair breeze and good sailing!

M. H. F.

Preface to the Revised and Updated Edition

SINCE *Sailing for Beginners* was launched in 1967, it has been bought by over 50,000 people, some of whom have kindly suggested improvements in various phases of the text. In addition, a number of changes in equipment to be carried by small-boat sailors have been made by the U. S. Coast Guard in the last few years.

As a result, this first revision of *SFB* contains both text changes suggested by perceptive readers and the pertinent regulations of the Coast Guard brought up to date. We have also included in our sailing pictures one of the many one-design daysailers that have become so popular in the past decade.

In shooting these new pictures on Chesapeake Bay, I am grateful to have had the skillful cooperation of Douglas W. McNitt, owner-skipper of the "420" *Tang,* and of his sister and crew, Katharine A. McNitt. Photographer Bob Grieser of the *Washington Star,* himself a sharp racing sailor, manned his camera with split-second timing.

An unexpected reward of writing a widely used book is chance encounters with some of its readers—for example going aboard a 44-foot motor-sailer and having its husband-wife crew tell me that *SFB* had given them confidence to buy their boat and, a year later, sail it transatlantic from England . . . or learning from another owner, at the launching of his new auxiliary cutter, that after reading *SFB* he was inspired to change from a powerboat and buy his first sailboat . . . or meeting a college girl of some sailing experience who said *SFB* had enabled her to sign on as crew for delivery of a boat to the Caribbean. My fond hope is that you may find the book equally helpful.

M.H.F.

Easton, Maryland
July 1980

You can learn more than two dozen facts and terms about sailing from this photograph; they're all in Chapter 1

1

Let's Go Sailing!

HERE ARE TWO YOUNG PEOPLE sharing the fun of a sport that has no equal on land. By themselves, away from crowds, they are enjoying the relaxing freedom of sailing. Using their skill to make the wind propel their boat, they have discovered an exciting world of outdoor adventure that will last them a lifetime.

This is what you can do, and more, once you have mastered the art of sailing.

It is not a difficult art to learn; today, even senior citizens are learning to sail expertly. But it does take some study and effort on your part. Vocabulary, for example.

To know what you're doing on the water and be able to give commands that will be understood instantly, you must know the correct nautical terms for the various parts of the boat and its equipment. Also you must be familiar with various words relating to winds and the different directions of sailing.

There's nothing unusual in this; every sport has its own vocabulary. If you were learning to ski or to fly a plane, you'd expect to learn new terms peculiar to those sports.

So it's important to equip yourself at the outset with a number of commonly used sailing terms. And don't be bashful about using them; on the water, one mark of a sailor is his ability to use correctly the language of the sea.

Yet even the learning can be fun.

Let's start with this picture, and see how much you can learn just by looking at it.

Three rules of safety

To start from the bottom, first notice the water—it's fairly smooth, not rough or boisterous. (The small wave at the front of the boat is caused by the boat pushing the water aside. The front of the boat, incidentally, is the *bow*—as in "ow"—and that wave is known as the *bow-wave*.)

A *smooth sea,* as sailors call it, usually indicates that the wind is not blowing too hard. Too hard for what? Too hard for a small boat to sail without danger of being blown over, or *capsized.* So this couple is observing Safety Rule No. I of small-boat sailing: DON'T GO SAILING IN STRONG WINDS OR ROUGH SEAS.

In another chapter we'll discuss how to judge the strength and direction of the wind

1

before you go sailing. But now let's look at the boat in the picture.

The first thing we notice is that, with only two people in this small boat, it isn't overcrowded: Each person has room to move around. The boat—known as a *420*—has been designed to carry two people safely; it is broad enough and heavy enough so that their weight shifting around isn't likely to cause a capsize.

But there is a limit to how many people any small boat can carry safely. It is of utmost importance not to go sailing with more than this limit. From this is born Safety Rule No. 2: NEVER SAIL IN AN OVER-CROWDED BOAT.

Looking at this couple, we see that the girl is wearing a life jacket. When racing, the boy also wears one. If, by mishap, the boat should be upset, they could both cling to it safely until rescued. This illustrates Safety Rule No. 3 of small-boat sailing: ALWAYS WEAR A LIFE JACKET IF YOU CAN'T SWIM, or when racing.

A basic vocabulary

Notice that both people are facing toward the bow—*ahead,* or *forward.* If they were facing the back of the boat—the *stern*—they would be facing *astern,* or *aft.* The girl is sitting about halfway between bow and stern, or *amidships.* (The word *amidships* is also used to indicate anything located on the boat's centerline.

The girl is sitting in the large, open section of the boat called the *cockpit.* Some boats—like the *Blue Jay,* shown in the sketches opposite and on the following pages—have a low rail around the cockpit, called a *coaming.*

Here, the boy is in command of the boat, so he is called the *skipper.* But the girl might also be skipper, as could anyone who had the knowledge and skill to be responsible for

the safety of the boat and her people. (We say "her" people, incidentally, because all boats are feminine.)

Both the girl and the boy are sailing the boat, which makes them the crew; no non-sailors, or *passengers,* are aboard.

You'll notice the skipper is steering with a steering stick called the *tiller,* or *helm;* both terms are correct. This makes him the *helmsman.*

The most noticeable fact about the boat itself is that she is a *sloop.* She's a sloop because she has a single vertical *spar* (pole) called a *mast,* and carries on it one large and one small *sail*—triangular cloths that capture the wind's force to drive the boat forward. The larger sail is the *mainsail* (pronounced mains'l); the smaller is the jib.

As the *Blue Jay* sketch opposite shows, a sail's forward edge is the *luff.* The mainsail's luff is attached to the mast. The sail's rear, or *after* edge, is the leech. The bottom edge, or *foot,* of the mainsail is attached to the *boom,* a horizontal spar that pivots at the mast in a fitting called a *gooseneck.*

Note on the sketch the three short strips from the leech into the mainsail. These are deep pockets sewn into the sail to contain light strips of wood or Fiberglas called *battens,* which hold the curved shape of the leech and keep it from sagging.

Each of the sail's corners has a name, starting with the top, or *head.* The lower, forward corner of the sail, where it is *made fast,* or *secured* to the boom, is the *tack.* The after corner, secured to the after end of the boom, is the *clew.*

The jib's three edges and corners have the same names as those of the mainsail: luff, leech, foot, and head, tack, and clew. The jib's luff, however, is secured by snaps to the *headstay,* a wire that runs from the bow up to a point on the mast. And the jib's foot is *loose-footed,* meaning not attached to a

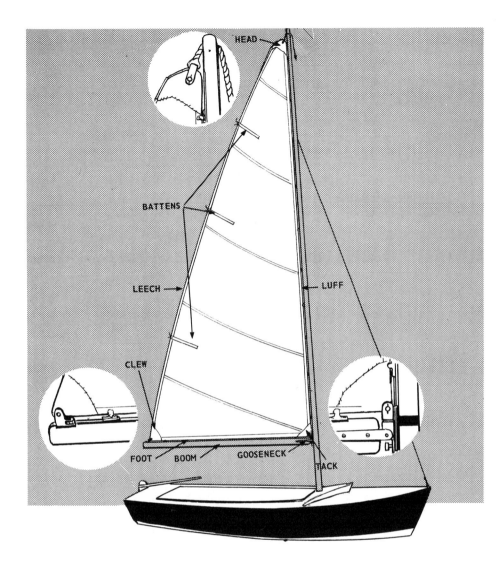

HEAD

BATTENS

LEECH

LUFF

CLEW

FOOT   BOOM   GOOSENECK   TACK

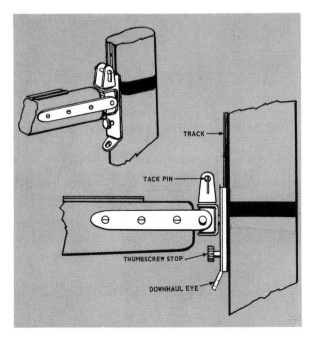

TRACK

TACK PIN

THUMBSCREW STOP

DOWNHAUL EYE

The Blue Jay, *like the* 420, *is a popular boat for both beginning and racing sailors. But because the* 420 *is dry-sailed—that is, hauled out after each usage—it lacks fittings carried by the* Blue Jay *and other boats that can be anchored or kept on a mooring. Since even a beginning sailor should know how to anchor or moor a boat, these* Blue Jay *sketches, and those that follow, will acquaint you with these fittings as well as other details common to the* 420 *and most small sailboats.*

Left: *Gooseneck fitting is universal joint that allows boom to swing freely for different angles of sailing*

3

boom. Notice that this jib has no battens; some jibs do.

The lines that look like seams on both mainsail and jib are just that. A sail is not one flat piece of cloth, but a series of cloths—usually cut and sewn to give the sail a curve, like an airplane wing standing on edge. To get this curve, each cloth, or *panel,* is carefully tapered and sewn to its neighbor.

We'll come back to the importance and purpose of the curve in a sail when we discuss how a sailboat is able to sail upwind, that is, *to windward.*

Let's look at the rest of the boat.

The whole body of the boat is the *hull.* Some of it floats above water, and is called the *topsides.* The part below water is the *underbody,* none of which can be seen in this sketch. The section of the hull from dead astern to 45° forward on both sides, is

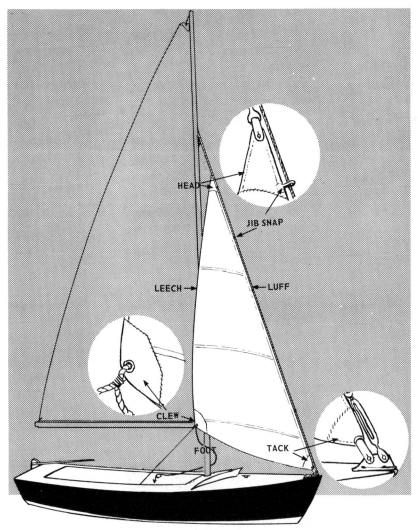

Besides providing secondary wind power for boat, the jib helps mainsail develop its maximum drive

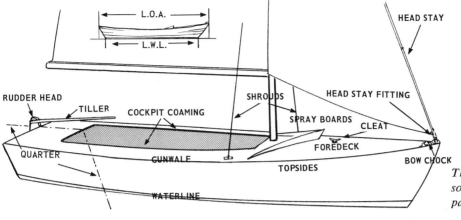

RUDDER HEAD · TILLER · COCKPIT COAMING · L.O.A. · L.W.L. · SHROUDS · HEAD STAY · HEAD STAY FITTING · SPRAY BOARDS · CLEAT · FOREDECK · QUARTER · GUNWALE · TOPSIDES · BOW CHOCK · WATERLINE

This diagram shows some of hull's principal parts and dimensions

the *quarter*. In old sailing ship days, the deck over this section—called the *quarterdeck*—was reserved as a promenade space for the captain and officers.

A boat's *waterline* is the level at which she floats, and is the dividing line between underbody and topsides. Her *waterline length* (abbreviated *LWL*), is the distance from the point where she floats forward, to the same point aft, measured along the boat's middle, or *centerline*. And her *length overall* (*LOA*), is the distance measured along her centerline from the tip of her bow to the stern.

Spreading across the topsides, and serving both as a surface to stand on and to keep water out of the boat, is the *deck*. The deck space forward of the cockpit is the *foredeck*, while the deck aft is the *afterdeck*. The afterdeck ends at the *transom*, the vertical end of the boat across the stern.

The distance from the edge of the deck, or *gunwale* (pronounced gunn'l), to the boat's waterline is her *freeboard*. Observe that the freeboard is greater forward than amidships.

Just forward of the mast, two *spray boards* meet to form a raised wedge that keeps spray from running over the foredeck and into the cockpit.

In this boat the mast is not fastened to the deck, but goes on through it and down into the bottom of the boat, where it fits into a slot called the *mast step,* which holds it securely.

Practically at the bow, on deck alongside the headstay, can be seen an oval-shaped fitting. This is a *chock,* specifically a *bow chock,* and its purpose is to keep a line in place when the boat is being towed, anchored, or tied up to a dock. The line will be made fast to the flat T-shaped fitting called a *cleat,* just forward of the spray boards in the center of the foredeck.

This boat is fairly *beamy,* meaning she is relatively wide in relation to her overall length. A boat's *beam* is her greatest width, measured from side to side. (The term *beam* is also used as a reference point amidships, at right angles to the centerline of the boat, and as a bearing—*on the beam,* or *abeam*—meaning at an angle of 90° to the centerline, from dead ahead.)

Just aft of the jib's leech, you can see a wire leading down from the mast through a hole near the outside edge of the deck. This wire is a *shroud.* Its job is to support the mast laterally, and there are two of them on this boat, one on each side. They are made fast below the deck to metal straps called *chain plates,* which are bolted into the topsides so as to distribute the strains from the mast to the hull. On many boats the chain plates are located at the outside edge

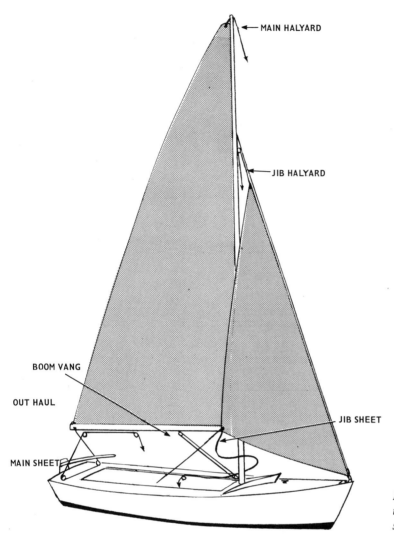

MAIN HALYARD

JIB HALYARD

BOOM VANG

OUT HAUL

JIB SHEET

MAIN SHEET

Running rigging includes all lines used to hoist, lower, and control sails

of the deck opposite the mast, and the shrouds lead to them without going through the deck.

Shrouds support the mast from side to side, *stays* (like the headstay), support the mast from front to back, or *fore-and-aft*. Stays and shrouds together are the boat's *standing rigging*.

What other information can we get from this sketch? A great deal.

We've learned something about the sails, and the mast, and the boom, but haven't discussed how the sails are controlled. This brings us to *running rigging*—all the lines by which sails are raised, lowered, and controlled.

In the sketch, at the *masthead* (top of the mast), you'll see part of the main *halyard,* the line used to *hoist* (raise) and *lower* (let down) the mainsail. This line runs over a *sheave* (grooved wheel) set in the masthead and continues down to a cleat on the side of the mast near the deck, where it is made fast. To lower the mainsail, you *cast off* (untie) the halyard from the cleat.

Also seen in the sketch is part of the jib halyard, which hoists the jib. It runs through a small *block* (pulley) on the forward side of the mast, under the headstay, and fastens to a cleat on the other side of the mast, opposite the main halyard cleat.

While we're talking about sides, this is a good time to cover the terms *port* and *starboard*. The *starboard* side of a boat is to your right as you face forward, toward the bow. In this sketch, the boat's starboard side is toward us.

The *port* side is the boat's left side, as you face the bow.

Notice that here the boom is not amidships, over the centerline of the boat, but is angled out over the starboard side, or *to starboard*. The jib, too, is set to starboard. This tells us the wind is blowing across the boat and into the sails from the port side. Under these conditions, the boat is said to be sailing *on the port tack*.

When the sails are set *to port* (over the port side of the boat), with the wind blowing into them from the starboard side, you are sailing *on the starboard tack*. To repeat, when the wind blows from the port side into the sails, you sail on the port tack. When it's on your starboard side, you sail on the starboard tack.

Note that the boat is tilted slightly toward us; her starboard side is lower in the water than her port side. This is because the pressure of the wind on her sails is causing her to tilt, or *heel*. The direction of the heeling is downwind, or *to leeward* (pronounced loo'ard).

To counteract this heeling tendency, you might want all or part of your crew to *windward,* meaning on the upwind side of the boat—like the skipper in the picture on page 1. His weight offsets the tilting pressure of the wind to let the boat sail more nearly level—*on an even keel,* as sailors call it. As a rule, a boat sails faster when she isn't heeled way over.

From time to time you may see a picture of a small boat racing, practically on its side, with the crew *hiking* (leaning) out to windward to keep the boat from capsizing. This is fun to marvel at, but the skipper would probably make better speed if his boat were more nearly upright.

We mentioned the boom angled out to starboard. Note the line from the outer end of the boom that leads down through a block on the port side, across to a block on the starboard side, back up to a block near the boom's end, then in along the boom to another block. This line continues to a block (not seen) in the cockpit, then up to the helmsman's hand.

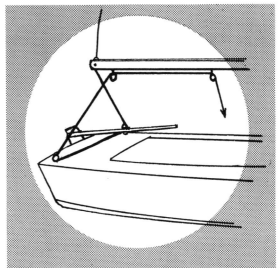

The mainsheet, which controls the mainsail, can be rigged in various ways. This method is called the "Crosby rig."

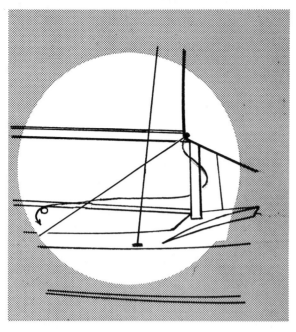

Left: *Jibsheets control jib's setting, and may be either removable or spliced permanently into jib's clew*

Below: *Jam cleats provide advantage of holding a line securely with single round turn*

This line controls the mainsail and is called the *mainsheet*.

A *sheet* is a line used to adjust the angle at which a sail is set. It is named for the sail it controls, as *mainsheet,* or *jibsheet*. Don't be confused and call a sail a sheet, a common mistake among novices.

Although the helmsman usually holds the mainsheet in his hand, there is a cleat handy in the cockpit to make fast to if he gets tired. Most small boat sailors prefer to hold the mainsheet, using it to *trim* the mainsail in, or *ease* it out, according to the force of the wind, which seldom blows steadily.

The jib on this boat has no boom, so two sheets are needed to control it, one to starboard, and one to port. The starboard jibsheet can be seen leading from the jib's clew down toward a block hidden under the lip of the cockpit, then it would lead to the jib tender's hand. The starboard jibsheet is used with the boat on port tack. Note the port jibsheet hanging slack from the jib's clew. It won't be used until the boat sails on the starboard tack, with the jib and mainsail set to port. Then the port jibsheet will control the jib, and the starboard jibsheet will be slack.

Although the sketch doesn't show them, on each side of the cockpit amidships is located a special kind of racing fitting known as *jam cleats*. They have tapered jaws so that a single turn of the line around the cleat, pulled snug, locks the line in place. The line is easily released instantly by unwinding the turn.

One last detail. At the masthead, many boats carry a small wind vane—a *masthead fly*. Its purpose is to show the direction from which the wind is blowing, to help the skipper trim his sails to obtain the maximum force from the available breeze.

Did you notice that *rope* wasn't mentioned anywhere in this chapter? To a sailor, rope means the large diameter, bulky line used for heavy duty, like towing or anchoring. Cordage under one inch in diameter—like sheets and halyards—is always called *line*.

We've now covered our first picture in enough detail to give you a general idea of what sailing is all about, and a good start on a seagoing vocabulary.

However, since our object is to put you at the tiller as soon as possible, let's get down to fundamentals and see exactly why and how the boat sails.

Summary

1. Safety Rule No. 1:
   DON'T GO SAILING IN STRONG WINDS OR
   ROUGH SEAS.
2. Safety Rule No. 2:
   NEVER SAIL IN AN OVERCROWDED BOAT.
3. Safety Rule No. 3:
   ALWAYS WEAR A LIFE JACKET UNLESS YOU
   CAN SWIM, OR WHEN RACING.
4. Checklist of nautical terms:

PARTS OF BOAT

afterdeck—Deck space aft.

amidships—In or toward the middle of a boat;
also, on the centerline.

block—A sheave fixed in a frame or shell for
lines to run through.

boom—A horizontal spar to which the foot of
a sail is secured.

bow—The front end of a boat.

bow chock—A fitting on the bow to hold a
line in place.

centerline—An imaginary line running lengthwise along the middle of a boat.

cleat—A T-shaped fitting for securing lines.

coaming—The rail around the cockpit.

cockpit—The open section aft of the mast.

deck—The horizontal, flat surface enclosing
the hull.

foredeck—Deck space forward.

gooseneck—A pivot fitting connecting the
boom to the mast.

gunwale—The outer edge of the deck.

hull—The body of a boat.

jam cleat—A fitting that secures a line with a
single round turn.

mast—The vertical spar on which the sails are
set.

masthead—The top of the mast.

masthead fly—A small flag or indicator at the
masthead, to show the direction of the wind.

mast step—The slot in which the butt of the
mast rests.

quarter—The section of the hull from dead
astern to 45° forward on both sides.

quarterdeck—The deck over the quarter.

sheave—A grooved wheel, or pulley.

spar—A wooden or metal pole to which sails
are secured; a mast.

spray boards—A pair of boards set into the
foredeck forming a vertical wedge to keep
spray from running into the cockpit.

stern—The back end of a boat.

tiller, helm—The steering rod.

topsides—The part of a hull above water.

transom—The vertical end of a boat, across
the stern.

underbody—The part of a hull below water.

waterline—The level at which a boat floats.

BOAT DIMENSIONS

beam—A boat's greatest width; also, a point
amidships, at right angles to the centerline.

freeboard—The distance from a boat's waterline to her gunwale.

length overall (LOA)—The distance, measured
on a boat's centerline, from the tip of her
bow to the stern.

waterline length (LWL)—The distance, measured on a boat's centerline, between the
points where she floats forward and aft.

DIRECTIONS

abeam, on the beam—At right angles to the
centerline, 90° from dead ahead.

aft—Toward the stern.

ahead—In front of the boat.

astern—Behind the boat.

dead ahead—In front of the boat, in line with
her centerline.

dead astern—Behind the boat, in line with her
centerline.

fore-and-aft—Lengthwise with the boat's centerline.

forward—Toward the bow.

port—The boat's left side as you face forward.

starboard—The boat's right side as you face
forward.

to leeward—Downwind, away from the wind.

to port—On the port side.

to starboard—On the starboard side.

to windward—Upwind, toward the wind.

SAIL TERMS

battens—Strips of wood or Fiberglas set in a sail's leech to hold its curved shape.

batten pockets—Deep pockets sewn into a sail to hold the battens.

clew—A sail's lower, after corner.

foot—The bottom edge of a sail.

head—A sail's upper corner.

jib—A headsail set forward of the mast on the headstay or jibstay.

leech—The after edge of a sail.

loose-footed—Not made fast to a boom.

luff—The forward edge of a sail.

mainsail—The sail hoisted on the after side of the mainmast.

panel—One of a sail's cloths.

tack—A sail's lower, forward corner.

SAILING TERMS

dry-sailed—Boat hauled out after each usage.

ease—To release a sheet to adjust a sail's angle.

heel—To tilt or lean.

hiking—Leaning far out to windward to offset heeling.

leeward—Downwind.

on an even keel—Boat parallel to the horizon.

port tack—Sailing with the wind coming over the port side, and sails set to starboard.

starboard tack—Sailing with the wind coming over the starboard side, and sails set to port.

trim—To pull in on a sheet to adjust the sail's angle.

windward—Upwind.

STANDING RIGGING

chain plates—The fittings on the hull to which shrouds fasten.

headstay—The fore-and-aft wire that supports the mast forward.

shrouds—Wires attached to the mast to give it lateral support.

stays—Wires attached to a mast to give it support fore-and-aft.

RUNNING RIGGING

halyards—Lines used for hoisting and lowering sails.

jib halyard—The line used to hoist and lower the jib.

jibsheet—The line used to control the jib.

main halyard—The line used to hoist and lower the mainsail.

mainsheet—The line used to control the mainsail.

sheets—Lines used to control the angle at which sails are set.

VERBS

capsize—To overturn.

cast off—To untie or release.

hoist—To raise.

lower—To let down.

make fast—To attach securely.

secure—To make fast.

GENERAL

beamy—Relatively broad in relation to length.

bow-wave—The wave produced at the bow by a boat's forward motion.

crew—Those who help work the boat.

helmsman—One who steers the boat.

line—Rope with a diameter of less than one inch.

passengers—Those who have no part in working the boat.

rope—Cordage with a diameter greater than one inch.

skipper—The person in command of a boat; the captain.

sloop—A single-masted boat having a mainsail and one jib.

smooth sea—Water with relatively small waves or no waves.

2

What Makes the Boat Go?

A LEAF DRIFTING on the water is the simplest kind of sailboat. Watching it, we quickly see what makes the boat go—*wind!* Wind blowing against the upturned curve of the leaf—its sail—pushes this miniature sailboat forward.

The leaf, however, has only two of the three elements needed for a complete sailboat: *a sail* for the wind to push against; and *a sailing platform,* or hull, to be moved by the wind's push against the sail. It lacks the important third element—*control*. The leaf has no way to change the angle of its sail to increase the wind's push against it, and no way to steer the hull across wind.

As a result, this incomplete sailboat must always drift downwind, directly to leeward.

Thousands of years ago men learned to make sailboats that, like leaves, would move before the wind. They probably started with something like a boy's toy sailboat, with its single square sail. Only they soon found they needed controls if they were to sail in any direction except straight downwind.

So early sailors, like the Phoenicians and Vikings, added to their boats some kind of steering device for the hull, and lines to the

A leaf, a simple sailboat, is always blown downwind

Like the leaf, toy sailboat goes only downwind

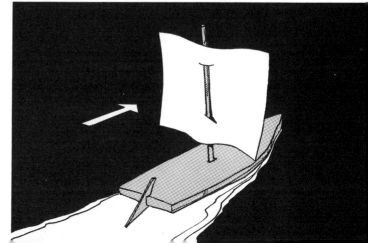

Above: *By adding braces and sheets to their square sails, Vikings were able to turn them to get maximum push from wind*

Below: *When you blow on luff of paper sail, sail does not flatten out but is pulled toward wind*

corners of their square sails to direct and control the wind's power.

They hung their great sails from horizontal spars called *yards,* which were hoisted up the mast by a halyard (from "haul yard"). The lines controlling the upper corners of the sail, attached to the end of the yards (the *yard arms*), were called *braces;* those to the lower, loose-footed corners were *sheets.* With sheets and braces, these bold sailors could trim their square sails to get the maximum push from the wind.

When *running,* or sailing before the wind, they swung the yard to bring the sail at right angles to the wind. Today, we trim our fore-and-aft sails the same way when running—at right angles to the wind.

It's easy to understand how the wind blowing into a square sail can push a boat before it, like a drifting leaf. But it's not so easy to visualize how a boat can sail upwind, against the wind. A simple experiment can help here.

Take an ordinary piece of letter-size paper (8½" x 11"), and cut it in half on the diagonal. This gives you two triangles that resemble the fore-and-aft sails used on most

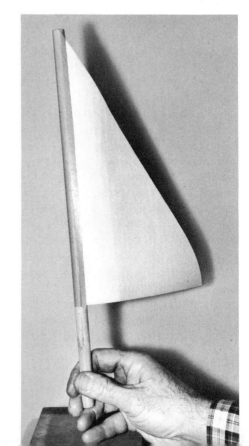

sailboats, lacking only the curved shape. To approximate that, tape one of the triangles to a length of ½-inch dowel, and roll the triangle's taped edge one revolution toward the point of the triangle, then release it. The triangle will take a curve like the illustration, giving you a paper "sail," with the dowel acting as a mast.

Hold the dowel in front of your lips so that the foot of the sail is about level with them, and blow vigorously at the luff of the sail. You will see the curved sail pull out toward you and remain pulled out as long as you keep blowing.

Instead of flattening out, as you might expect, the sail is pulled forward, *toward* the wind. The effect is similar to the lifting power given a glider's curved wing by wind rushing over it. And it is apparent that if a sheet were added to the sail to control it, this lifting power could be harnessed to pull the boat forward.

Without getting involved in a welter of technical details, this gives a general idea of how a sailboat can move upwind.

As a practical matter, it isn't possible to sail directly into the wind, except for very short periods. But when you have developed some skill as a helmsman, you should be able to trim your sails so as to sail within about 45° of the wind.

Sailing to windward, as close to the wind as possible, is called sailing *close-hauled.*

If the boat is steered too directly toward the wind, or if the sheets are not trimmed in close enough, the wind will blow equally on both sides of the sail, causing it to flutter, or *luff.* This destroys the lifting power of the wind, and the boat loses *headway* (forward motion).

Hence the skill of the helmsman is most important in getting a boat to sail to windward. By delicate adjustments of his sheets and steering, he keeps his sails as full as pos-

BOB GRIESER

13

sible, without luffing, and so captures the maximum lifting power of the wind.

Sailing close-hauled is also known as sailing *on the wind,* or *full-and-by,* meaning with "sails full" and "by the wind."

How the jib works

For sailing to windward, the jib is a most valuable sail. The wind blowing across its curved luff produces, of course, the same kind of lifting power as on the mainsail. But more important is the effect of the wind rushing off the after end of the jib into the slot between the jib and mainsail.

When the jibsheet is properly trimmed, the slot increases the speed of the wind rushing across the mainsail's luff, and gives it greater lifting power. Because of this, the boat not only makes greater speed, but is also able to sail closer to the wind.

If the jib is *overtrimmed,* that is, hauled in too tight, the air rushing from it hits the mainsail at an angle, instead of flowing smoothly across. This creates a backwind that causes the mainsail to luff and reduces the wind's lifting power.

A general rule for trimming sheets when sailing close-hauled, is to keep the leeches of the jib and mainsail about parallel to each other.

With this background on how sails capture the wind's power, let's see how this power is controlled on the boat to convert it into forward motion.

Summary

1. Wind blowing from astern, pushes against a sail and drives the boat forward, as in a drifting leaf.
2. Three elements, however, are needed for a complete sailboat: (1) a sail, (2) a sailing

BOB GRIESER

Above: *Luffing occurs when wind starts to blow on both sides of sail's leading edge*

Right: *A properly trimmed jib speeds flow of air through slot between mainsail and jib and helps mainsail develop maximum power*

BOB GRIESER

platform, or hull, and (3) control. Without control, a boat can sail only downwind.

3. Early sailors, like the Phoenicians and Vikings, added lines to the corners of their square sails to control and trim them.

4. Wind blowing from ahead, rushes across the curved surface of a fore-and-aft sail and pulls the boat *toward* the wind. The effect is like that of wind over a glider's wing, which produces the lifting power.

5. A good helmsman, with a properly designed boat, should be able to trim his sails so as to sail at an angle of about 45° from the wind's direction. Thus, with a north wind, he should be able to sail either northwest or northeast.

6. The chief value of the jib is in sailing to windward. When trimmed correctly, it speeds the flow of air through the slot between the jib and mainsail, and increases the wind's lifting power on the mainsail.

7. When the jib is overtrimmed, it reduces the mainsail's power by backwinding it, causing it to luff. Proper trim is to have the leeches of jib and mainsail about parallel.

8. Checklist of nautical terms:

PARTS OF BOAT

yard—The horizontal spar from which a square sail is hung.

yard arms—The outer extremities of a yard, to which braces are secured.

RUNNING RIGGING

braces—Lines secured to a yard for controlling its angle in relation to the wind.

SAILING TERMS

by the wind—Sailing close-hauled.
close-hauled—Sailing as close as possible to the direction of the wind without the sails luffing.
full-and-by—Sailing close-hauled.
on the wind—Sailing close-hauled.
overtrimmed—A condition when sheets are hauled in too close for sails to capture the full power of the wind.
running—Sailing before the wind.

VERB

luff, luffing—To cause the wind to flow equally on both sides of a sail, making it flutter and shake.

GENERAL

headway—Forward motion of a boat.

3

The Sailing Hull

A SAILBOAT, any sailboat, is simply a hull able to carry one or more people, and equipped with various controls to harness the wind's power and direct the boat's course. You have controls for the wind on the sails, for the wind on the boat, and for steering.

Controls for the wind on the sails

We have already learned that sails are raised and lowered by halyards. Though not controls in the sense of adjusting the sails for use of the wind's power, halyards can be considered emergency controls to get rid of wind power. If the wind is blowing so hard it cannot be handled safely by other controls, halyards can be released to lower the sails, and relieve the boat of much wind pressure.

With all sails lowered, a boat is said to be sailing *under bare poles*. This, however, is an extreme measure, and should not be used if the boat can possibly be sailed. It robs her of headway which, as we shall see, is needed for proper steering.

The chief control for the wind on a sail is the sheet, the line that adjusts its angle to the wind. When sailing close-hauled, sheets

When sailing under bare poles, boat has minimum headway, hence less control for steering

17

When sailing close-hauled, sheets are trimmed in to harden curve of sails for maximum lift

are trimmed in to bring sails close to the boat and harden their curve, so as to get the maximum forward lift from the wind.

When *reaching* (sailing across the wind), sheets are eased out to let sails ride at a wider angle from the boat and capture more of the wind's push.

In running before the wind, the sheets are eased out until the sails are at right angles to the wind's direction, for maximum push.

Incidentally, although it might seem that running would be the fastest point of sailing, most boats actually go faster when reaching.

Steering

Before looking at the controls for the wind on the boat, it's good to have a thorough understanding of how a small sailboat steers, which is *opposite* to any vehicle you've ever steered on land.

Large sailboats are usually equipped with a steering wheel that works like an automobile's, turning the boat's bow in the same direction the wheel is turned. Small sailboats,

Above: *When reaching, sheets are eased somewhat to let sails receive some of wind's push*

Right: *In running, mainsail is kept at right angles to wind for maximum push*

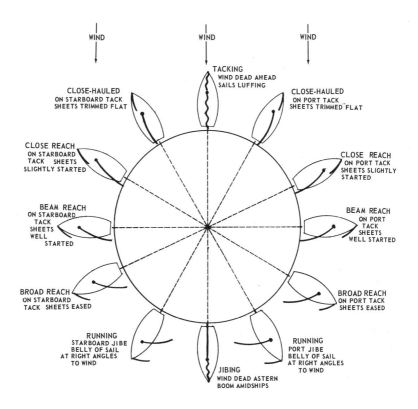

WIND   WIND   WIND

TACKING
WIND DEAD AHEAD
SAILS LUFFING

CLOSE-HAULED
ON STARBOARD TACK
SHEETS TRIMMED FLAT

CLOSE-HAULED
ON PORT TACK
SHEETS TRIMMED FLAT

CLOSE REACH
ON STARBOARD
TACK SHEETS
SLIGHTLY STARTED

CLOSE REACH
ON PORT TACK
SHEETS SLIGHTLY
STARTED

BEAM REACH
ON STARBOARD
TACK
SHEETS
WELL
STARTED

BEAM REACH
ON PORT
TACK
SHEETS
WELL STARTED

BROAD REACH
ON STARBOARD
TACK SHEETS EASED

BROAD REACH
ON PORT TACK
SHEETS EASED

RUNNING
STARBOARD JIBE
BELLY OF SAIL
AT RIGHT ANGLES
TO WIND

RUNNING
PORT JIBE
BELLY OF SAIL
AT RIGHT ANGLES
TO WIND

JIBING
WIND DEAD ASTERN
BOOM AMIDSHIPS

Above: *This diagram shows approximate angle to wind at which sails should be trimmed on each of various points of sailing*

Below: *The tiller steers boat by controlling side-to-side angle of rudder*

however, are steered by a *tiller,* a wooden or metal stick or rod connected to the head of the *rudder,* a movable underwater blade fastened to the boat's stern. The effect of the tiller on the rudder is like that of a pencil held horizontally—when you push one end, the other end moves in the opposite direction. And since the bow moves in the same direction as the rudder, this means it moves *opposite* to the direction of the tiller.

When the boat is at rest, not moving, both tiller and rudder are in line with the centerline, amidships. When you push the tiller away from the centerline—to the left, for example—the rudder moves in the opposite direction, to the right. This produces little

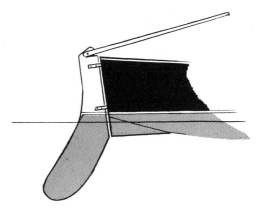

change in the direction of the boat, however, until the boat has headway.

Then, the pressure of the water flowing against the rudder blade pushes the stern away, causing the bow to swing in the same direction as the rudder. Etch this in your memory: Tiller to the *left* sends rudder and bow to the *right;* tiller to the *right* sends rudder and bow to the *left*.

If this seems confusing at first, be assured it's only a temporary condition. Once you actually begin to sail a boat, you'll be pleasantly surprised to find how quickly your reactions become automatic. You'll push the tiller *left* to swing the boat *right,* or vice versa, as naturally as you blink your eyes.

The central fact to keep firmly in mind is that rudder and bow work together, and the tiller opposite to the bow. This is important, because under the Coast Guard's Pilot Rules, all steering instructions to the helmsman must be given in terms of the rudder, not the tiller.

"Right rudder!", for example, is the command to the helmsman when the skipper wants the boat's bow to go to the right. *"Left rudder!"* is used to send the boat to the left. For safety's sake, adopt this routine in all your sailing.

It's easy to see that if there is a lot of pressure against the rudder, as when the boat is moving rapidly ahead, any change in the tiller's position will swing the bow farther in the opposite direction than when the boat is moving slowly. With little headway, a boat *answers her helm* (changes direction) sluggishly. This emphasizes the need to keep your boat moving as smartly as possible under all conditions, since control through steering depends on speed through the water, and vanishes when your headway ceases. *Steerageway* is the slowest forward speed at which a boat will answer her helm.

When steering in close quarters, as in a crowded anchorage, keep in mind that when your bow turns in one direction, your stern

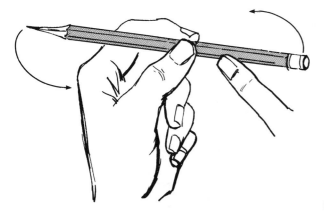

When you push tiller in one direction, rudder moves opposite

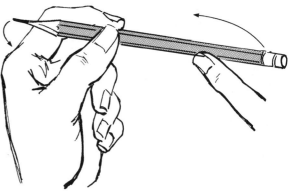

When boat's pivoting point is forward, stern swings more than bow

swings *in the opposite direction,* though not necessarily the same amount.

If your boat has more weight forward than aft, she will pivot around a point forward of amidships, and the stern will swing through a longer arc than the bow. To illustrate, hold a pencil horizontally just ahead of its midpoint, push the shorter end sideways and notice how much greater an arc the long end covers.

With her weight distributed equally forward and aft, a boat's pivoting point will be amidships; bow and stern will swing the same distance. When the balance of weight is aft, the pivot point will be aft and cause the bow to cover a greater arc than the stern in turning.

Wherever your boat's pivot point is located, when sailing between or close to other boats, or in rounding buoys, be sure to allow enough room for your stern to swing clear as the bow comes around.

Steering astern. Sometimes it happens that you must steer your boat while she is going *astern,* or backward. In this situation, *steer exactly opposite to when going ahead.*

In other words, when your boat has *sternway* (backward motion), to make her bow go to the *right,* you push the tiller to the *right;* to send the bow *left,* you push the tiller *left.* This simple rhyme may help you remember:

> *Going astern, in any weather,*
> *Bow and tiller work together.*

It's doubly important to remember this procedure, because most of your steering will be done with the boat going ahead; you will find it highly unnatural to push the tiller opposite to your normal practice. This will be particularly true since, when the situation occurs that gives you sternway, you will probably be excited and eager to have the bow swing in the correct direction as quickly

as possible. But you'll do all right if you keep a firm grip on the basic rule: *When going astern, push the tiller in the same direction you want the bow to swing.*

Controls for the wind on the boat

The wind has two effects on a boat: *leeway* and *heeling.* Leeway is the amount a boat drifts to leeward as a result of the wind's pressure against it. *Heeling,* as we have already seen, is the tilting or leaning of the boat to leeward caused by the wind's pressure against sails and hull.

Controlling leeway. How much leeway a boat makes and how much she heels depend on her hull shape and the resistance her underbody offers to sideways pressure. A drifting leaf, having no underbody, presents no lateral resistance to the wind's push; its entire progress is leeway. On the other hand, because it has no underwater projection resisting the wind's sideways push, the leaf doesn't heel—it slides off to leeward as the wind blows.

Most single-hulled sailboats have an underbody designed to reduce leeway either by means of a centerboard, or a keel, or a combination of both.

A *centerboard* is a strong, usually weighted, wood or metal fin that can be lowered vertically on the centerline below the boat to increase her *draft,* or depth below the waterline. Greater draft gives a boat increased resistance to sideways pressure. The centerboard is housed in a narrow box called the *centerboard trunk,* and is raised and lowered by a line called the *centerboard pennant,* attached to one end of the centerboard.

The word *"keel"* has two meanings, of which the first refers to the backbone, or principal fore-and-aft structural member of a hull. In a boat of deep draft, this keel may have lead or iron set into it at its deepest part

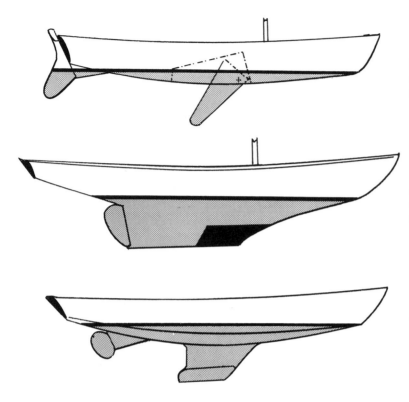

Centerboard, by providing lateral resistance, helps boat stay on course

Ballast keels are shaped to fit as an integral part of boat's underbody

Fin-bulb keels are separate projections bolted on to provide lateral resistance and stability

to increase its weight, or it may be fitted with a metal shoe. The second meaning of *keel* refers to a permanent, immovable vertical projection underwater on the centerline. It may be either built or molded into the boat's backbone, or fastened on by *keel bolts*. The effect of deep draft and of the permanent vertical projection is the same—resistance to sideways pressure.

Some boats are built with a slotted keel, through which a centerboard can be lowered to increase the boat's draft and lateral resistance when sailing to windward.

Controlling the angle of heel. For a quick picture of what happens to a boat when the wind pushes against her sails from the side, hold a pencil vertically near the bottom so that it pivots between thumb and forefinger, and press against the top, as in the sketch. The top of the pencil tilts in the direction of your push, while the bottom pivots up toward your pushing finger.

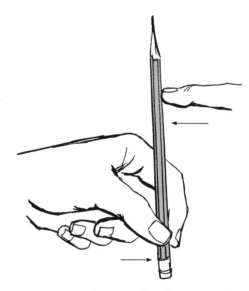

Pressure in one direction at pencil's top sends bottom in opposite direction

With a boat, when the wind blows from the side, the water holds the hull as your fingers held the pencil. Mast and sails are pressed downwind, and the hull heels over so that its windward side rides higher. If the wind blows hard enough, and the boat continues on the same course without easing sails off to spill some of the pressure, she may even be knocked flat in the water, *on her beam ends.*

There are, however, three influences helping to keep her on her feet: (1) *The beam of the boat itself.* Her width provides her with a certain amount of resistance to heeling; a broad, beamy boat resists the wind's heeling force better than a slender, narrow hull; (2) *The weight of the boat's keel or centerboard.* The farther over a boat heels, the more gravity pulls on the weight in the bottom of the keel or centerboard to bring the boat back upright; (3) *Ballast.* This is either fixed or movable weight used to give the boat greater stability.

THE EFFECT OF BEAM It takes more force to heel a floating box, which is broad and shallow, than a floating bottle, which is deep and narrow. A beamy, shoal-draft catboat will heel less than a narrow sloop of deeper draft, in the average sailing breeze. This does not mean, however, that the catboat is a safer boat to sail. On the contrary, she may require more skillful handling to prevent a capsize when the breeze becomes heavy.

Because she has a high initial resistance to heeling, the catboat may remain relatively upright, taking the full force of the breeze, until the wind becomes so strong that it overcomes her underbody's hold on the water, then suddenly knocks her flat.

The narrow, deep boat, on the other hand, though heeling more readily than the beamy, shoal-draft type, in the very act of heeling spills some of the wind. The farther she heels, the more she relieves herself of the wind's

pressure. At the same time, as her angle of heel increases so, too, does the righting effect of any weight built into her deep draft.

THE EFFECT OF BALLAST *Fixed ballast* is any weight fastened in place to increase

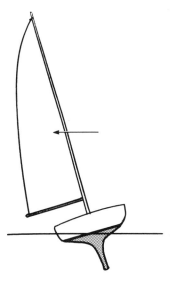

Right: *As wind pressure forces mast and sails downwind, windward side of boat rises*

Below: *Deep, narrow boat heels more than beamy, shoal-draft type in average sailing breeze*

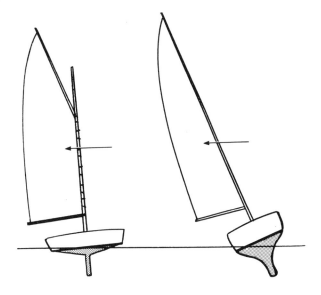

Crew of log canoe hikes out to windward to offset wind's heeling pressure

the boat's *initial stability,* or built-in resistance to heeling. This ballast may be inside or outside the hull. Inside ballast might be pigs of lead or iron bolted to the inside bottom (the *bilge*) planking of a wooden boat, or metal shot or punchings molded in the

24

resin of the bilge or in the keel of a fiber-glass boat. Outside ballast might be a metal shoe set into a boat's keel, or a heavy weight built into a boat's centerboard. My old 29-foot Chesapeake Bay skipjack sloop, for example, had a great bar of iron bolted into the heel of her 9-foot-long wooden centerboard. This performed the double duty of sinking the board rapidly when it was lowered, and providing additional stability when the board was down.

Movable ballast is any weight that is shifted as needed to offset the wind's heeling pressure, and increase the boat's stability. In the late nineteenth century a class of extreme racing yachts known as "sandbaggers," which carried an enormous spread of sail, required their crews to scramble out on the windward side of the boat when it was blowing hard, each man lugging a heavy bag of sand. The extra weight was needed to keep the boats from capsizing.

Today, Chesapeake Bay log canoes race with their crews sliding in and out to windward on long *hiking boards* to keep their sporty craft upright in a strong breeze. And many small, high performance racing boats like the one-design Flying Dutchman class are equipped with a trapeze slung from the mast, to let the crew swing well out to windward from the boat, as a counterweight to heeling. In a similar fashion the sailing efficiency of every sailboat, large or small, is affected by how the skipper arranges the side-to-side and fore-and-aft distribution of his principal movable ballast—the weight of himself and his crew.

Athwartships trim is the term used to describe the side-to-side balance of a boat, the angle she makes with the horizon when looking at her head on. At rest, when properly balanced and with no one on board, she should ride level, on an even keel, with her mast at right angles to the horizon. If she does not, and *lists* (heels) to one side or the other, her fixed inside ballast may have to be shifted to bring her back level. Or if she has heavy gear (like anchors) placed where it produces a list, it may be corrected by relocating the offending weight closer to the centerline.

Although her athwartships trim should be on even keel when at rest, a boat usually goes faster when sailing if heeled at a slight angle, to get her down to her *sailing lines,* the point at which she has been designed to sail most efficiently. The exact angle varies from boat to boat, and must be found by experimenting with your trim under different weights of breeze. In general, however, centerboard boats begin to lose efficiency when their angle of heel exceeds about 5°; most keel boats can take more heel and still sail effectively.

Because of her beam, underbody (centerboard or keel), and fixed ballast, each boat has a certain amount of initial stability. If she has a high initial stability, she does not heel readily and is said to be *stiff.* But a boat with a low initial stability goes off an even keel at the slightest heeling pressure, and is called *tender* or *cranky.* Once you start sailing, you'll quickly learn whether your boat is stiff or tender.

It's an important fact to know. For it tells you how much you can depend on the boat itself to resist heeling in various weights of breeze, and how much you will have to help it stay upright by shifting your own weight and that of your crew to windward when the breeze freshens.

Fore-and-aft trim. Though not a control in the sense of being a tangible piece of her gear, like a sheet or centerboard, a boat's *fore-and-aft trim* has a vital effect on her behavior and performance. This is the angle at which she rides in relation to the horizon, when viewed from the side. If her bow tilts down, she is said to be trimmed *by the head;* if her stern, she is *by the stern.* As a rule, she should be neither, but ride level, on an even keel.

When Sir Isaac Newton drafted his Third Law of Motion, he could have been thinking of small-boat sailors, it affects their operations in so many ways. The law, in a nutshell, states: *To every action there is an equal and opposite reaction.* It applies with great emphasis in establishing a boat's fore-and-aft trim.

When you step into either end of a small boat, that end goes deeper in the water and the opposite end rises an equal amount. If it's a very small boat, like a rowing pram or dinghy, your weight in the extreme end might be enough to force it under water and cause the boat to fill, or *swamp;* the sad result of neglecting to remember the critical importance of fore-and-aft trim.

Apart from its influence on how a boat behaves in other ways, her fore-and-aft trim has a direct effect on her steering qualities because of its influence on the relative position of the boat's underwater pivoting point and the central point above water where the wind's pressure is concentrated. Technically these two spots are known respectively as the *Center of Lateral Resistance* (CLR), and the *Center of Effort* (CE).

To visualize the CLR, it can be located approximately by cutting a piece of cardboard in the shape of the boat's underwater profile and finding the spot where the cardboard will balance on a pencil's point. This is not entirely accurate, because it takes no account of the actual distribution of ballast inside and outside the hull, but it does give a picture of the fact that the boat has a point

Boat's Center of Lateral Resistance may be located approximately by balancing on pencil point a piece of cardboard cut in shape of her underwater profile

CENTER OF LATERAL RESISTAN

Stepping into extreme end of any small boat may cause it to swamp or capsize

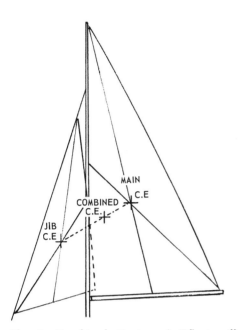

Sloop's Combined Center of Effort will be found somewhere along line joining CE's of jib and mainsail, with its location dependent on relative areas of sails

will be proportional to the relative areas of the mainsail and jib.

But these roughly determined CLR and CE points will serve to demonstrate a principle that is easily stated: *In adjusting a sailboat's fore-and-aft trim, the Center of Effort should be located aft of her Center of Resistance, so that she will point into the wind by herself when the tiller is let go.*

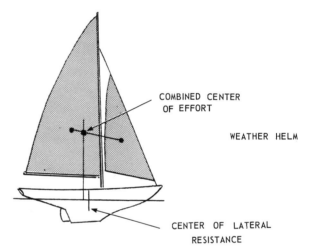

When Combined Center of Effort is located aft of Center of Lateral Resistance, boat will have weather helm

under water where all her resistance to sideways pressure is concentrated. She tends to pivot around this point. And the pivoting point can be moved forward or aft by shifting ballast—fixed or movable—forward or aft, preferably on the centerline.

The Center of Effort (CE) is simply the point where all the wind pressure on the boat exerts its total heeling effect. To find the CE for any triangular sail, draw lines from any two corners to the midpoint of the sides opposite—where the lines cross will be the CE. Alternately, you can cut a cardboard triangle to the shape of the sail and find the spot at which this triangle balances on a pencil point, as described above.

On a sloop the combined CE will be found along a line joining the CE's of the jib and mainsail. Its distance from the mainsail's CE

A boat trimmed this way is said to carry a *weather helm,* since the helmsman must keep his tiller angled slightly *to weather* (toward the wind), to hold her bow off, countering the boat's tendency to head into the wind. The safety value of this tendency is apparent. It means the boat has a head start in turning toward the wind to spill it under emergency conditions.

Sometimes, however, you can have too much of a good thing. A small amount of weather helm is welcome, with the tiller angled out a couple of degrees to weather in

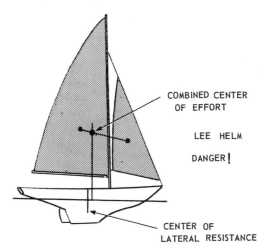

COMBINED CENTER
OF EFFORT

LEE HELM

DANGER!

CENTER OF
LATERAL RESISTANCE

Should Combined Center of Effort be forward of Center of Lateral Resistance, boat will carry lee helm, a potentially dangerous condition

the average sailing breeze. But if the Center of Effort is so far aft of the Center of Lateral Resistance that the helmsman must keep a large windward angle on his helm, the boat's speed is lowered by the increased drag of the rudder. Also, a heavy weather helm can become an arm-pulling, back-breaking nuisance in a breeze of any weight.

To correct an overly strong weather helm, the fore-and-aft trim should be changed to bring the CE and CLR closer together on a fore-and-aft line. This can be done in several ways:

Raking (tilting) the mast forward moves the CE forward. Raising the centerboard some, or shifting ballast aft on the centerline, moves the CLR aft. The CE can also be moved forward by increasing the size of the jib or other headsails, or by cutting down the area of the mainsail, or by doing both.

Some boats have such a pronounced weather helm, it seems almost incurable, short of surgery. My 29-foot skipjack—which had a 42-foot mast that raked aft about 15°, and a 27-foot main boom—carried enough weather helm to give a strong man a workout in even a moderate breeze. The problem was, these boats were designed and built to drag for oysters under sail—to move her CLR aft far enough to lighten her helm,

I'd have had to lug an oyster drag!

The opposite side of the coin from a boat that carries weather helm is one whose Center of Effort is located forward of her Center of Lateral Resistance, forcing her to carry a *lee helm* to hold the boat on course. This condition should be avoided as you would a fire extinguisher filled with gasoline; in an emergency, it could mean disaster. For unlike the weather helm boat, a boat trimmed with a lee helm tends to point *away* from the wind when her tiller is released.

In a squall, this tendency could easily send the boat into an *accidental jibe,* a situation when, with the stern pointed upwind, the wind gets on the same side of the boat as the mainsail and swings the boom across the boat to the other side, like a giant baseball bat. An accidental jibe can result in cracked skulls, people knocked overboard, a broken mast, a broken boom, or a capsize.

A lee helm is particularly dangerous when running before the wind, because a relatively small change of direction by either the boat or the wind can put the wind on the same side as the mainsail and trigger an accidental jibe.

Correcting a lee helm. Knowing that a helm is caused by a CE located forward of the CLR, raking the mast aft will move the CE aft. Lowering the centerboard to its full depth will move the CLR forward, as will shifting ballast forward on the centerline. Increasing the size of the mainsail and reducing the area of the jib will also move the CE aft.

There is much more at stake in this adjustment of fore-and-aft trim to get rid of a tendency to point off the wind than there is in correcting an overly strong weather helm. The latter is a matter of speed, convenience, and comfort; elimination of a lee helm is a matter of critical safety.

Keeping weight out of the ends. The technical process of determining the exact location of a boat's Centers of Effort and Lateral Resistance is properly the work of a naval architect. Any boat owner, however, can make a few simple adjustments himself and determine their effectiveness on the basis of his own experience at the tiller. There is one basic axiom he can start with: *Keep weight out of the ends of a boat.*

Anyone who has ever raced a small boat to windward and had a man go forward for any reason, knows how the boat's speed drops at once when the 150 pounds or more of extra weight forward throws the fore-and-aft trim out of balance. All weight forward of the mast tends to hold the bow down; extreme weight may cause the boat to bury her nose when going to windward and take water aboard.

In the same way, weight aft tends to hold the stern down. When running before the wind, excess weight in the stern may result in the boat being *pooped*—boarded by a following sea that climbs over the transom and pours aboard.

This is why sailors who take their boats offshore, where they meet the most severe conditions of wind and sea, are careful to keep weight centered more or less amidships, out of the ends of the boat, and their fore-and-aft trim level with the horizon. Sailors who face the less exposed conditions of inland and coastal waters will find it profitable to adopt the same practice.

Two safety valves

Sometimes you get caught out with more wind power than you want or can safely use.

It may come on gradually, as when a wind keeps increasing in strength until it threatens **to overwhelm you. Or it may hit you suddenly in the form of a violent squall that** heels you over dangerously. Regardless of how it comes, when it arrives you want a way to get rid of it *fast,* yet keep your boat moving safely.

Since the way to spill wind power is to get the wind to blow equally on both sides of the sail, you have two excellent safety valves. They can be used separately or, depending on the strength of the wind, both at once:

Safety Valve No. 1—PUSH THE TILLER TOWARD THE BOOM, to turn the boat into the wind.

Safety Valve No. 2—LET SHEETS RUN, to send sails out and spill the wind.

Pushing the tiller toward the boom (which is always to leeward when sailing), sends the bow in the opposite direction—to windward, and so brings the boat with the wind more directly over the bow, to blow more equally on both sides of the sails, thus reducing its power to make the boat heel. If you turn straight into the wind, all pressure on the sails is spilled, they shake violently, and your boat quickly loses her headway.

Usually, however, you can ease pressure and keep sailing comfortably by turning only far enough toward the wind to produce a slight luffing in the sails. This avoids the violent shaking—which may break battens in a sail and cause it to tear—and also keeps the boat *footing* (moving ahead), so that you maintain steerageway.

Letting sheets run, the second safety valve, produces the same effect as heading the boat toward the wind—it spills pressure by allowing the wind to blow more equally on both sides of the sail. It has the great advantage of speed in dumping excess wind power, compared with the slower action of the tiller, but it has a disadvantage in tending to kill the boat's headway. Since, as we have seen, any loss in headway reduces steering control, sheets should be eased only if there is not time to spill pressure by turning toward the wind.

As a quick, temporary parry of the wind's thrust, however, letting sheets run is an excellent safety measure. The term "run" should be defined; it seldom means letting go more than a foot or so of any sheet, even to handle a violent puff. If when the puff is past you trim sheets again and continue to sail your course, you will avoid losing too much headway.

In comparing the relative merits of the two "safety valves," another factor in favor of using the tiller first is that it gains distance to windward. Rather than merely parrying the puff, as you do when you let sheets run, you use the extra strength of the breeze to sail higher against it, picking up extra yardage toward any objective lying upwind.

Now we're ready to take a look at the wind itself.

Summary

1. Effect of wind on sails is controlled by
   a. **Halyards**—Cast off in extreme emergency to lower sails and relieve wind pressure; sailing under bare poles.
   b. **Sheets**—The normal control, for adjusting the angle of the sails to the wind.
2. Usual sail trim:
   a. **Close-hauled**—Sheets trimmed to bring sails close to boat, to harden the curve of the sail.
   b. **Reaching**—Sheets eased out some, sails at wider angle to boat.
   c. **Running**—Sheets eased out until sails are at right angles to the wind.
3. Steering ahead:
   a. Push tiller *opposite* to the direction you want the bow to go.
   b. Rudder and bow swing in the same direction.
   c. All steering orders to the helmsman are in terms of the direction the bow is to swing, e.g., "Right rudder!" means "Steer the boat to the right."
   d. In turning, bow and stern swing in opposite directions. Be sure the stern has room to swing clear when in close quarters.
4. Steering astern:
   a. Push tiller *toward* the direction you want the bow to go.
5. The leeway effect of wind on a boat is controlled by:
   a. **A centerboard**, lowered to provide more lateral resistance, or
   b. **A keel** projecting vertically underwater to resist sideways pressure, or
   c. **A combination** of keel and centerboard.
6. The wind's heeling effect on a boat is controlled by:
   a. **Her beam**—Breadth of beam increases resistance to heeling.
   b. **Her underbody**—Weight in keel or lowered centerboard helps keep the boat upright.
   c. **Ballast**—Fixed ballast, inside or outside the hull, makes the boat more stable. Movable ballast is placed to windward on the boat to help her stay upright as wind pressure increases.
7. A boat's athwartships trim should be on an even keel when she is at rest, with no one on board.
8. Most boats sail better with a few degrees of heeling angle; keel boats with more heel than centerboarders.
9. A boat's initial stability is determined by her beam, underbody, and fixed ballast.
10. Fore-and-aft trim should have the boat level with the horizon when she is at rest with no one aboard.
11. A sailboat's tendency to head upwind or downwind when her helm is released, depends on the relative positions of her Center of Effort (CE) and Center of Lateral Resistance (CLR), and can be changed by her fore-and-aft trim.

12. **A weather helm** is a desirable safety factor, and exists when the Center of Effort is aft of the Center of Lateral Resistance.

13. A too-strong weather helm can be corrected by bringing the Centers of Effort and Lateral Resistance closer together, fore-and-aft.

14. **A lee helm** is a dangerous quality in a sailboat, the result of her CE being forward of her CLR. It can result in an accidental jibe. It can be corrected by moving the CE aft of the CLR.

15. A general rule of fore-and-aft trim is to keep weight out of the ends.

16. In case of squall or violent wind pressure, a sailboat's two safety measures to spill wind power are:
    a. **Push the tiller toward the boom,** to turn the boat into the wind.
    b. **Let sheets run,** to send sails out and spill the wind.

17. Checklist of nautical terms:

PARTS OF BOAT

bilge—The inside, bottom of a boat.

centerboard—A strong, usually weighted, wood or metal fin lowered vertically on the centerline to increase lateral resistance and reduce leeway.

centerboard pennant—A line attached to one end of the centerboard for raising and lowering it.

centerboard trunk—The narrow box housing the centerboard.

hiking boards—Movable supports pushed out from a boat's side to let her crew put their weight farther to windward.

keel—The fore-and-aft structural backbone of a boat; also any additional permanent, vertical underwater projection bolted to or molded as part of the structural keel to increase resistance to leeway and for greater stability.

rudder—The boat's underwater steering blade; a movable blade at the stern, connected to the tiller, by which a boat is steered.

tiller—The boat's steering rod or stick, fastened to the rudder head for turning the rudder.

BOAT DIMENSION

draft—The depth to the lowest point of a boat below her waterline; on a centerboard boat, specified as *Draft with board up* and *Draft with board down.*

DIRECTION

to weather—To windward.

SAILING TERMS

accidental jibe—A situation with the boat's stern facing into the wind, when the wind shifts to the side on which the mainsail is set, causing the boom to sweep violently across the boat.

cranky—With little resistance to heeling; tender.

lee helm—With the tiller to leeward. A boat carries *lee helm* when the tiller must be kept to leeward to hold her on course.

reaching—Sailing across the wind; the point of sailing between close-hauled and running.

sailing lines—The theoretical point in heeling at which a boat sails best, with least resistance to the waves.

stiff—With a high resistance to heeling.

tender—With little resistance to heeling; cranky.

under bare poles—Sailing before the wind with all sails lowered.

weather helm—With the helm to weather. A boat carries *weather* helm when the tiller must be held to weather to keep her on course.

VERBS

foot, footing—To move ahead; keeping the boat moving.

list—To heel as a result of some other influence than wind or sea; also the condition, as a *list to starboard,* meaning an angle of heel to the right.

rake—To tilt from vertical on a fore-and-aft line; also the condition, as *the rake of her mast,* meaning the angle of tilt forward or aft.

swamp—To sink by filling with water.

GENERAL

answer her helm—Change direction in response to the tiller.

athwartships trim—The side-to-side balance of a boat.

ballast (**fixed**)—Heavy weights fastened inside or outside the bottom of a boat to increase her stability.

ballast (**movable**)—Weight, including people, shifted around to offset temporary heeling pressure of wind or sea.

by the head—Fore-and-aft trim with the bow lower than the stern.

by the stern—Trimmed fore-and-aft with the stern lower than the bow.

Center of Effort (**CE**)—The point on a boat above water at which the heeling pressures are focused.

Center of Lateral Resistance (**CLR**)—The point on a boat's underbody where all her resistance to sideways pressure is concentrated.

fore-and-aft trim—The angle at which a boat rides in relation to the horizon, when viewed from the side.

initial stability—A boat's built-in, basic resistance to heeling.

leeway—The downwind drift of a boat, caused by wind or sea.

"Left rudder!"—A command to the helmsman to steer the boat to the left.

on beam ends—Heeled over so far that the boat's deck beams are vertical.

pooped—Boarded by a following sea.

"Right rudder!"—A command to the helmsman to steer the boat to the right.

steerageway—Enough forward motion for a boat to answer her helm.

sternway—Backward motion.

4

How to Judge the Wind

WE KNOW THAT WIND is what makes the sailboat go—wind blowing from behind the boat, wind blowing across the boat, even wind blowing toward the boat. We depend on wind power to move our boat.

This makes two facts about the wind important to us every time we go sailing: Which way is the wind blowing? and How hard?

Finding the wind's direction

You know, of course, that wind blows from one direction toward another, and is named for the direction from which it blows. A *north wind* blows from the north toward the south, a southwest wind from the southwest toward the northeast, and so forth.

But even though you may have heard a radio weather broadcast that gave a wind direction and velocity for your area, you'll want to make your own check on the spot before you hoist sail. Weather vanes, flags, smoke, clouds, tree leaves, waves, your face, and a wetted finger can all help you find which way the wind is blowing.

Weather vanes are made so that the pointer swings *into* the wind, to tell from

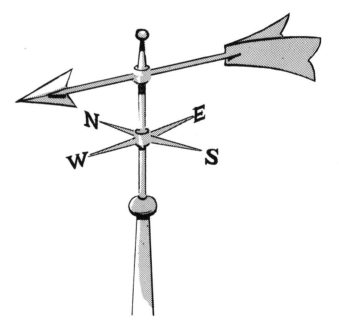

Weather vanes point to direction from which wind is blowing

which direction the wind is blowing. When you watch a weather vane in a strong breeze, notice how the pointer keeps shifting; it's seldom at rest. This shows that the wind rarely flows uniformly from one direction. Rather, it blows in puffs and gusts of varying strength and direction, though its general direction will average north, east, south, west, or some point between. A masthead fly acts like a weather vane.

Flags are lifted by the wind, and stretch out in the direction the wind is blowing.

Smoke in the air usually does the same. At the dock look around you and toward the horizon for smoke from chimneys or distant stacks. It will be stretched downwind from its source.

Clouds also tell which way the wind is blowing because they, too, are propelled by the wind. Observe how they are moving in the sky; notice which way they are drifting. Though there may be a slight difference in direction between the wind aloft and on the water, clouds give a general indication of where the wind lies.

Waves can give some clue to wind direction, since they usually run downwind. By watching them, you can at least determine roughly which direction is downwind and which upwind. If the waves are small, or the water is calm, you may be able to see little dark ruffled patches hurrying across the surface. These *catspaws* are actually small puffs of wind. Observe which direction they are coming from—catspaws often indicate that a new, steady breeze is about to set in from the same direction.

Your face is a valuable aid to telling wind direction, once you have learned how to interpret the wind pressure blowing against it. Try facing the direction you think the wind is blowing from; your face should feel some pressure against it, depending on the strength of the breeze. If you are standing in the open, away from buildings that might change the wind's direction, the wind comes from the

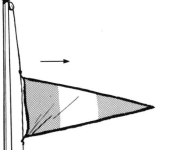

Flags stretch out in direction wind is blowing

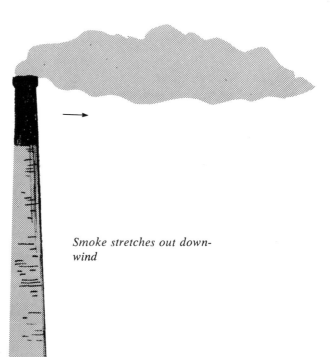

Smoke stretches out downwind

Above: *Clouds drift in direction wind is blowing*

Right: *Waves usually run downwind*

direction that makes most pressure on your face.

A wetted finger, held high, will tell which direction the wind is from in very light airs, when the breeze is hard to find. Your finger will get cool on the upwind side. Even a slight breeze will cause the moisture on your finger to evaporate, and so cool it. Be sure to wet the *whole* finger, not just lick one side!

Estimating the wind's strength

Today, continuous marine weather broadcasts from the National Weather Service of the National Oceanic and Atmospheric Administration make it possible for you to know before leaving home what kind of weather the day is likely to bring. Two VHF-FM radio frequencies are used, 162.55 MHz and 162.40 MHz, and the broadcasts can usually be received 35 to 40 miles from the transmitting stations.

A free folder, "The NOAA VHF Radio Weather," lists the latest station locations. To order it, write to National Weather Service, Att. W#112, 8060 13th Street, Silver Spring, Md. 20910, and ask for their latest Folder No. NOAA/PA 70035.

These VHF-FM broadcasts, which are repeated continuously around the clock, cover both land and marine forecasts. For land areas, the wind velocities are usually given in miles per hour (mph), as "Winds from the North to Northwest at eight to ten mph." For marine forecasts, however, the velocities are given in *knots,* as "For coastal waters from Block Island to Manasquan Inlet, including Long Island Sound: West to Northwest winds of ten to fifteen knots . . ."

A knot is a unit of speed measurement meaning "one nautical mile per hour." Since the nautical mile is 6076.1 feet, as opposed to the statute mile of 5280 feet, you must multiply the speed in knots by 1.15 to obtain the approximate speed in statute mph. Thus, 10-15 knots would be, in land terms, 11½ to 17¼ mph, though as a practical matter, no broadcast would attempt to predict velocities of less than whole numbers.

In any event, until you have had some experience in sailing your particular boat, the information on the wind's speed is not very meaningful. There is a direct relationship between the wind's speed and its pressure against your sails, of course, but it takes time and experience to learn exactly how much wind your boat can handle safely.

At this point, to know that a breeze of eight miles an hour exerts a pressure of .183 pounds per square foot, or that one of 16 miles has a pressure of .732 pounds is interesting but not vital. It is much more important to realize that a small boat cannot sail in as strong winds as a large boat. You don't have to be an expert to know that an 8-foot sailing dinghy may be in danger of capsizing in a breeze that a 45-foot schooner will find delightful sailing.

A guide to wind speed for safe sailing

As a starting point in building your knowledge of what winds are safe for small-boat sailing, this table may be useful. The suggested maximum speeds for each size boat are approximations of conditions for *safe, comfortable* sailing, not racing.

A careless skipper might capsize an able boat in a flat calm, while a skillful sailor might weather a storm in a rowboat.

Recall, for example, one of the greatest feats of seamanship on record—Captain Bligh's handling of the 23-foot open longboat in which he and nineteen companions were set adrift from H.M.S. *Bounty* by mutineers in 1789. Battling giant seas whipped by easterly gales, for forty-one days the doughty captain kept his overladen craft afloat, and successfully navigated his crew to safety over 3600 miles of open sea.

SUGGESTED MAXIMUM WIND SPEEDS FOR SAFE SAILING

Size of Boat (LWL)	Max. Desirable Wind Speed	U. S. Weather Bureau Term	Signs to Look for on Land	Signs to Look for on Water
8 to 12 feet	**8 to 12 knots**	Gentle	Leaves and small twigs in constant motion; wind extends light flag.	Small waves begin to break; occasional whitecaps seen.
13 to 18 feet	**13 to 18 knots**	Moderate	Wind raises dust and loose paper; small branches are moved.	Waves getting longer and bigger whitecaps fairly frequent.
19 to 26 feet	**19 to 24 knots**	Fresh	Small leafy trees begin to sway; crested wavelets form on lakes, ponds, and rivers.	More whitecaps than clear water; moderate-sized waves.

Note: *This table is only a guide, and the author assumes no responsibility for any boat or skipper using it. Too many variables affect the safety of a boat in a breeze, not the least of which are the skill of the skipper and the seaworthiness of his boat.*

Summary

1. Each time before you go sailing, determine the wind's direction and strength, and plan your outing accordingly.
2. Wind is named for the direction from which it blows.
3. Weather vanes and masthead flies show the direction the wind is from. So does your face, or a wetted finger.
4. Flags, smoke, clouds, and waves all show the direction in which the wind is blowing.
5. An easy way to learn to judge wind speed is to hold a hand out of a car window at different speeds, up to 40 miles per hour (mph).
6. As a rough rule of thumb, a small sailboat should be able to sail safely and comfortably if she avoids sailing in wind speeds greater than the number of feet in her waterline length (LWL). That is, a 10-foot boat should avoid winds over 10 knots; a 15-foot boat not sail in winds over 15 knots, etc.
7. Checklist of nautical terms:

GENERAL

catspaws—Dark, ruffled patches on the water, caused by wind hurrying across the surface, usually during a calm.

knot—A speed of one nautical mile per hour.

mph—Abbreviation for "miles per hour."

nautical mile—A unit of measurement that is 6076.1 feet long, as opposed to the statute mile of 5280 feet.

5

Six Useful Knots

WHEN YOU ARE SAILING you're continually using lines of various kinds and for various purposes—*halyards* to hoist sails, *sheets* to control them, *dock lines* for tying up at a dock or float, *mooring lines* for securing a mooring, *anchor lines* for anchoring. So before you go on the water and start sailing, obviously you should know how to make a line fast *properly*.

"Properly" means so that it will hold securely, yet be easy to cast off when you want to let it go. This requires knowing how to tie the right kind of knot for each of five main situations: making a line fast to a cleat, to itself, to another line, to a ring of some kind, and to a post or piling.

Any knot won't do. It may hold all right but not untie readily. On the water, lines often get wet and shrink, tightening knots. If you've used the wrong kind of knot, it may jam in an emergency when you want to let the line go in a hurry, and cause a capsize or other trouble. But when you use the right knot for each purpose, you *know* it will hold securely yet always be easy to let go.

Six knots will equip you to handle practically every sailing situation where you must make a line fast. Later, you may want to add others to your repertory, but for the time being, these six will do nicely:

1. Half-hitch (Overhand Knot)
2. Clove Hitch (Two Half-hitches)
3. Figure-8 Knot
4. Reef (Square) Knot
5. Bowline
6. Halyard Hitch

First, supply yourself with a six-foot length of clothesline or heavy cord and learn how to tie each of the six correctly. Then practice them over and over until you can make each one instantly, without hesitation. When you think you have them down cold, let a couple of days go by without touching a line. Then see if you can still tie all six quickly and right the first time; you may get a surprise.

You don't really *know* a knot until you can tie it automatically, without thinking about the different steps to make it. Your goal should be to *know* all six of these.

In the following descriptions the *standing part* of the line means the part closest to the end already made fast, or to the main body of the line; the *end* is the free end you use to form the knot or secure the line; and the *bight* is a loop between the standing part and the end. Incidentally, you'll learn more quickly and gain confidence, too, by always making the knot the same way—if you're right-handed, hold the standing part in your left hand, facing up, with the bight toward you, and work with the end in your right hand, using your right index finger to guide the end as you form the knot. The illustrations are all made right-handed.

If you're left-handed, hold the standing part in your right hand, facing up, with the bight toward you, and let your left hand work the end, using your left index finger to guide it.

1. The Half-hitch (Overhand Knot)

The half-hitch and overhand knot are formed the same way—the simplest form of tie—except that the half-hitch is attached to or around something, while the overhand knot is made in its own line. By itself, the half-hitch is useful as a temporary fastening to secure the end of a line that has no strain on it. But the overhand knot, by itself, is not included in our list of useful knots because, under strain, it easily jams so tight it can be freed only by cutting. You've probably tied an overhand knot many times; it will serve to familiarize you with the use of knot-tying terms.

To tie: Pass the end over the standing part, forming a bight, then push the end through the bight and pull tight.

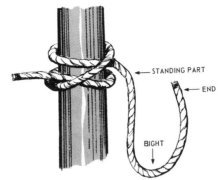

Standing part of a line leads to end made fast; bight is a loop; and working part is free end

LARRY KEAN

Above: *Knot-tying should always be done the same way—for most people this means holding standing part in left hand and working end in right*

Left: *Overhand knot is easily tied but jams so tight it may have to be cut to free it*

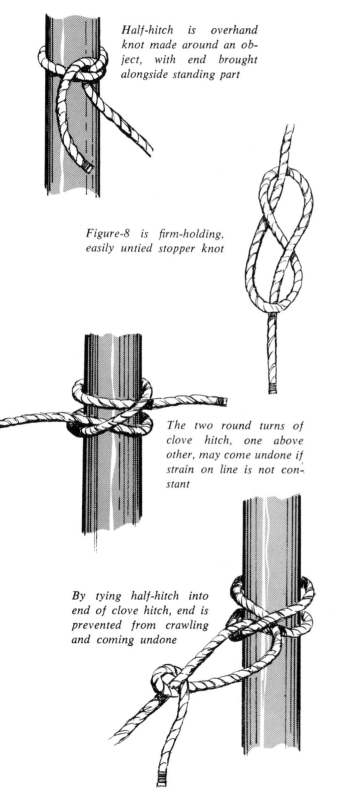

Half-hitch is overhand knot made around an object, with end brought alongside standing part

Figure-8 is firm-holding, easily untied stopper knot

The two round turns of clove hitch, one above other, may come undone if strain on line is not constant

By tying half-hitch into end of clove hitch, end is prevented from crawling and coming undone

The half-hitch is made exactly the same way, but the end is passed around something before crossing over the standing part, so that the object is enclosed in the bight; then the end is pushed through the bight and brought up alongside the standing part.

2. The Figure-8 Knot

This provides an easily untied stopper lump, and is chiefly used to prevent the end of a line from going through a block. You tie a Figure-8 in the end of each sheet, for example, to keep it from slipping through its blocks and getting away, should you accidentally let it go while the sail is putting a strain on it.

To tie: Pass the end over the standing part, behind it, then down across itself, through the bight, and pull tight.

3. The Clove Hitch
(Two Half-hitches)

The clove hitch and two half-hitches are both formed the same way, except the clove hitch is made around a post or some other round object, while two half-hitches is a clove hitch made around the line's own standing part.

Both have the advantage of being quickly made and holding securely under strain, though the clove hitch may come adrift if the strain is not constant. Alternate tightening and slackening of a line secured by a clove hitch may cause the end to "crawl" and eventually undo the hitch.

To tie: A clove hitch is two round turns, one above the other. Keep a tension on the standing part by holding it with one hand, and with the working hand pass the end around the post or other object, and back under the standing part to make a *round turn.* Above this first round turn, pass the end around the post again and back under itself to make a second round turn, directly over the first, and pull it tight. If you wish to prevent the end from "crawling," tie in a half-hitch around the standing part and pull it tight.

The clove hitch is widely used in tying boats to a float or dock, where vertical posts, or *bitts,* are often provided for mooring purposes. Sometimes *ring bolts* are furnished, instead—heavy rings of iron or steel, bolted to dock or float, for holding a line. Then, rather than a clove hitch, it's better to pass the line's end through the ring and tie in two half-hitches, one above the other. This, you will notice, is really a clove hitch around the line's own standing part.

Two half-hitches is also useful when you want to tie up to a big piling and your line isn't long enough to go around it twice to make a clove hitch. Usually you have enough line to go around the piling once, and can then secure the line with two half-hitches.

4. The Reef (or Square) Knot

This is an excellent knot for tying together two lines of the same diameter; it will not slip under strain.

To tie: Treat the end of one line (either one) as though it were the standing part, and the other end as "the" end. Then make two overhand knots, one on top of the other, as follows: Pass "the" end over the standing part, down around it and back up. Bend the standing part toward "the" end, to form a bight, pass "the" end over the standing part, through the bight, and pull tight.

Some sailors prefer to use this formula for tying a reef knot: "Right over left, then left over right," which translates: "Pass the end of the line in your right hand over the end in your left hand, then the end now in your

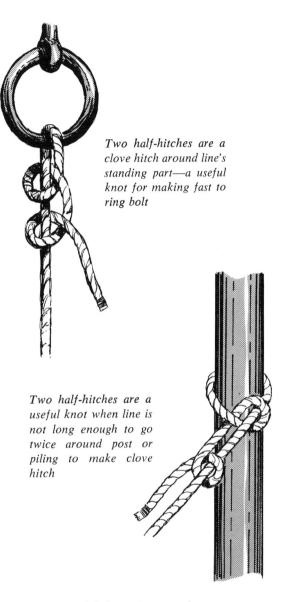

Two half-hitches are a clove hitch around line's standing part—a useful knot for making fast to ring bolt

Two half-hitches are a useful knot when line is not long enough to go twice around post or piling to make clove hitch

Most useful for tying together two lines of same diameter, reef knot will not slip under strain, is readily untied

left hand over the end now in your right, and pull tight." The result will be exactly the same as the method above, so use whichever instruction you find easier to follow. The important thing is to be able to make the knot correctly each time.

Note the square, symmetrical appearance of the properly made reef knot, like two interlocking loops. When you pull on the two lines, the knot snugs up, with each end lying alongside its standing part. Yet a reef knot is easily untied by holding the end and standing part of one line firmly in your right hand, and the end and standing part of the other firmly in your left hand, and pushing them toward each other to force the loops apart.

Inexperienced sailors often fail to make the two overhand knots of the reef knot in the correct order, and end up with a *granny knot,* a treacherous knot that's unpredictable in two ways, both bad—either it slips and will not hold, or it jams so tight it has to be cut to free the lines. You can tell a granny knot by its twisted, involved appearance. And when you put a strain on it, if it doesn't slip but jams, the ends go out at right angles to the standing parts.

The reef knot gets its name from *reefing,* the process of reducing sail area in heavy weather by tying down a portion of the sail to its foot. *Reef points*—short lines sewn to both sides of the sail—are passed under the foot of the sail and tied together with reef knots to hold the reefed portion securely.

5. The Bowline

This well-named "king of knots" is used whenever you want a loop that will not slip: to tie a halyard to a *snap shackle,* (a fitting used in the head of a sail for hoisting it); to secure the *outhaul* to the outhaul fitting for stretching the foot of the sail along the boom; to make a line fast around a mast for towing;

Aptly called "king of knots," bowline provides loop that will not slip, yet is easily untied

and dozens of other places. Even to slip over the head and under the arms of a man overboard, to haul him back to safety!

To tie: With the standing part in one hand, form a bight of the desired size. With your working hand, place the end over the standing part and pinch them together, with your index finger on the end and your thumb underneath the standing part, your hand facing down. Step 2: With your index finger, force the end down and into the bight, at the same time turning your working hand face up. This surrounds the end with a small loop of the standing part. Step 3: Hold this loop with your other hand, and with your working hand lead the end behind the standing part, across in front of it, and down through the small loop. Step 4: Hold the end and the side of the bight together with your working hand and pull the standing part with your other hand to tighten the bowline.

This method works, it never fails. You'll tie it quickly in a squall on the blackest night, where you can't see your hands, and know

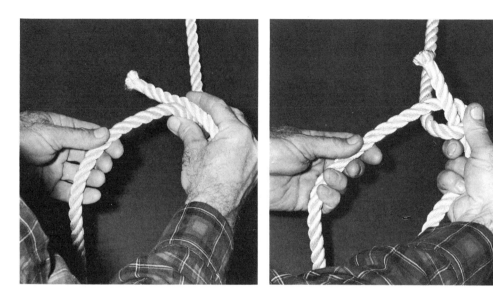

STEP 1—*Pass end over standing part, with thumb underneath, index finger on top, and hand facing down . . .*

STEP 2—*Force end into bight and turn hand up . . .*

STEP 3—*Lead end behind standing part and back through loop . . .*

STEP 4—*Hold end and side of bight and pull on standing part to tighten knot*

BOWLINE COMPLETED—*Loop will not slip*

you've made a loop that will not slip. An eight-year-old can learn it in five minutes. Resists, as you would the devil, anyone who tries to teach you any other way to make the bowline; the other methods are not *certain*. I know—I've used them!

Making fast to a cleat. Halyards and many other lines are usually made fast to cleats. Cleats are also provided on most boats for securing sheets, though as we have seen, many skippers prefer to hold sheets by hand, for faster adjustment as the breeze shifts.

In making fast any line, if possible always use a cleat positioned so that one horn is angled away from the line leading to it, to prevent jamming when the line is made fast

and a strain comes on it. This procedure should be used even with jam cleats, since the cleat is meant to do the jamming, not the line against the cleat.

For an ordinary cleat, a line is secured by leading the end around the horn that isn't angled out, taking a round turn, two cross turns, and finishing off with two more round turns.

To make fast: Pass the end of the line under the first cleat horn (the one not angled out), and take one round turn completely around the cleat, pass under the first horn a second time, up and across the top of the cleat and down under the opposite horn, back up across the top again and down under

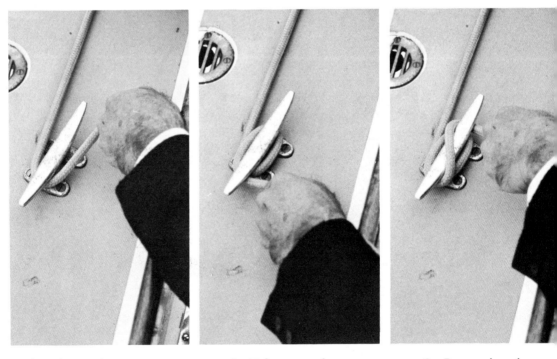

Making fast to cleat, STEP 1—*Lead end around far horn of cleat . . .*

STEP 2—*Take a complete round turn . . .*

STEP 3—*Pass end under far horn again and make first cross turn . . .*

the first horn, then take two round turns completely around the cleat, and pull tight.

If this seems a long-winded process, take heart; in actual practice you'll take less than five seconds to make a line fast this way, though it took you three times as long to read about it!

How to make a locking round turn. Although in making fast halyards it's a good small-boat safety measure to finish with two simple round turns—which can be cast off quickly in an emergency—for docking and other lines not apt to require rapid releasing, it is more secure to finish instead with a locking round turn around one horn of the cleat.

To make fast: The procedure is identical to that described above for securing to a cleat, up to the point where the two cross turns have been completed. Then, instead of taking two round turns, lead the end up and across the cleat and down under the opposite horn, then up again and under itself right at the horn—which makes a locking round turn—and pull tight.

The advantage of this method for making fast is, that any increase in strain on the cleated line tends to lock the final round turn even more securely. Also, there is little likelihood of the locking round turn coming off accidentally, as sometimes happens with simple round turns, especially with new line.

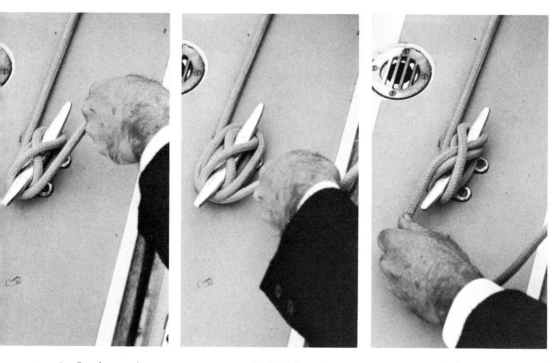

STEP 4—*Lead second cross turn back under far horn once more . . .*

STEP 5—*Finish with two round turns*

STEP 5 (*alternate*)—*Instead of two round turns take third cross turn and lead end back under itself to make locking round turn on horn of cleat*

45

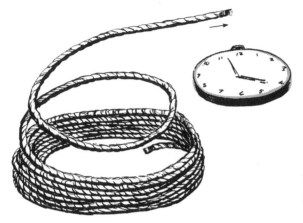

Three-stranded line for small boat use must be coiled clockwise to prevent kinking

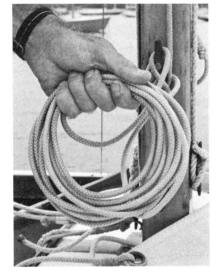

Halyard hitch, STEP 1—*Coil halyard about six inches from cleat . . .*

STEP 2—*Reach through coil and take hold of standing part coming from cleat*

STEP 3—*Bring loop of standing part through coil, twist it, and drop over top of cleat*

6. The Halyard Hitch

When making fast a halyard after hoisting sail, you always have the problem of stowing the extra line represented by the length of the sail's luff; too much, as a rule, to wind around the cleat. Instead of leaving it on deck, where it may get tangled or go overboard, it's smart seamanship to coil it up and hang it on the cleat with a *halyard hitch*.

In the following description of how to make this handy hitch, note that the line *must* be coiled *clockwise,* even by left-handed sailors. This is because most lines in small-boat use are composed of three strands that have been twisted together in a clockwise direction. If the line isn't coiled in the same direction, it will develop kinks and twists, and get *fouled* (tangled) when uncoiling. *Clockwise,* of course, means the way a clock's hands move—to the right.

To tie: After the halyard is made fast to the cleat (as described above), about six inches from the cleat take the standing part in your left hand and with your right hand form a series of uniform, clockwise coils, taking each coil in your left hand as it is made, until all the excess line has been coiled and is in the left hand. Now reach your right hand *through* the coil, take hold of the standing part and bring it *back out* through the coil, form a loop, twist and drop this loop over the cleat. The coil will then hang neatly under the cleat, ready to be cast off and uncoil smoothly when you wish to lower sail.

Summary

1. A properly made knot is one that holds securely, yet is easy to untie.
2. The three parts of a line are the standing part, end, and bight.
3. In tying knots it is good procedure to hold the standing part in your least skillful hand, and work the end with your other hand; e.g., a right-handed person would hold the standing part in his left hand.
4. A **half-hitch** is useful as a temporary fastening to hold the end of a line having no strain on it.
5. Use of the **overhand knot** as a stopper is not recommended if there is time to tie a **Figure-8 knot**.
6. The **Figure-8 knot** is easily tied in the end of a line as a stopper and is easy to untie.
7. A **clove hitch** holds well under constant strain, but may come undone under alternating stress and slack. It can be made more secure by tying in a half-hitch.
8. **Two half-hitches** is a useful knot for tying a line to a ring or around a piling too large for more than one turn of line.
9. The **reef knot** is used to tie together two lines of the same diameter, as, for example, reef points. It will not slip under strain.
10. The **granny knot**, or "false reef knot," is dangerous because it may either slip or jam.
11. The **bowline** provides a quickly tied loop that will not slip.
12. In making fast to a cleat, try to have the line lead so that one horn is angled away from the direction of the standing part.
13. Halyards and sheets (when made fast), are secured to a cleat by a round turn, two cross turns, and two more round turns, pulled tight.
14. Lines not apt to require rapid releasing can be secured to a cleat by a locking round turn, instead of the final two round turns.
15. In making a **halyard hitch**, the coils must be laid up *clockwise*.
16. Checklist of nautical terms:

SAIL TERMS

reefing—Reducing a boat's sail area in heavy weather by tying down a portion of the sail to the foot.

reef points—Short lines attached to both sides of a sail for tying together under the sail's foot in reefing.

snap shackle—A U-shaped metal fitting, closed by a spring-loaded pin, often used to attach the halyard to the head of a sail.

GENERAL

bitts—Vertical wood or metal posts, used for securing lines.

fouled—Tangled.

locking round turn—A round turn in which the end crosses under the standing part, on a cleat, so that it is "locked" in place when a strain comes on the standing part.

mooring—The place where a boat is made fast, which may be at anchor, or alongside a float or dock; also, the act of making a boat fast.

ringbolts—Strong iron or steel rings, bolted to a dock or float, for securing lines.

round turn—A loop in a line in which the end crosses the standing part.

6

Making Sail and

Getting Under Way

FINALLY, WE'RE READY to go sailing! We start with the process known as *making sail,* which includes boarding the boat, getting the sails out of their bag, securing them to mast and boom, and hoisting them. With sails up, casting off from mooring or dock is called *getting under way*.

It takes a lot of words, unfortunately, to spell out each of these steps so that every detail is perfectly plain. But don't let this dampen your ardor. As in making fast to a cleat, you'll be able to do the various acts in a fraction of the time it takes to read about them. In a class of novices, for example, I once had three ten-year-olds who could board a boat at its mooring and regularly make sail and get under way in less than three minutes!

Preliminaries

Before you board. You wouldn't go out, of course, unless you knew it was going to be a good day for sailing—a reminder to get a local weather forecast before going out in *any* boat. You want to sail, not be drenched by a sudden rain squall or caught in a thunderstorm.

Also, you'd not go sailing without having all necessary equipment on the boat (pp. 225-229), including a jug of drinking water, in case the wind should fail. Finally, before going out you'd leave word with some responsible person about when you expected to return.

Boarding a boat. As with most phases of sailing, there's a right way and wrong way to board a boat. One of the commonest mistakes is not to have at least one hand free for holding on; as sailors say, "One hand for yourself and one for the ship." Novices often try to step on board carrying bundles and packages in both hands—shortcut to a dunking.

Another common error is failure to step *into* the boat as close to the centerline as possible. If you step on the gunwale—the outer edge of the boat—you may cause it to heel sharply and so lose your balance. Avoid, too, the example of those who *jump* aboard boats—and sometimes go right through the bottom of a dinghy!

Looking around. Let's assume you're

The Blue Jay *sloop—a Sparkman & Stephens design—is typical, wholesome centerboarder, excellent for beginning sailor*

going sailing in a small centerboard sloop, something like the one in the illustration. This boat is a wholesome, contemporary model, able and seaworthy, ideal in many ways for the beginning sailor.

If the boat you actually sail differs in some details, no matter—the *principles* of sailing are the same. You can still use the procedures described in this and the following chapters.

It makes no difference, for example, whether or not your boat has *lock shackles,* as this one has, for securing her halyards to the sails—you can attach your halyards with bowlines, and many people do. Either way, the lines are properly secured.

Perhaps you sail a *dinghy* or a *catboat,* or some other type that has no jib, making your

sailing that much simpler: in making sail and getting under way, merely omit the actions pertaining to the jib.

In the same way, if you're sailing a keel boat, instead of one with a centerboard, it's also a simpler operation—skip the procedures pertaining to the centerboard.

Note that the various procedures are described, for the most part, as though you were sailing alone, or *single-handed.* This is to avoid the confusion of having to switch back and forth from the skipper's functions to those of the crew. It also has the advantage of equipping you to sail by yourself, by instructing you, the skipper, in every step of making sail and getting under way.

In actual practice it's generally easier to sail a small sloop with two people, one acting as skipper, the other as crew. The skipper, besides taking the tiller and being in command, usually raises and lowers the mainsail, handles the mainsheet, and performs all functions in the after end of the boat—whence, incidentally, the term *afterguard* to denote a boat's officers as opposed to her crew. The crew raises and lowers the centerboard, bails the boat if necessary, and performs all work in the forward end of the boat, including letting go the mooring and, later, picking it up.

Now, let's step aboard. . . .

After you step carefully into the cockpit, take a moment to look around and study the boat's layout.

Looking forward, you note that where the mooring line leads through the bow chock, it is protected from chafe by a *parceling* (wrapping) of heavy canvas, lashed around the line. Then you observe that the *eye* (loop) spliced in the end of the mooring line, has been secured around the cleat on the

foredeck, and is held in place by the *pennant* (light line) of the *pick-up buoy,* the round float with the boat's name on it.

This pennant, which is attached to the eye of the mooring line, has been made fast to the cleat by a round turn, two cross turns, and a locking round turn.

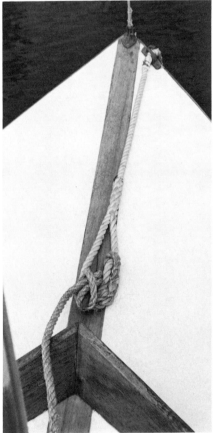

Above: *Use pick-up buoy's pennant to secure mooring eye to bow cleat*

Left: *Permanent mooring line should be protected against chafe where it runs through bow chock. Note smooth metal plate under line to prevent chafe.*

On the starboard side of the mast, near the deck, you see that the end of the main halyard terminates in an overhand knot securing it to a cleat—the main halyard cleat. The jib halyard leads to a similar cleat on the mast's port side—the jib halyard cleat.

The other end of the main halyard, you notice, has been secured to the outhaul fitting on the outboard end of the boom, to keep the line from slapping against the mast. (On boats whose halyards are not long enough to reach the boom end, the halyard may be secured to the gooseneck tack pin.) The jib halyard's other end has been secured below the headstay turnbuckle to keep the line free of the mast. Some boats have shorter jib halyards which must be secured at the mast, with a separate lashing around a shroud to prevent the line slapping against the mast.

Turning your attention amidships, you see the long, vertical housing of the centerboard trunk in the center of the cockpit, with the top of the centerboard visible, ready to be lowered by the centerboard pennant, which is secured to a cleat on top of the trunk.

Making sail

1. Lower the centerboard. At this point, take your first action in making sail—uncleat the centerboard pennant, lower the center-

Right: This boat's main halyard is secured by overhand knot led through cleat; Figure-8 knot is preferable

Above: Secure main halyard shackle to outhaul fitting when boat is at rest, to keep halyard from slapping against mast

Right: Secure jib halyard shackle to headstay fitting when halyard is not in use, to keep it free of mast

board all the way, and make fast the pennant again—with a round turn, two cross turns, and a locking round turn. Lowering the board will help stabilize the boat while you're moving around getting on sail.

2. Rig rudder and tiller. With the centerboard down, you're ready to *rig* (put in place) the rudder and tiller, which have been lying on the cockpit *sole* (floor). On this particular boat, rudder and tiller are bolted together with a hinge that lets the tiller swing vertically, for convenience when rigging the rudder. It's an awkward piece of gear to handle, however, with its only recommendation the fact that rudder and tiller cannot become separated accidentally, unless something breaks. Perhaps this virtue justifies its clumsiness.

An easier type of rig to stow and handle is that of separate rudder and tiller. Assembled for use, a removable locking pin holds the tiller in place to a fitting on the rudder head.

In any event, rig rudder and tiller at the stern by slipping the two rudder *pintles* (pins) into the *gudgeons* (sockets) bolted amidships on the transom. If the rudder has a catch to prevent it lifting out of the gudgeons, be sure to lock the catch.

Note that this boat's *boom crutch* (support) is to one side of the boat's centerline so that the tiller can be rigged without removing the crutch, which stays in place until the mainsail is hoisted.

3. Check the bilge. Now that rudder and tiller are out of the cockpit, you can lift the cockpit floorboards and check the bilge for water. If it has rained, or if the boat has *made water* (leaked) since she was last used, it should be sponged out or pumped dry. Loose water in a boat is dangerous when sailing because it is *uncontrollable* movable ballast. It moves to leeward the instant the boat heels, and increases her angle of heel— the exact opposite of the effect wanted from

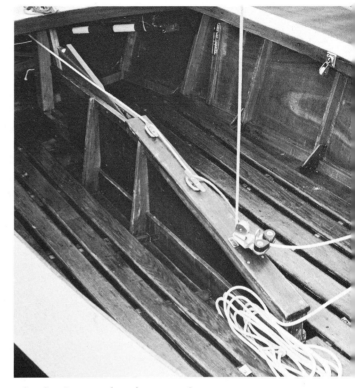

This boat's centerboard pennant leads forward to block under foredeck, then back to jam cleat on top of centerboard trunk, and is made fast to second jam cleat for extra security

Rudder pintles fit into gudgeons on transom to let rudder swing freely

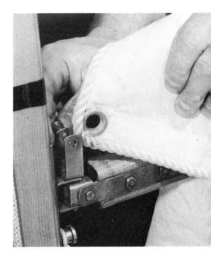

Left: *Jib sheets may be removable or—as here—secured permanently to jib's clew*

Below: *First step in setting mainsail is to secure its tack cringle to gooseneck shackle*

movable ballast. Good seamanship demands a dry bilge at all times.

4. Secure loose gear. If you've brought on board with you any loose gear like picnic hampers, lunch boxes, coolers, etc., secure them belowdeck before making sail. Make them fast so that they'll stay put even if the boat should heel sharply while you're under way.

5. Rig and clear sheets. Before getting the mainsail out of the bag and *bending* (fastening) it on, rig and clear the mainsheet. It has been cleated down to take the slack out of it while the boat has been at rest; now uncleat it, remove any twists or turns that might hinder it from running smoothly through its blocks, and pull some of the excess sheet through the blocks to provide plenty of slack for the boom to swing freely and spill the wind when you hoist the mainsail.

If you fail to do this, and hoist the mainsail with the sheet holding the boom fast, you may not be able to raise the sail fully. Then it may fill with wind before you have it properly set, and start the boat sailing before you're ready to cast off.

The jibsheets are next. On this boat, they are spliced into the jib's clew, so take the jib out of the sailbag and place it on the foredeck, with the clew aft. Now lead the starboard jibsheet back to its amidships block or *fair-lead* (guide fitting), then to its jam cleat on the starboard side of the cockpit. Do the same with the port jibsheet, on the port side, to its block or fair-lead and jam cleat.

6. Clear the halyards. Check both main halyard and jib halyard to be sure they are clear *aloft* (above the deck), with no twists around headstay or shrouds to make them jam when hoisting.

7. Bend on the mainsail. In hoisting sail,

with one exception that will be covered later under getting away from a dock (page 100), you always work from aft to forward, i.e., hoist the mainsail before the jib. This keeps the boat balanced properly, since any wind pressure on the mainsail will tend to force the boat into the wind and spill it. If the jib were hoisted first, any wind pressure on it would tend to drive the boat's head off the wind, possibly starting the boat to sail, making it harder to hoist the mainsail.

Accordingly, pull the mainsail out of its bag, dump it on the cockpit sole, and locate its *headboard*—the reinforcement in the head of the sail to which the halyard makes fast. Now unshackle the main halyard from the outhaul fitting, and secure the shackle to the headboard.

Run your hands down the luff to remove

any twists and locate the metal ring in the tack—the tack *cringle*—for securing the tack to the gooseneck fitting on the boom. Pull the pin out of the jaws of the fitting, insert the cringle between the jaws, and replace the pin to make fast the tack.

Next, run your hands along the foot of the sail to take out any twists and find the cringle at the clew. Feed the slides of the foot onto the boom's sail track starting with the slide nearest the clew cringle and continuing in order until all are on the track. (Some boats have slotted booms, instead of slide track—the bolt rope of the foot is fed into the slot evenly, starting with the clew end of the sail). You're now ready to secure the clew to the outhaul fitting and stretch the foot of the sail.

Cast off the outhaul from its cleat to give

Stretch foot of sail "hand tight" before making outhaul fast

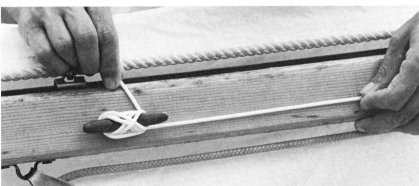

Use locking round turn to secure outhaul to its cleat

slack for the outhaul fitting. Pull the pin from the fitting, stretch the sail's foot out on the boom to the jaws of the fitting, insert the clew cringle between the jaws, and replace the pin to secure the clew. Now, with one hand pulling on the sail and the other pulling on the outhaul, stretch the foot of the sail until it is perfectly straight and fairly taut. You don't have to stretch it bar tight; "hand tight" will do. Make fast the outhaul with a round turn, two cross turns, and a locking round turn, followed by as many round turns as needed to secure ·the spare line.

To fit the luff of the sail on the mast, open the locking latch on the mast's slide track and feed the sail slides of the luff onto the track, starting with the slide nearest the tack cringle and continuing in order until you have all slides on. Close the latch to hold them fast. (On masts with a sail slot instead of slide track, feed the bolt rope of the luff in evenly, starting with the head of the sail.)

8. Insert the battens. With the mainsail made fast, battens are inserted. Unless they

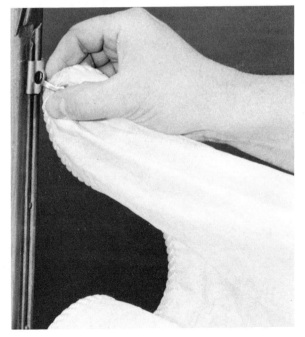

are sewn into a sail, they should always be removed when the sail is stowed in its bag, to avoid one breaking and tearing the sail.

Most sails today are made with the batten pockets so cut that the batten can be slipped in and held securely without being tied. Former practice was to lash each batten in its pocket with a small line through a hole in the batten's end and through two small *grommets* (sewn rings) in the pocket opening, and tying a square knot. In heavy breezes, however, battens often came loose with this method, then might break and tear the sail.

Battens, incidentally, should be perfectly smooth, preferably varnished, and slightly shorter than the pocket, to avoid stretching it. Since the battens are often of different lengths, it saves time in making sail to have each batten numbered by marking pen for its particular pocket.

To insert battens, slide each one fully into its pocket and pull the opening together over it, so the batten won't slip out, even if the sail should shake violently.

9. Slacken the downhaul. If your boat is equipped with a downhaul on the gooseneck for stretching the luff of the mainsail, at this point cast it off. The mainsail is now ready to hoist.

10. Hank on the jib. Before you run up the mainsail, prepare the jib, too, for hoisting. Locate the head—the narrowest corner of the sail—which is fitted with either a cringle or wire eye to take the halyard. In *hanking on* (attaching) the jib, you'll probably find it more convenient to kneel on the foredeck, which is too narrow on most small boats for comfortable standing. Cast off the jib halyard from its cleat, and release the jib halyard shackle from the headstay fitting.

Starting with slide nearest tack cringle, feed luff slides onto mast track in order

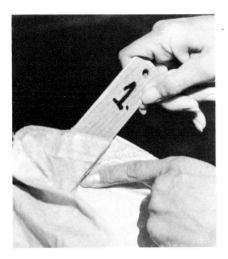

Slip each batten into its correct pocket and pull pocket over to hold it in securely

Attach the shackle to the head cringle, then run your hand down the luff to remove any twists, and locate the tack cringle.

Secure this to the bow fitting with a shackle. Now, starting with the jib *hank* (snap hook) nearest the tack cringle, attach each of the hanks to the headstay in order, being sure none is skipped. The jib is now ready to hoist.

11. Prepare to cast off—decide which tack. While you're still on the foredeck, prepare the mooring line for letting go by casting off the pennant of the pick-up buoy from the foredeck cleat. This leaves the eye of the mooring line still around the cleat, yet easily

Above: *Secure jib halyard shackle to jib head cringle. Note that this boat's halyard is of wire.*

Secure jib tack cringle to headstay fitting with a shackle. Snap hooks are not recommended for this use.

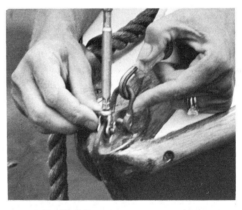

Right: *Jib hanks fitted with end pull pin lock securely and are nonfouling*

lifted to drop overboard when you're finally ready to cast off. The pick-up buoy's pennant, of course, is permanently attached to the eye.

At this time decide whether you will cast off on the starboard or port tack, based on wind direction and the course you want to steer. In making this decision, take a moment to study the local water traffic. Until you've developed some confidence in handling your boat, avoid sailing toward any area where a lot of boats are moving around if you can sail where it's less crowded. Also, if you have a choice, plan always to sail upwind for the first half of your outing. If the breeze should get light later, it's easier to run back to your mooring before the wind than to try to sail upwind against a fading breeze.

12. Hoist the mainsail. Before hoisting, make a final check to be sure the sail is all clear to run up freely, and will not get caught under the deck or snagged on a cleat. Take the end of the main halyard and slowly pull it in, hand over hand, until the mainsail slides up its track to the top, as high as it can go, and *belay* (secure) the halyard, using a round turn, two cross hitches, and two more round turns.

13. Remove and stow the boom crutch. Lift the boom out of its crutch, and let it swing free. Stow the crutch under the deck, out of the way.

14. Coil down the main halyard. With the boom free to swing and spill the wind, finish coiling down the main halyard and hang it over its cleat with a halyard hitch. It is important to make up the halyard right away. In your eagerness to get under way, you may be tempted to let it go until later—*don't.* You'll soon find all that halyard on deck or in the cockpit is a menace to safe footing. Also,

it may get badly fouled and prove an embarrassment if for any reason you should want to lower sail in a hurry. Make it standard practice to coil down each halyard as soon as it is secured.

15. Take up on the downhaul. Pull on the downhaul until a vertical wrinkle develops in the luff. Cleat the downhaul and secure it with a round turn, two cross turns, and a locking round turn.

Let the mainsail swing free, spilling the wind, while you hoist the jib.

16. Hoist the jib. Check to see that the sail is all clear and will go up freely. Also be sure both jibsheets are free from their jam cleats; otherwise you may not be able to hoist the jib all the way up. Take the end of the jib halyard and pull it in smartly, hand over hand, until the luff is stretched tight. Secure the halyard around its cleat, as you did the main halyard, finishing off with a halyard hitch.

Getting under way

Casting off—starboard tack. Take the slack out of the mainsheet to bring the boom under control; take the slack out of the port jibsheet, leaving the starboard jibsheet loose. Lift the mooring eye off the foredeck cleat, remove the mooring line from the bow chock, and pull the pick-up buoy aft *outside the shrouds* on the starboard side, forcing the bow to the left to help the sails fill. As the jib fills, drop the pick-up buoy overboard, trim jibsheet and mainsheet to get the boat moving at speed, and steer your desired course out of the anchorage.

Casting off—port tack. Take the slack out

When casting off, pull pick-up buoy aft outside shrouds to force boat's head off on desired tack

of the mainsheet to bring the boom under control; take the slack out of the starboard jibsheet, leaving the port loose. Lift the mooring eye off its cleat, remove the mooring line from the bow chock and pull the pick-up buoy aft *outside the port shrouds,* forcing the bow off to the right. As the jib fills, drop the pick-up buoy overboard, trim jibsheet and mainsheet to get the boat moving at speed, and steer the desired course out of the anchorage.

Two cautions: (1) As you sail out of the anchorage area, avoid sailing close ahead of any anchored boat—your centerboard or rudder may foul on its mooring line and bring you to a halt. If you should get hung up this way, quickly pull up your centerboard or rudder to clear it. Unless you can clear it promptly and maintain headway, lower your mainsail *at once* to prevent the possibility of an accidental jibe if your bow should swing away from the wind; (2) Avoid sailing too close behind any anchored boat—its wind shadow may rob your sails of their power, causing you to lose headway and maneuverability.

SUMMARY

1. Always get a local weather forecast before going sailing.
2. Have all necessary equipment on board, including drinking water.
3. Leave your estimated return time with someone responsible.
4. In boarding a boat, have at least one hand free for holding.
5. Always step *into* a small sailboat, never on the gunwale; don't jump.
6. A mooring line should be protected against chafe at the bow chock, by parceling.
7. The mooring line's eye should be secured to its cleat with the pennant of the pick-up buoy.
8. In a centerboard boat, the first action in making sail is to lower the centerboard fully.
9. Next, rudder and tiller are rigged.
10. The bilge is then sponged out or pumped dry.
11. Loose gear is secured so it will stay fast on an angle of heel.
12. Then the mainsheet is uncleated, and ample slack given to let the boom swing freely when the mainsail goes up.
13. Port and starboard jibsheets are rigged next.
14. Main and jib halyards are checked aloft to be sure they lead clear.
15. The mainsail is attached to its halyard, the foot is bent to the boom and is stretched with the outhaul, then the luff is bent to the mast.
16. Battens are inserted.
17. The downhaul on the boom is cast off.
18. Before hoisting the mainsail, the jib is attached to its halyard, the jib tack cringle is made fast to the bow fitting, and the jib hanks are secured on the headstay.
19. The pick-up buoy's pennant is uncleated and the decision made whether to start on the port or starboard tack. The first course should be upwind, if possible.
20. Then the mainsail is hoisted, its halyard is secured, and the boom crutch is re-

moved and stowed. The halyard is coiled down with a halyard hitch.
21. A strain is taken on the downhaul to produce a vertical wrinkle in the mainsail's luff, and the downhaul is secured.
21. Next, the jib is raised, and its halyard secured and coiled down with a halyard hitch.
22. In casting off on the starboard tack, the pick-up buoy is hauled aft, outside the shrouds, on the starboard side before being dropped, forcing the bow to the left. Port jibsheet and mainsheet are trimmed to get the boat sailing. Similar procedure, with directions reversed, is used to cast off on the port tack.
23. Sailing out of the anchorage area, care should be taken not to pass close ahead of anchored boats or too close behind them.
24. Checklist of nautical terms:

PARTS OF BOAT

fair-lead—A block or ring that guides a line and keeps it from chafing.

gudgeon—A supporting socket at the stern to hold a rudder's pintle.

pintle—A strong pin attached to the rudder, for insertion in a gudgeon.

sole—The floor of an enclosed space.

DIRECTION

aloft—Above the deck.

SAIL TERMS

cringle—A short piece of line spliced to form an eye around a metal thimble, in the bolt rope of a sail.

grommet—A ring made by laying up a single strand of line around itself three times.

hank—A hook or ring for securing a sail to a stay.

headboard—The reinforcement in the head of a mainsail, to which the halyard is attached.

RUNNING RIGGING

downhaul—A line attached to the gooseneck

to stretch the mainsail's luff; also, a line attached to a sail to lower it quickly.

VERBS

belay—To secure; make fast.

bend—To make fast one piece of gear to another, as a sail to a boom or mast, or a line to another line.

make water—To leak.

rig—To fit or put into place; also (noun), the arrangement of a boat's mast, sails, and rigging.

GENERAL

afterguard—A boat's officers.

boom crutch—A support for a boom when at rest.

catboat, cat rig—A boat with one fore-and-aft sail, set on a single mast stepped near the bow.

dinghy—A small rowboat, often cat-rigged, with a single sail and centerboard.

eye—A loop spliced into a line, rope, or wire.

parceling—Material wrapped or sewn around a line to protect it against chafe.

pennant—A short piece of line or wire, usually fitted at one end with a thimble; also called *pendant;* also, a long, narrow, triangular flag.

pick-up buoy—A float attached by a short pennant to the mooring line eye, for ease in picking up the mooring.

Close-hauled on starboard tack, with sails trimmed to keep boat moving without luffing. Jib halyard should be taken up tightly to minimize luff sagging to leeward.

7

Sailing to Windward
and Tacking

YOU ARE FINALLY FREE TO SAIL and are headed upwind, on the starboard tack. The breeze is brisk, from the north, jib and mainsail are both full, and the boat is moving nicely, with a slight angle of heel to port. You have decided to sail as close as possible to the direction of the wind so as to *make good* (complete) a course to a buoy that lies about a mile north of your mooring.

General considerations

Keeping weight to windward. Except in very light airs, to sail efficiently upwind requires keeping your weight (and that of your crew) more or less to windward, to offset the heeling pressure of the wind on sails and hull. By contrast, in light airs, when there's little heeling pressure, you may even want to put some of your weight to *leeward* to heel the boat down to her sailing lines and give the sails a better draft.

But more often than not the wind pressure tends to heel the boat over farther than she should go to sail her best, and must be countered. You'll quickly learn how far to put your weight to windward to offset different strengths of breeze for your boat.

Reducing leeway with centerboard. Your course directly to windward demands that you sail close-hauled, a point of sailing in which it is important to reduce leeway to a minimum. Since you are trying to convert as much of the wind's energy as possible into forward motion, anything you can do to increase the boat's underwater lateral resistance will reduce her leeway, and make her move to windward more efficiently. Accordingly, if you have not already lowered your centerboard to its full depth, you now uncleat the centerboard pennant, lower the full board, and resecure the pennant.

Trimming the sails. The essence of trimming sails correctly to get the maximum forward drive is to remember two facts: (1) When you point the boat too close to the wind, you lose drive as the wind begins to blow more equally on both sides of the sails and they start to luff, and (2) The same thing happens when you ease sails out too far. So trimming becomes a matter of gauging how close you can steer the boat and trim the sails to keep moving well, without either luffing or *pinching*—sailing so close to the wind that the luff begins to tremble and the boat doesn't foot.

Look aloft to the masthead fly and see

where the wind lies. Then, since you're on the starboard tack, try to steer about 45° to the left of the indicated wind direction. To trim sails, start with the jib, because the trim of the mainsail is affected by the wind coming off the jib. Ease out the port jibsheet until the jib starts to luff, then trim it in just a hair beyond the point where the sail is firm again; keep it trimmed that way.

Whether or not you make the jibsheet fast is a matter of personal preference. If you're sailing single-handed, you may find it more convenient. This is when jam cleats are very handy, since one round turn holds the sheet securely, yet leaves it free to be cast off with a single motion. On ordinary cleats, make sheets fast with a round turn,

This cam cleat holds mainsheet securely yet ready for instant release by lifting end clear of cams

two cross turns, and two round turns pulled tight, *never* with a locking round turn. It's preferable, of course, if you have crew, to have the jibsheet held by hand, to save time in keeping its trim adjusted to the shifting of the breeze.

Follow the same procedure to trim the mainsail. If it is not already luffing as a result of trimming the jib, ease out the mainsheet until the mainsail begins to flutter at the luff, then trim back just enough to make the sail firm again. Most small sailboats become *pinched* (overtrimmed) when sailing close-hauled if the main boom is trimmed in beyond the corner of the transom. Bringing it in closer usually makes the boat straighten up and lose speed; leaving it out farther may keep her from pointing as high as she might.

Wherever your boom trims best, however, make it a practice to keep it there by holding the mainsheet in your hand, *not cleating it.* This is an essential safety precaution since, as we have seen, one of our two emergency measures for spilling excess windpower is to let the sheet run, which we probably would not have time to do if it had to be uncleated. So imperative does the United States Naval Academy consider this practice that the instruction book for midshipmen, *Elementary Seamanship,** has this statement standing by itself at the head of the chapter on Sailing: "It is a Universal Rule in Small Boat Sailing that the Main Sheet should *Never* be Belayed in Any Weather."

Many small-boat sailors modify this doctrine slightly by leading their mainsheet through a spring-loaded fitting called a *cam cleat,* which takes the strain off the sheet yet permits instant easing or trimming as long as the sheet is held.

Apart from safety considerations, you'll

* U.S. Naval Institute, Annapolis, Md.

sail your boat more effectively by holding the mainsheet. With tiller in one hand and mainsheet in the other, you feel the boat's life. Your skill in making sensitive adjustments of the two controls determines her response and performance. This is the thrill and deep satisfaction of helmsmanship.

Testing the wind. When sailing to windward, a good helmsman doesn't trim his sails once and forget them—he keeps testing the wind. He knows that most breezes are constantly changing both direction and force, so he stays alert, trying to work ever closer to the wind. Holding his sheets secure, he edges his tiller gently toward the boom, scanning the luff of his jib for the first sign of a flutter as the boat points higher. He may be able to gain only a few degrees to windward before the jib begins to soften and he has to *fall off* (point away from the wind) to get the sail firm again. But each degree higher he can steer, saves time and distance in making good his windward course.

If his course is already high enough, he tests his sails while holding his course constant. First he eases out the jib an inch or so at a time, to see if it will take extra sheet without luffing. If he can gain a slightly fuller sail without his heading being affected, his speed will probably benefit. Should the jib take more sheet, he repeats the process with the mainsail. For any sailor who takes pride in his helmsmanship, such testing of the wind is important. For the racing sailor it is indispensable if he is to get top performance from his boat.

Tacking to make a windward mark

The wind is blowing from the north, your destination buoy lies north, yet the closest you can sail to the wind is an angle of about 45°, or roughly northwest, as you sail on the starboard tack. It's apparent that you'll never reach the buoy by continuing to sail only on that tack.

However, if you sail *northwest* for ten minutes on the starboard tack, then swing the boat around and sail at an angle of 45° to the wind on the port tack—or *northeast*—for ten minutes, your course made good for the twenty minutes will be *north*. By repeating this zigzag process, you'll soon reach the buoy lying to windward, your *windward mark*. Changing course upwind like this is called *tacking*. It is also known as *going about,* or *coming about.*

The theory of tacking is simple: if you've been sailing on one tack, with the wind coming over that side, you steer into the wind, then beyond its eye so that it now blows

To reach goal directly to windward, sail zigzag course—close-hauled first on one tack; then on other

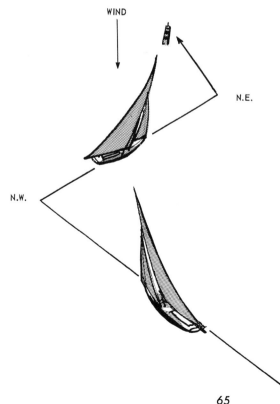

WIND

N.E.

N.W.

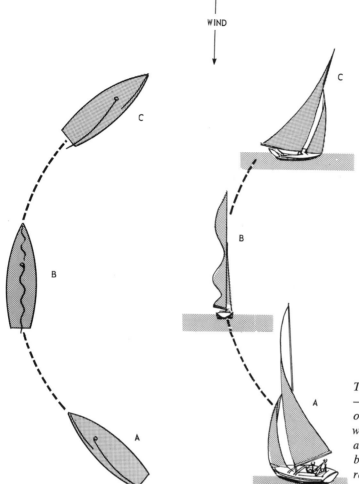

WIND

Tacking, from starboard to port —with boat sailing close-hauled on starboard tack, push tiller toward boom, shoot boat into wind, and before losing headway swing boat over on port tack. Jib is released and reset on new tack as bow swings over.

across the boat from the other side, and start sailing on the other tack. There are, however, several details in tacking that are worthy of your close attention.

How to tack. One essential detail in tacking is to have your boat moving fast enough through the water, with enough momentum to turn against the wind and whatever sea may be running, and swing over on to the new tack.

Let's assume you're still sailing close-hauled on the starboard tack and want to go about on the port tack. First, be sure the boat is footing as fast as possible. When you feel you have enough headway and are ready to go about, prepare to release the port jib-sheet, clear the starboard jibsheet for making up on the new tack, and get ready to shift your weight to the new windward side. If you have crew, these actions are taken when

you give the command of preparation, "Ready about!"

To tack, push your tiller smartly toward the boom and point the boat into the wind, with the command, "Hard alee!" to your crew. As the boat rounds up, the boom comes in toward the boat, and jib and mainsail start luffing. You and your crew shift your weight toward the centerline. For a few seconds you're headed directly into the wind, with sails shaking, as you use some of your headway to steer straight upwind—*into the eye of the wind*—thereby gaining perhaps a boat-length or more of valuable windward distance. (Every 10 feet you gain directly to windward saves more than 14 feet of close-hauled sailing!)

This heading directly into the wind is called *shooting,* and some boats shoot better than others. Keel boats—having deeper, heavier hulls as a rule—shoot better than centerboarders. Dinghies and catamarans (twin-hulled craft), having relatively little weight below the surface to give them momentum, and a great deal of windage above, shoot hardly at all, and have to be spun around on the new tack as quickly as possible. And, of course, wind and sea conditions affect how far a boat can shoot and still have enough headway to swing over on the new tack.

The relative carry of your boat should be determined under a variety of conditions, especially if you keep her on a mooring that must be picked up under sail each time you come in. Practice the shooting out in the clear, away from other boats, by dropping a buoyant cushion over the side as a marker and making practice approaches to it.

Regardless of how far your boat shoots to windward, in our example here, before your forward motion and steerageway are lost, push your tiller smoothly to the left to swing the boat's bow through the eye of the wind and off to the right. This brings the wind **over your port bow, and causes the jib to fill**

BOB GRIESER

Wait until jib is aback before releasing port jibsheet and making up starboard jibsheet on new tack

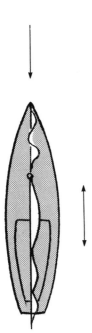

When caught in irons, your headway is gone . . .

Without headway, you cannot steer, and may be hit by knockdown puff . . .

on the wrong side, or *aback*. Now release the port jibsheet to let the jib swing over to starboard, trim the starboard jibsheet, and as the main boom swings across to the starboard side, settle your weight to windward (the port side), and start sailing close-hauled on the port tack.

The hazard of being "in irons." The key to successful tacking lies in estimating how far to shoot your boat into the wind before swinging over on the new tack. If you swing too early, you lose a lot of windward distance that your boat's momentum would have given you free. But if you wait too long, and use up too much headway, you may *miss*

stays—not have enough momentum to carry you through the eye of the wind—and be forced to fall back on the old tack.

Even worse than missing stays, though, is getting caught *in irons*. This is the situation when you've lost all headway, are dead in the water, and can neither swing on to the new tack nor fall back on the old. Being caught in irons is embarrassing at any time, but in heavy weather may be dangerous. When you no longer have steerageway, you are at the mercy of any violent puff of wind, because you cannot spill its pressure by steering into it. Unless you take prompt corrective action, the boat will start drifting backward, gathering sternway, and leaving you vulnerable to being *knocked down* (blown over).

To get out of irons, back jib promptly, holding clew well out to windward until bow swings over on new course

In this situation, your best procedure is to *back the jib* promptly by slacking off both jibsheets and holding the clew of the jib well out to windward on one side, to force the bow off the wind, to leeward. As soon as the bow swings in the desired direction, trim the jibsheet on the leeward side and sail the boat so as to pick up speed again. With speed, you regain maneuverability.

When you are caught in irons and have sternway, it helps to *shift the rudder,* that is, reverse your helm. If, for example, you have been caught in irons trying to go from starboard tack to port tack, with your tiller pushed well over to the left, quickly pull your tiller well over to the right. This will send your rudder to the left, and as the boat drifts backward, the pressure against the blade will help force the bow to the right, especially if, at the same time, you have the jib backed to port.

From this brief discussion you can see that when tacking in a heavy breeze, or when you have any doubt about how far your boat can safely shoot without losing headway, it's better to swing on to the new tack a little too soon rather than too late. You'll never get caught in irons if you keep your boat moving ahead fast enough to create water pressure for your rudder to work against.

Laying the mark. As you tack back and forth toward your windward goal, you soon make enough progress to feel your next tack will bring you to the buoy. The question is, At what point should you make this final tack to be certain of *laying the mark*—that is, sailing past the buoy, slightly to windward of it?

Since your boat tacks through an arc of about 90°—in going from close-hauled on one tack to close-hauled on the other—you should wait until the buoy bears at least 90° from ahead, or abeam, before thinking of the final tack. Generally it's better to have the mark bearing slightly *abaft* (aft of) *the beam* before trying to lay it. For although you may

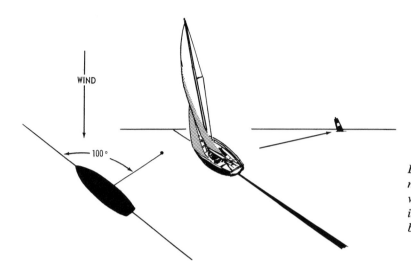

WIND

100°

Before trying to lay a mark when going to windward, wait until it is about 10° abaft the beam

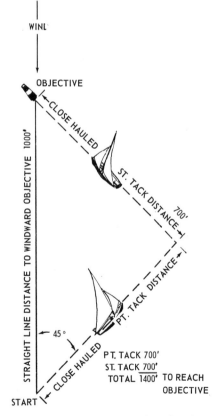

WIND

OBJECTIVE

CLOSE HAULED

ST. TACK DISTANCE

700'

PT. TACK DISTANCE

STRAIGHT LINE DISTANCE TO WINDWARD OBJECTIVE 1000'

45°

CLOSE HAULED

PT. TACK 700'
ST. TACK 700'
TOTAL 1400' TO REACH
OBJECTIVE

START

Assuming a boat can sail within four points (45°) of wind, to make 1000 feet directly to windward, she must sail a total of 1400 feet—or 14 feet of close-hauled sailing for each 10 feet of windward distance

be able to tack through an arc of about 90° under the most favorable conditions, wind and sea will usually cause your boat to make some leeway and add a number of degrees to your tacking arc.

By waiting until the mark is about 10° past abeam, depending on wind and sea conditions, you'll be more certain of arriving at the buoy on its weather side and not be forced to sail below it. Laying a course this way, to pass to weather of a mark rather than to leeward, is good seamanship; it gives you some insurance against being *headed*— getting a shift of the wind that might force you to sail lower before reaching the mark.

The importance of windward distance. What altitude is to an airplane pilot, windward distance is to the sailor—something to be jealously hoarded and frugally dispensed. In going to windward, as we have noted, it takes more than 14 feet of close-hauled sailing to make good 10 feet toward your objective. So every foot of windward distance is 40 per cent more valuable than distance across wind or downwind, when your goal lies to windward.

Once you have gained enough windward distance to be comfortably to weather of your mark, you can sail directly for it, without further tacking. But until that point is reached, only the careless sailor would relax his effort to use every possible puff and all his skill to sail closer to the wind. The prudent sailor even continues to sail a little high of his mark until he has reached a point where nothing but a major shift of the breeze could keep him from reaching his objective. Not until then does he ease sheets and *bear off* (sail more free).

Summary

1. When sailing to windward, weight must usually be kept to windward, though in very light airs it may be needed to *leeward* to get the boat down to her sailing lines.
2. When sailing close-hauled, full centerboard is used.
3. To trim sails when close-hauled, the boat should be pointed about 45° off the wind and the jib trimmed first, then the mainsail.
4. To trim a sail, ease its sheet until the sail begins to luff, then trim back slightly till the sail is firm again, and hold it. Overtrimming results in pinching, and reduces a boat's speed and performance.
5. A sheet is made fast to an ordinary cleat with a round turn, two cross turns, and two round turns pulled tight, *never* with a locking round turn.
6. Most small-boat skippers prefer not to cleat any sheets. As a basic safety measure, the mainsheet should not be cleated, though cam cleats are safe provided the sheet is still held in hand for instant easing or trimming.
7. When sailing close-hauled, the main boom is trimmed approximately over the corner of the transom.
8. Sailing to windward, a good helmsman keeps testing the breeze by pointing higher or by easing sheets.
9. By tacking, it is possible to make good a course directly to windward.
10. In tacking, it is essential to have enough headway to carry the boat through the eye of the wind and over to the new tack.
11. The command of preparation for tacking is "Ready about!"
12. The command of execution for tacking is "Hard alee!" given by the skipper as he pushes the tiller to leeward, toward the boom.
13. In tacking, if the breeze and sea are not heavy, some of the boat's headway should be used to shoot straight upwind.
14. Keel boats shoot better than centerboarders, and light craft shoot hardly at all. A boat that shoots poorly should be spun from one tack to the other as quickly as possible.
15. When shooting, enough momentum should be maintained to swing the boat over to the new tack.
16. In tacking, the jibsheet for the old tack is not released until the jib is aback; it is then cast off and the sail trimmed on the new tack by the other jibsheet.
17. When a boat is caught in irons and begins to make sternway, she may be knocked down by a violent puff because she cannot turn into it.
18. The fastest way to get a boat out of irons is to back the jib.
19. When in irons, with sternway, another measure is to shift the rudder.
20. When tacking to lay a mark to windward, wait until the mark bears about 100° from dead ahead before tacking.
21. It is good procedure to steer high of a weather mark.
22. It takes more than 14 feet of sailing close-hauled to make good 10 feet of distance directly to windward.
23. Checklist of nautical terms:

DIRECTIONS

abaft—aft of.
abaft the beam—Aft of abeam; more than 90° from dead ahead.

SAILING TERMS

back the jib—To hold the jib's clew out to

windward, causing it to fill on the wrong side, so as to force the bow over in the opposite direction.

bear off—To point the boat away from the wind; fall off.

coming about—Changing tacks by bringing the bow into and across the wind.

fall off—To point the bow away from the wind; bear off.

going about—Coming about; tacking.

"Hard alee!"—Command of execution in tacking, when the tiller is pushed to leeward to point the boat into the wind.

in irons—Caught without steerageway in tacking, unable to swing either on to the new tack or back on the old.

knocked down—Blown over; knocked flat.

lay a mark—To fetch or arrive at an objective to windward.

make good—To actually complete.

miss stays—To fail completion of a tack because of insufficient headway, and being forced back on to the old tack.

"Ready about!"—Command of preparation in tacking.

tacking—Changing tacks by bringing the bow into and across the wind so that it blows on the boat's other side; coming about; going about.

VERBS

pinch—Either to steer a boat so close to the wind that she virtually stands still, or to overtrim her sails and produce the same effect.

weather—To pass to windward of.

GENERAL

cam cleat—A spring-loaded fitting that holds a sheet securely yet permits instant trimming or easing if the end of the sheet is held in hand.

shift the rudder—To send the rudder to the opposite side.

weather mark—A buoy or other turning point to windward.

windward mark—In racing, the turning point that lies to windward.

8

Reaching

SAILING ACROSS THE WIND is *reaching*, also called *running free* under the *Inland Navigation Rules* (page 145). With the wind anywhere between five points (56¼°) aft of the bow and two points (22½°) forward of the stern, it is the fastest point of sailing.

Kinds of reaches. When you sail across the wind at an angle just short of being close-hauled, you are sailing a *close reach*. With the wind more nearly abeam or on the beam, your point of sailing is called a *beam reach*. And with the wind abaft the beam, but not so far aft as to come over the quarter, it's a *broad reach*.

Let's assume that after sailing to windward close-hauled, in a series of starboard and port tacks, you finally make your weather mark on the port tack and want to sail to another buoy that lies some distance off to your right, about halfway between dead ahead and abeam, or *broad on the starboard bow*.

Since the course is no longer so nearly upwind, some of the boat's leeway now represents useful distance toward your objective; hence you no longer need to minimize leeway by using full centerboard. As you point the bow slightly high of this second

buoy and ease sheets a trifle for the new course, you should also raise the centerboard about one-quarter. You'll notice the boat's speed pick up as she feels the greater power from the eased sheets, and starts to take the waves at an easier angle.

Also, with the boat presenting herself more broadly to the wind, you'll experience greater rolling motion from the sea, and find you must keep your weight well out to windward to offset both it and the increased heeling pressure of the wind.

This is glorious sailing! At the same time, it gives you the greatest variety of possibilities for a change of course without tacking. When you are sailing toward your objective on a reach, for example, if the wind should shift to come more ahead, you can always *sharpen up* (trim sheets and point higher) to sail close-hauled on the same tack, with full centerboard down, and still make your destination. Or, if the wind should shift the other way, and come from astern, you can ease sheets until you are before it, and run for your mark. No other point of sailing offers so wide a range of choices without tacking.

This makes reaching especially good for

In reaching, you sail across wind, with angle changing from close *to* beam *to* broad *as you bring wind farther aft*

WIND

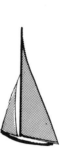

WIND

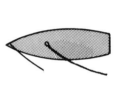

CLOSE REACH   BEAM REACH   BROAD

5 POINTS (56¼°)
CLOSE-HAULED

CLOSE HAULED

CLOSE REACH

WIND

BEAM REACH

RUNNING FREE
(REACHING)

BROAD REACH

RUNNING

2 POINTS (22½°)
WIND AFT
(RUNNING)

practice when you are learning to sail. By choosing an objective that lies across the wind from your starting place, as you sail toward it you can concentrate on the effect of different adjustments of the sheets, tiller, and centerboard. Alternately you can *harden up* (sail closer to the wind), and *run off* (sail before the wind), gaining confidence and familiarity with your craft from the repeated adjustments for each point of sailing.

Tacking on a reach. If you should want to tack while sailing on a reach, it is important first to trim sheets and sharpen up until the boat is sailing close-hauled. Unless you do, and try to head the boat directly into the wind from a reach, with sheets eased and

Reaching provides good practice in sailing because of many alternative courses that can be sailed without tacking

boom out, you may heel the boat so far over that her boom will drag in the water, robbing your rudder of control, and causing water to pour over the lee rail into the cockpit. You may also lose so much headway in rounding up directly from a reach that you miss stays or get caught in irons.

So make it standard procedure in tacking from a reach to sail close-hauled a short distance before coming about. The transition should be made smoothly to maintain full headway, with sheets trimmed in gradually and the boat pointed higher a few degrees at a time. In general, sudden trimming of sheets and abrupt tiller movements are marks of the novice. Under normal sailing conditions a boat, like a horse, responds better to deliberate, unhurried handling.

Summary

1. Reaching (running free) is the fastest point of sailing.
2. In reaching, some leeway is useful, so about one-quarter less centerboard is used for a close reach, and one-half for a beam or broad reach.
3. Sheets are eased slightly for close-reaching, and more for beam and broad reaches.
4. The rolling motion of the waves is more evident when reaching, and weight must be kept well to windward.
5. Of all points of sailing, reaching offers the widest range of sailing angles without tacking. Hence, the beginning sailor has no better practice than reaching toward a mark, alternately to sharpen up and run off, familiarizing himself with the relationship of sheets, tiller, and centerboard on each point of sailing.
6. In tacking from a reach, it is important first to sail close-hauled, and the change from reach to close-hauled should be made smoothly, with gradual movements of the tiller and trimming of sheets. Abrupt tiller movements and jerking of sheets mark the novice.
7. Checklist of nautical terms:

DIRECTION

broad on the bow (starboard, port)—Bearing halfway from dead ahead to abeam.

SAILING TERMS

beam reach—A point of sailing when the wind is abeam or nearly abeam.
broad reach—Sailing with the wind well abaft the beam, but not yet over the quarter.
close reach—A point of sailing between close-hauled and a beam reach.
harden up—To trim sheets and sail closer to the wind; sharpen up.
running free—reaching, under *Inland Navigation Rules.*
run off—To ease sheets and run before the wind.
sharpen up—To trim sheets and sail closer to the wind; harden up.

9

Sailing Downwind and Jibing

SAILING DOWNWIND is *running*—not to be confused with *running free* (page 145). A sailboat is running when her wind is aft, from any direction within two points (22½°) of dead astern on either side. Changing course downwind by pointing the stern into and past the eye of the wind, to bring it on the other side, is *jibing*—the opposite of tacking. Running with the wind aft on the starboard side is sailing on the *starboard jibe*; with the wind aft on the port side, is sailing on the *port jibe*.

Running

Running may seem to be the simplest point of sailing, but in a strong wind it can, in fact, be the most difficult. One reason is the constant danger of an accidental jibe. This is a subject worth reviewing.

In running, you try to capture the wind's push by having it blow squarely against your sail. The square-rigged Viking ship did this by swinging its yard to keep the great square sail at right angles to the wind. However, to get a triangular, fore-and-aft mainsail at right angles to the wind, you must ease sheets until the boom is well out from the boat on

one side, with the wind coming across the stern from the other.

This is the nub of the problem, because a square sail and a fore-and-aft sail react quite differently if the breeze happens to shift suddenly from one side of the stern to the opposite side, as it might when running in squally weather, or before a heavy sea that caused the stern to *yaw* (swing wildly off course).

With the square sail, such a sudden change in the direction of the wind involves only a simple slackening and retrimming of sheets and braces to swing the sail at right angles to the new direction. But the fore-and-aft sail, caught by an accidental jibe, swings violently across the boat the instant the breeze stops blowing into it from the opposite side and blows on the side where it is set. And the boom sweeps across the deck like a club, endangering the crew and the safety of the boat by its ability to break a mast or even cause a capsize.

Broaching to of the boat after the jibe is one other possible result. This is a slewing around, broadside to wind and sea, as the bow of the boat completes a 180° turn back into the wind, after the boom has swung over. Broaching to can capsize a boat or fill it with water.

It can be caused by carrying too much sail before the wind, as well as by an accidental jibe. In effect, it is like a case of weather helm that has gotten out of control —the boat refuses to answer her helmsman's efforts to hold her bow off the wind, and rounds up sharply in spite of him. It is an even worse situation than trying to tack from a reach, because here the boom is farther out from the boat, and the rounding up happens so fast there is no time to trim it in.

As a result, the boom drags in the water, along with the mainsail, and the combined weight tends to pull the boat over on its side. Wind and sea pushing against the boat broadside help overturn her.

The first defense against broaching to when running, is to *shorten sail*—to reef or otherwise reduce sail area—at once if the boat starts to require unnaturally strong

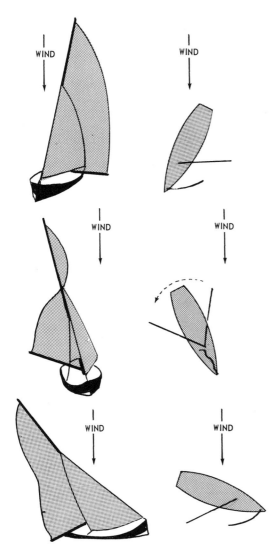

In running, ease out main boom until sail is at right angles to wind coming across boat's opposite quarter

An accidental jibe occurs when wind suddenly blows on same side where mainsail is set and boom swings violently across boat

Broaching to heels boat sharply over, broadside to wind; can cause her to fill or capsize

weather helm, an indication that she wants to round to. A second defense is to move all weight well aft and raise the centerboard almost all the way up, to bring the Center of Lateral Resistance as far aft as possible. Another defense is to tow a bucket astern, or a long bight of anchor line to act as a drag. But above all, stay alert on the helm, to check instantly every tendency of the boat to round up. If you mind your helm as you would a horse that wants to run away, she'll never get a proper start for broaching to. But once she gets going, she'll go all the way.

How to prevent an accidental jibe. The importance of knowing exactly where the wind is at all times, when running, cannot be overemphasized. Keep an eye on the masthead fly, or on light ribbons tied to the shrouds about shoulder-high, as wind indicators. Develop a sensitivity to how the wind blows on the side and back of your neck. And especially, *watch the jib*—it gives the first indication of when you are beginning to sail *by the lee* (with the wind and sails on the same side), by lifting from the side where it is set and flopping over to the other side.

When any of these signs report that the wind is coming too far astern, the surest way to avoid the dangers described above is to push the tiller *toward the boom* and turn the boat to bring the wind well over the quarter opposite to the boom, particularly if running before a heavy sea. In short, don't try to run directly downwind, with the wind dead aft. The closer you bring your stern to the direction of the wind and sea, the smaller your margin of safety against an accidental jibe.

For example, the experience of Sumner A. Long's 57-foot aluminum yawl *Ondine,* while running directly before a heavy wind and sea in the 1963 Transatlantic Race, is instructive.

A breaking sea got under *Ondine's* stern [wrote crewman Norris D. Hoyt in his account

of the race] when the boat was making 18 knots on a surfing run and swung her around in a broach that lifted the rudder out of the water as though a giant had picked the whole boat up by the stern. Then a cross sea swung her 160° in the other direction in a full jibe. The boom slammed inboard, tagged the backstay and jackknifed up it to a 70° angle.*

Only the fact that *Ondine* was built so enormously strong saved her from crippling damage; nothing carried away, and they went on to win the race. But their tactic of running dead off before a heavy sea and wind of nearly gale force is not recommended for beginning sailors.

How to control rolling. Running before a big sea sometimes causes a boat to roll from side to side so deeply that she threatens to dip her boom in the water. This is an accident emphatically to be avoided. The drag of the submerged boom end can take control away from the rudder and cause the boat to spin off the wind in an accidental jibe, followed by broaching to. For this reason, many experienced sailors lower full centerboard when running in heavy weather, to dampen the boat's rolling motion by increasing her lateral resistance. It also helps her resist the tendency of the sea to make her yaw.

An additional precaution is to break up the rhythm of the rolling by careful use of the tiller. As the boat starts to swing deeply to one side, check the swing with the tiller. When she responds, steer her on a straight course. Try to avoid large movements of the tiller, since they bring correspondingly large movements of the rudder and accentuate the rhythm of swinging. Alertness at the helm is the key to safe running in a heavy sea. Whence, it follows, no one should be put on the tiller who is tired or slow in his reactions.

* *Sports Illustrated,* August 5, 1963.

The boom vang—a line from underside of boom to low point forward—serves to steady boom and hold it down to present maximum sail area when running before wind

Jibing

The controlled jibe. Having started our discussion of sailing downwind with a full treatment of its potential problems, we're better equipped to appreciate and learn how to enjoy its very real pleasures. The controlled jibe is one of them.

Simply, it's the opposite of a tack—instead of changing course in an upwind direction by bringing your bow into the wind's eye and through it, you change course downwind by bringing your stern into the eye of the wind and past it, to the other jibe.

In tacking, it is essential that the boom be trimmed in close-hauled before putting the bow into the wind; in jibing, it is *imperative* that the boom be trimmed exactly amidships, on the centerline, when the stern is brought into the wind.

"Stand by to jibe!" is the command of preparation for a controlled jibe. The main-

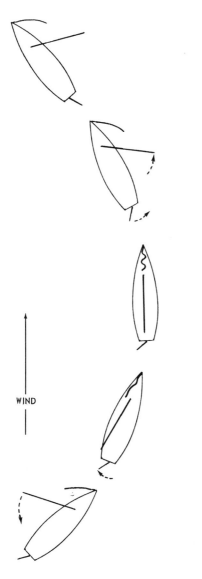

WIND

This sketch shows steps in controlled jibe, in which secret is to have boom amidships exactly when stern is in wind's eye, then paying out sheet smoothly as you head boat on new course

sheet is made ready for trimming in to bring the boom amidships when the jibe begins, jibsheets are cleared to be ready for reversing when the jibe is completed. In running, the weight distribution is kept aft of amidships, with little angle of heel, so weight need not be shifted in jibing.

"Jibe-ho!" is the command of execution, at which the mainsheet is trimmed in slowly while the boat is gradually steered more downwind, and the jib is *let fly* (cast off). Trimming of the mainsheet and the steering should be worked together and so timed that you have your boom amidships as the wind comes over the stern from dead aft.

At this point it's a good idea to take a round turn with the mainsheet on an ordinary cleat to prevent it getting away when the sail fills on the opposite jibe, and the sheet must be *paid out* (eased off) for the new course. With boom amidships and the wind dead aft, carefully move your tiller to head the boat toward the new course, sending the stern through the eye of the wind to bring it over the other side. This causes the boom and sail to flop gently across the boat's centerline, opposite to the side from which the wind is now blowing.

Now steer a new course that will bring the wind well over the quarter opposite to the boom, paying out mainsheet steadily and smoothly as you approach the course, to let the boom swing full away from the boat, with the sail at right angles to the breeze. Trim the leeward jibsheet and sail the new course.

Because timing is so important in working your tiller and boom together, practice the routine of jibing in light airs at first—when the wind action is gentler and mistakes may be made without hazard—before attempting to jibe in stronger breezes. Properly executed, the controlled jibe is a great timesaver when sailing downwind—it enables you to change course without having to head your boat back into the wind, and tacking. The operation, however, demands good control of your boat at all times.

When not to jibe. When in doubt, because of heavy weather or rough seas, don't attempt to jibe. Change course by the longer method of going about, bringing your bow around into the wind and tacking, then bearing off to make the new course.

Since it will be blowing hard when you use this alternative, execute it by trimming sheets carefully to sail from a run, to a broad reach, to a beam reach, to a close reach, and then close-hauled, before tacking. The secret is to coordinate tiller action and sail trim to take the boat successively through each point of sailing, back into the wind.

Avoid, on the one hand, swinging the bow around so rapidly into the wind that the boom is still well out from the boat and drags in the water, with all the dangers of broaching to. And on the other, avoid trimming the boom so fast that you have it in flat while the boat is still more or less broadside to the wind, a sure invitation to a capsize.

Making a mark directly downwind. As you gain experience in sailing, and confidence in handling a boat, you'll find yourself able to sail more directly downwind without danger of jibing accidentally. In the beginning, however, and under heavy wind and sea conditions even after you are experienced, you will find it safer to run for a mark to leeward on a zigzag course similar to one sailed in making a windward mark, except that the zigs and zags are made by bringing your stern into the wind each time, in a series of controlled jibes.

The zigzag course has another advantage besides safety over the straight downwind course, an advantage of particular interest to racing sailors—though longer, it may take less time to sail. Most boats sail faster with the wind at an angle across the stern than with it dead aft.

One reason is, when sailing directly before the wind, the jib is practically useless and is usually sheeted in flat on the same side as the boom. Blanketed from the wind by the mainsail, it hangs forward, waving loosely like so much drying laundry. As soon as you sail a bit higher, however, the jib comes out of the mainsail's wind shadow and begins to fill again, adding its power to the boat.

Another factor favoring a zigzag course downwind, especially in light airs, is the possibility of a boat running ahead of her wind when sailing dead off. This is quite evident when sailing with a *spinnaker,* a large parachute-shaped headsail designed for running. Frequently a boat sailing under spinnaker in light air, with the wind coming over her

Tacking downwind— sailing zigzag course by series of controlled jibes —is safe and fast way to fetch mark to leeward

quarter, will beat a boat of the same class with an identical sail but with the wind astern, because the second boat's spinnaker collapses and loses its power periodically as the boat runs ahead of her wind.

A final consideration in running at an angle off the wind, is comfort. When you run directly with the wind, you minimize any cooling effect the breeze might have. This is painfully evident when the breeze is light to start with, as it often is in the summer on such waters as Long Island Sound and Chesapeake Bay. If your downwind course happens to place the sun anywhere aft of abeam, so that you get no shade from the mainsail, running dead off can be a most uncomfortable point of sailing. You sit in the cockpit in the sun's glare and broil.

Under these conditions, sailing a zigzag course gives some slight relief by bringing the wind diagonally across the stern, instead of dead aft, and lets you feel the breeze. It's not quite the equivalent of a long, cool drink but, as the old lady said, " 'Tis better than a poke in the eye with a sharp stick."

The converse holds, of course, for cold weather sailing. Then, you might want to sail as nearly before the wind as possible to keep warm. Usually, though, you're dressed for the weather and will probably prefer the zigzag course for its other advantages.

Use of the boom vang. The small boat in the photograph carries a *boom vang*—a line that runs from the underside of the boom to the mast at deck level. This serves to hold the boom down and thereby present maximum sail area when running before the wind.

"Winging out" the jib. Experienced sailors sometimes *wing out* the jib on the opposite side from the mainsail, to get it to draw when running dead off. Using a *whisker pole*—a slender staff with a fitting at one end to engage the clew of the jib, and one at the other to brace the pole against the mast—the clew is held out from the boat, with a strain kept on the jibsheet to hold the whisker pole firmly in place. This is also known as sailing *wing and wing.* "Winging out" makes the jib draw, but removes its ability to warn of sailing by the lee. Hence, in the interest of safety, novice sailors should defer using the maneuver until they are no longer novices.

Summary

1. Running before the wind has three hazards in strong breezes—
   a. The accidental jibe.
   b. Broaching to.
   c. Rolling.
2. **The accidental jibe** is best avoided by steering a course that keeps the wind well over the quarter opposite to the boom. The jib gives the first warning of sailing by the lee when it lifts from the side where it is set and swings past the centerline to the other side.
3. **Broaching to** can be avoided by shortening sail, by moving weight aft, by raising the centerboard, by towing a bucket or other drag, and above all, by alert helmsmanship.
4. **Rolling the boom under** can be prevented by lowering full centerboard and by skillful use of the helm to break the rhythm of rolling.
5. **The controlled jibe** is used to change course downwind.
6. In the controlled jibe, it is *imperative* that the main boom be trimmed exactly amidships, on the centerline, at the moment when the stern is directly into the wind.
7. Jibing should not be attempted under conditions when loss of control might be dangerous.
8. To change course downwind without jibing, the boat must be *put about* (tacked) by sailing successively through the various points of sailing.
9. To make a mark that lies directly downwind, it is safer and usually faster to sail

a zigzag course with a series of controlled jibes.

10. In running dead off, any cooling effect of the breeze is reduced.

11. "Winging out" the jib when running should be avoided by novices.

12. Checklist of nautical terms:

SAIL TERMS

spinnaker—A large-area racing sail, shaped like a three-sided parachute, set ahead of the boat when sailing off the wind.

SAILING TERMS

by the lee—Running with the wind on the same side as the main boom.

controlled jibe—Changing course downwind by bringing the stern into and past the eye of the wind, with boom under control.

"Jibe-ho!"—Command of execution for a controlled jibe.

let fly—To cast a sheet off quickly.

port jibe—Running with the wind aft to port and main boom out to starboard.

put about—To change course by tacking.

shorten sail—To reduce sail area by reefing or by setting fewer or smaller sails.

"Stand by to jibe!"—Command of preparation for a controlled jibe.

starboard jibe—Running with the wind aft to starboard and main boom out to port.

wing and wing—Running with jib set on one side and mainsail on the other.

wing out—To set the jib on the opposite side from the main boom.

wung out—When the jib is set on the opposite side from the main boom.

VERBS

jibe—To change course by bringing the stern into the eye of the wind and past it, to make it blow from the other side.

yaw—To swing wildly off course when running.

GENERAL

broaching to—To slew around broadside to wind and sea while running.

carry away—To break or part.

pay out—To ease off or give more slack.

vang—A line rigged to hold down or steady a boom.

whisker pole—A pole used to hold the jib out on the opposite side from the main boom when running dead before the wind.

10

Picking Up a Mooring and Securing the Boat

WHEN YOU THINK of picking up a mooring, think of parking a car in a garage—you approach the opening slowly, with minimum speed, ease into place, and stop. Yet people who wouldn't dream of driving into a garage at speed and slamming on the brakes to keep from going through the wall, often try to pick up a mooring with their boat making full headway, sailing across the wind or downwind.

If they approach the mooring on a reach and the man on the foredeck is successful in his attempt to snatch the pick-up buoy as the boat flashes by it, he either stretches his arms an inch or two trying to hold it or has the buoy dragged from his hand by the boat's forward momentum. Sometimes, by a miracle, he manages to secure the pennant of the pick-up buoy over the foredeck cleat; then all hell breaks loose.

The boat may have so much headway that she stretches out her mooring line and actually drags the mooring along before it pulls her to a stop unless, in the meantime, she has rammed into a nearby boat. Or if the mooring is a heavy one, when the mooring line has reached the limit of its stretch, the boat may fetch up like a yo-yo and heel sharply

over as her bow comes around into the wind. Or the foredeck cleat may pull out.

The skipper who approaches his mooring on a run has even more action. *His* foredeck man has the same problem of holding on to the pick-up buoy as his friend on the reaching approach, with the added possibility of being tossed overboard. For if he succeeds in securing the pick-up buoy's pennant to the foredeck cleat, unless his skipper has managed to get the mainsail down (highly unlikely!), the chances are the boat will broach to when she fetches up on the stretched-out mooring line.

From this little drama in two acts, it's easy to draw the moral: *Always approach your mooring so that when you arrive at the pick-up buoy your boat has little or no headway.*

When you dropped your mooring to start sailing, back on page 58, your bow was headed upwind, and your first point of sailing was to windward, close-hauled. Unless you have an unusual *current* (underwater stream) running through your anchorage, this same point of sailing is used when you pick up your mooring, which should lie to windward as you approach it.

Have little or no headway on your boat when you reach your pick-up buoy

Even without the unhappy examples above, the reason for an upwind approach should be reasonably clear, now that you know about shooting a boat into the wind to kill her headway. When your close-hauled course brings you directly to leeward of your mooring, near enough so that you can shoot into the wind and fetch the pick-up buoy with a *little* headway to spare, you're ready to push your tiller smartly toward the boom and make the pick-up. This brief summary gives you the big picture, but there are a few details of preparation to make before shooting for the pick-up.

Picking up a mooring

Look around as you approach the mooring area. While still some distance away, locate your pick-up buoy and see whether or not it is clear and free to be picked up. Or has the wind moved other boats over near your mooring, so that you have less maneuvering room than when you left? If it seems more crowded, sail past the mooring once or twice to see the best way to come up to it. Don't be in a hurry.

Also, notice how other sailboats are lying and whether or not they are heading into the wind. Usually they will be. If they are not, there may be a current running through the anchorage, strong enough to offset the wind's effect. In such a case, as you approach your mooring you will have to head *up current* instead of upwind, using the current's flow against the boat's underbody to kill your forward motion in the same way shooting into the wind stops the boat.

Strike (remove) the jib. Unless you are sailing alone, or the wind is very light and you are trying to hoard every possible ounce of energy to get back home, the jib is not needed for picking up your mooring, and is better *struck* (removed) at this point, to clear

the foredeck. Your command to your crew can be *"Strike the jib!"*

To lower the jib, clear its coiled halyard so that it will run freely when released. Hold the uncleated leeward jibsheet in one hand, putting a strain on the jib's clew. With the other hand, cast off the jib halyard but keep control of it as you let it go on the run, to get it down quickly, at the same time pulling on the leeward sheet to keep the sail from going overboard.

With the jib on deck, it should be taken off by reversing the procedure described for setting it (page 56)—unsnap each of the jib hanks, starting with the top and working down; unshackle the tack cringle from the bow fitting and secure the shackle in place; unshackle the halyard and make its shackle fast to the headstay fitting, and then bring the sail aft to stow in the sailbag. If the jib has removable battens, remove them before stowing the sail. Take a light strain on the jib halyard and secure it to its cleat, coiling up any spare line with a halyard hitch.

When you are sailing single-handed, it is better to leave the jib up until you have picked up your mooring. With it you have somewhat greater maneuverability, which you need, since you have no one forward to seize the pick-up for you, and will probably have to keep the boat sailing until you are practically on top of your mooring.

Prepare to sail close-hauled. If you have been running downwind toward your mooring area, plan to round up in as long an arc as possible below your mooring, to have enough time to go through the necessary steps of trimming your mainsheet from a run to close-hauled. A long arc also has the advantage of maintaining more of your momentum, enabling you to shoot farther when you finally head into the wind. Be sure the centerboard is down all the way.

Should you find that your pick-up buoy has been boxed in by other boats swinging close to it, so that a long arc is not feasible, you'll probably have to round up in a tight turn. In this situation, don't sail too far below your mooring, because the tight turn will kill most of your momentum, and you'll want some steerageway until you make the pickup. Also with her jib off (assuming you're not sailing single-handed), your boat will not shoot as far as she does under mainsail and jib.

Rounding up in a tight turn from a run takes some lively sheet handling to avoid dragging your boom and broaching to. In a spot like this it's a great help to have at least one other person in the boat to trim the mainsheet. If you're sailing single-handed, a good stunt is to steer with the tiller between your legs, leaving both hands free to handle the mainsheet; the jibsheet can be left eased off and presents no problem.

As you approach the point where you will begin your final turn, whether a long or tight arc, give your crew a command of preparation: *"Stand by to round up!"* The coil of the main halyard should be cleared for lowering.

Round up and shoot! With the command of execution, *"Helm's alee!"*, push your tiller toward the boom to swing the boat around into the wind, while your crew trims the mainsheet at a pace gauged to the radius of the arc you must travel to fetch your

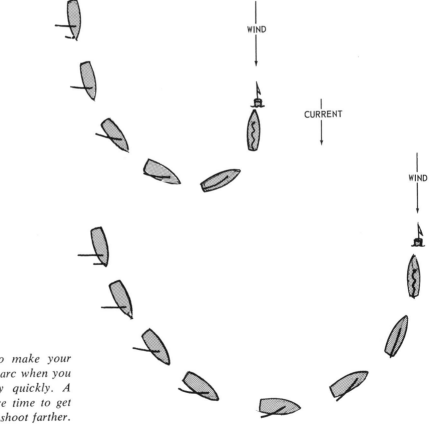

In rounding up to make your mooring, use tight arc when you must kill headway quickly. A long arc gives more time to get ready and lets you shoot farther.

mooring. With the boat directly in the wind, mainsail luffing and you steering to bring the pick-up buoy slightly on the bow where the chock is located, have your foredeck man *lie* on the foredeck to pull the buoy's pennant aboard.

If you have gauged your approach correctly, the boat will still have a touch of headway—as insurance against her failing to shoot as far as you had expected. But if she has too much headway, work the tiller rapidly from side to side to kill it. Should this not slow the boat down enough, sail off and make a new approach. Otherwise you risk a sudden jibe if you hold on to the mooring, unless the mainsail has been lowered promptly.

Pick up and secure mooring. The instant the pick-up buoy pennant is aboard *and made fast,* lower the mainsail by casting off the main halyard and pulling on the luff to help the slides down the track. Get out the boom crutch, fit it in place, and lift the main boom into it, taking care to have the mainsheet clear.

With mainsail down (but not off), finish securing the mooring line. Lead it through the bow chock, drop the eye over the foredeck cleat, and lash the pennant of the pick-up buoy to hold it, with a round turn, two cross turns, and a locking turn.

Putting the boat to bed

Perhaps you are finished sailing for the day. If so, follow the reverse procedure of making sail (pp. 52-58) in putting the boat to bed before you go ashore.

Remove and stow the mainsail battens. Examine each batten pocket for signs of wear or broken stitching.

Remove and stow the mainsail. Slacken the outhaul to permit releasing the clew cringle from the outhaul fitting. Then re-

secure the outhaul. Stow the mainsail in the sailbag foot first, with the headboard pushed in last.

Make up the main halyard. Snap the halyard shackle into the outhaul fitting, take a slight strain on the halyard and secure it, making up any spare halyard with a halyard hitch. If your halyard is too short to reach the end of the boom, secure the shackle to the gooseneck tack pin and rig a lashing to a shroud to prevent slapping.

Remove and stow the jibsheets (if they are not spliced into the jib). Make them up in two neat clockwise coils and stow them in the sailbag. The sailbag is now ready to go ashore with you.

Make up the mainsheet. Remove all slack and cleat the mainsheet. Make up the balance in a neat clockwise coil and hang it on any convenient cleat with a halyard hitch.

Check the bilge. Bail or sponge out any water the boat might have taken aboard during the sail; don't leave it till next time. By drying the bilge each time, you're better able to tell if she should develop a leak before you take her out again. Also, you'll be able to *get under way* (off the mooring) that much faster next time.

Unship (remove) rudder and tiller. Stow them on the cockpit sole as far outboard as possible, out of the way. Be sure to lash them (and any other loose gear) to the boat. Small boats often capsize at their moorings —unsecured gear floats away.

Raise and secure the centerboard. Coil the pennant neatly and hang it on its cleat with a halyard hitch.

You have now properly put the boat to bed, and are ready to go ashore.

To this point, we have assumed that you were finished sailing for the day, and wanted to secure the boat and her gear for overnight or longer, until you could sail her again.

Suppose, however, you have been sailing in the morning and want only to go ashore

Lash rudder and tiller securely to floorboards when you put boat to bed

for lunch and sail again in the afternoon. How do you tie up the boat so that you can leave her for a few hours without putting her completely to bed, yet secure enough so you won't worry about her going *adrift* (loose from her mooring) or any gear coming loose if the wind should come on to blow before you get back? The procedure is given below.

Securing a boat for a short time

As soon as you have picked up your mooring:

Lower the jib (if you have been sailing single-handed and still have it up). Uncleat its halyard and let it go *by the run* (completely free) to get the sail down quickly. But do not take the jib off; leave it on its stay. Unsnap the jib halyard from the head cringle and hold the shackle while you unsnap the top two jib hanks from the head-

stay. This gives you a couple of feet of loose sail near the head. Pass this loose head of the sail *under* the foot of the sail, bring it up and resecure the two hanks to the stay again. Resnap the halyard into the head cringle, take a slight strain, and make it fast. This binds up the jib in a neat furl that cannot come undone without unsnapping the top two jib hanks. Take a strain on both jib-sheets to keep the jib's foot taut, secure them and make up each end with a halyard hitch over its jam cleat.

Lower the mainsail. Uncleat its halyard and let the sail down by the run, pulling on the luff to help the slides down the track. But do not take the mainsail off. With main-sheet slack, lift the boom into the boom crutch, taking care not to catch the main-sheet between crutch and boom.

Slack the outhaul. Uncleat it, give it some slack, and resecure.

Secure the mooring line. If the eye of the mooring line is not already over the fore-deck cleat, bring it through the bow chock and drop it in place over the cleat. Check to see that the parceling is at the right spot to prevent chafe. Lash the mooring line in place with the pick-up buoy's pennant, with a round turn, two cross turns, and a locking round turn.

Furl the mainsail. To furl (roll up) the mainsail is simple, but to keep it furled, you should have handy several *sail stops.* These are five- or six-foot lengths of inch-wide canvas or nylon webbing, to pass around the boom and sail to hold it in place. Unroll the stops and space them out along the boom about three feet apart, passing each stop between the sail and the boom, letting the ends dangle evenly on both sides of the boom.

Next, pull all the sail over so that it hangs on one side of the boom, either side. Place yourself on that same side and pull the sail out from the boom to form a big pocket.

89

Hang sail stops about t...
feet apart, passing them
tween sail and boom

Bring stops under boom
then tie on top of furled
with bowknots, and tuck

Furled mainsail can be la...
quickly and easily by u...
mainsheet and series of ...
line hitches

Stretch the pocket aft as much as possible. Fold the sail into the pocket and roll it in and up toward the boom, pulling steadily aft to smooth it. Slap the sail down with your hands, to flatten it as you roll, driving the air out. Keep rolling in toward the boom until all the body of the sail is enclosed in the pocket, and it looks like a long white sausage.

Roll the sausage up on top of the boom and make it fast with the sail stops, passing the ends of the stops under the boom so they cross each other, bringing them up on top of the rolled sail. Tie an overhand knot in each stop, pulling it down as tight as you can, and finish with a bow knot, as though you were tying a pair of shoelaces. Tuck the bows between the sail and the boom.

Instead of the sail stops, you can lash the sail with one end of the mainsheet, if you wish, using a series of *marline hitches*. The marline hitch is an overhand knot made around the boom and sail with the continuous end of the line. To secure the sail this way, take all the available slack of the mainsheet and tie a clove hitch with it around the outboard end of the boom and sail, with the long end of the mainsheet facing forward, on top of the sail.

About three feet from the end of the boom, hold the standing part of the mainsheet (closest to the end of the boom) in one hand, pass the end around and under the boom, back on top of the sail and make an overhand knot, and pull it snug. Three feet farther forward on the boom, repeat the process, and so on, until you have the sail snugly held by several marline hitches. Secure the end by tying two half-hitches in the standing part after you have formed the final marline hitch.

More convenient than the mainsheet for securing in this fashion is a *heaving line*— a light line about 35 feet long that should be kept on board for *heaving* (throwing),

when you want to get a line across to someone at a distance, as on a float, or a dock or another boat. Secure one end of the heaving line with a clove hitch around the furled sail at the *forward* end of the boom, and work aft with a series of marline hitches, and make fast.

Coil down all lines. With the mainsail furled and *shipshape* (neat and orderly), make up any loose lines, starting with the main halyard. Secure it to its cleat and make up any slack with a halyard hitch. If you have not used the mainsheet for furling, take

This tiller is lashed to boom crutch

the slack out of it and make it fast, with a halyard hitch to hang up the slack. Unless you are sailing single-handed, your jib and jibsheets have already been stowed. If you are alone, and the jib is still on, you have already secured and made up the jibsheets. Make up the end of the jib halyard and hang it with a halyard hitch.

Bail the boat. If the boat has made any water, either from spray or leaking during your sail, sponge it dry or bail it before you go ashore.

Lash (secure) the tiller. Since you will be sailing again shortly, there is no need to un-ship rudder and tiller. But the tiller should be lashed amidships—on the centerline—to keep the rudder from working side to side while you're ashore. Using a short piece of line, make a clove hitch around the end of the tiller in the middle of the line. Take a strain on one end and secure it on a cleat to port, and a strain on the other end and secure it on a cleat to starboard, so that the tiller is held firmly in place amidships. If you haven't used your mainsheet for furling, you can use the end of it to secure the tiller, making it fast with a tension on both sides.

Raise the centerboard. Haul it all the way up and secure the pennant to its cleat on the centerboard trunk. Make up the slack with a halyard hitch.

The boat is now properly secured to be safe while you are gone; you can go ashore with an easy mind.

Summary

1. Picking up a mooring is like parking a car —you approach the opening at minimum speed, ease into place, and stop.
2. The approach should be made so as to arrive at the pick-up buoy with little or no headway.
3. Unless there is a current in the anchorage that is stronger than the wind, the approach should always be made with the mooring upwind.
4. Before making the approach, the pick-up buoy should be sighted and the approach planned; don't hurry.
5. Unless sailing alone, the jib should be *doused* (lowered) before making the approach.
6. When returning to the mooring from upwind, use a long arc of approach if possible.
7. When prepared to round up, a command of preparation is given: "**Stand by to round up!**"
8. At the command of execution, "**Helm's alee!**", the foredeck man *lies* on the foredeck, to take aboard the pick-up buoy.
9. In shooting for a mooring, it is desirable to have a little spare headway as insurance.
10. If the boat has too much headway, rapid working of the rudder from side to side may slow her down enough to still pick up the mooring safely.
11. But if the boat is moving too fast, do not attempt the pick-up; sail off and make another approach.
12. When the pick-up buoy pennant is aboard and *fast* (made fast), the mainsail is lowered and the boom set in the boom crutch.
13. The mooring line is then brought aboard and secured with the pick-up buoy's pennant, prior to putting the boat to bed.
14. Before going ashore, the boat is put to bed in reverse order from making sail:
    a. If the jib has not been lowered and stowed during the approach, it is now doused and stowed in the sailbag, with removable battens taken out and stowed separately.
    b. Remove and stow the mainsail battens.
    c. Remove and stow the mainsail in the sailbag, with headboard in last.
    d. Make up the main halyard.
    e. Remove and stow the jibsheets (if not spliced to the jib's clew).
    f. Make up the mainsheet.
    g. Check the bilge; sponge, bail, or pump it dry.

h. Unship the rudder and tiller, and stow them.

i. Raise and secure the centerboard.

15. For a short absence from the boat, the following routine will keep the boat secure and safe:

a. Lower the jib and furl it with its head wrapped around the foot.

b. Lower the mainsail, set the boom in its crutch, and slacken the outhaul.

c. Secure the mooring line with the pennant of the pick-up buoy.

d. Furl the mainsail, using sail stops or a series of marline hitches.

e. Coil down all loose lines.

f. Bail the boat.

g. Lash the tiller.

h. Raise the centerboard.

16. Checklist of nautical terms:

SAIL TERMS

sail stops—Lengths of flat, strong material for securing a furled sail.

SAILING TERMS

"Helm's alee!"—Command of execution for rounding up into the wind.

"Stand by to round up!"—Command of preparation for rounding up, prior to shooting for the mooring.

"Strike the jib!"—Command to lower and remove the jib.

VERBS

douse—To lower quickly.

furl—To roll up tightly.

heave—To throw or cast.

lash—To bind securely.

strike—To lower and remove, as a sail or a flag.

unship—To remove a piece of gear from its regular position.

GENERAL

adrift—Floating free; not tied up.

by the run—Released fully; let go freely.

current—Horizontal movement of water; a horizontal stream or flow.

fast—Made fast; secured.

heaving line—A length of light line, sometimes with an elaborate knot at one end to give it weight, for heaving at a distance.

marline hitch—A lashing overhand knot, usually made in series with the continuous end of a line, for furling sails.

shipshape—Neat and orderly; seamanlike.

under way—Formerly "under weigh," meaning no longer anchored or made fast to the shore; in *Navigation Rules,* also means "not aground."

up current—Against the direction of a current's flow.

11

Approaching and Leaving a Dock or Float

THE IMPORTANT DIFFERENCE between the approach to pick up a mooring and the approach to tie up at a dock (or float) is—go *long* of a mooring and *short* of a dock.

In other respects the approach to each is similar. But whereas when you arrive at your pick-up buoy you should have a little headway to spare, your headway should be killed completely *before* you fetch dock or float, if you must approach it head-on. The extra headway does your boat no damage at the mooring—you can pick up the buoy and carry it ahead with you a few feet while the remaining momentum is spent. But docks and floats are not so portable; many smallboat sailors have proved this beyond question. If your approach to them must be head-on, far better to be short a few feet than long six inches.

In tying up at docks and floats, there are some problems not met with in picking up a mooring. This summary of procedures covers the most important, with the word "dock" used to indicate both dock and float.

Approaching a dock

Note, incidentally, that no mention is made here of entering or leaving a slip. This

is a deliberate omission. To enter or leave a slip under sail alone can be a demanding exercise for the expert; for the novice it can be a disaster and, accordingly, is not recommended.

Take a look around as you get within approach distance. Note the wind direction and condition of current, if any. Observe traffic around the dock and which way boats tied up to it are heading; you'll probably want to tie up facing the same way.

Since you will want to make your approach upwind (or up current, if it is stronger), try to find an open spot on a side of the dock that faces upwind, if possible. This is the ideal situation because you can then shoot into the wind on a course parallel with the dock face and coast to a stop close enough to get a line ashore on the nearest cleat, piling, or *bollard* (mooring post).

If no side of the dock faces upwind, or if no mooring space is available on that side, next most preferable is a *berth* (mooring spot) on the leeward face of the dock, where the wind off the dock will keep your boat from rubbing against it. In approaching this side, however, you must ease sheets well out to kill headway, so as to be dead in the water before you fetch the dock face, using the last of your momentum to swing one bow parallel to the dock a foot or so out to let your foredeck man get a bow line ashore.

Except as a last resort, avoid tying up on the windward face of a dock, particularly if there is any sea running. Even with *fenders* (portable bumpers) to protect the boat, its movement against the dock puts a strain on lines and gear. And the problem of getting away again can easily become sticky. If there is a heavy wind *and* a big sea, do not attempt to tie up to a dock's windward face. It's better seamanship to anchor and row in to the dock's leeward side, where you can certainly squeeze a dinghy in, even though there might not be room for your boat.

If weather and sea conditions are not wild, and you have no choice but to tie up on the windward side, one method is to make your approach in a long curve, lower all sail while still some distance off and, with the last of your headway, coast in parallel with the dock face to get a line ashore. This approach calls for a good *seaman's eye*—the ability to judge your boat's carrying qualities—because even without sail on, she will carry her headway a lot farther across the wind than when shooting. Before attempting the approach, be sure there's ample sea room beyond the dock, so that if you are going too fast to stop when you reach the dock face, you'll still have space to turn back into the wind, raise sail, and sail off to make another approach.

A second method to tie up to a windward dock face is to anchor close enough upwind of it so that you can *veer* (pay out) anchor line and let the wind carry your boat down to the dock. Like the first method, however, this also calls for a seaman's eye in gauging (a) how far your boat will shoot into the wind before she loses all headway so that you

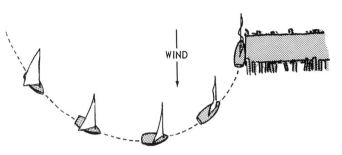

Whenever possible, tie up to dock face that lets you head directly upwind

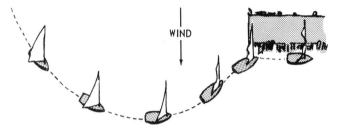

In approaching leeward dock face, use last of headway to swing boat parallel with dock

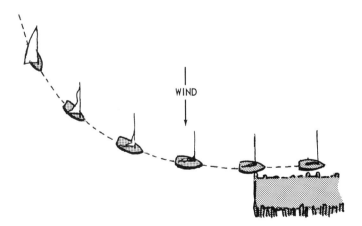

Best approach to windward dock face is to lose momentum and drift down on it. Avoid windward dock face in heavy weather.

95

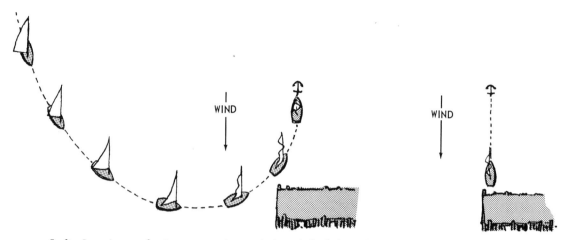

Left: *In using anchoring approach to windward dock face, it is essential to have anchor securely caught before you pay out line to carry you down*

Right: *When using anchoring approach, leave someone on board to tend anchor if you do not tie up to dock*

can let go your anchor, and (b) where your boat will fetch up when her anchor is securely caught—will the dock be within range of the rest of your anchor line?

Assuming that your judgment is correct, and the boat comes to rest within easy drifting distance of the dock, it is essential to remove the rudder to avoid damaging it, since you will be approaching the dock stern first. You may not actually want to touch or lie alongside the dock face in this approach, but merely get close enough to put someone ashore with a line to secure the boat's stern, to prevent its swinging away from the dock if the wind should shift. In using this approach it is advisable to have someone remain on board to tend the anchor line in case the anchor should start to *drag* (pull loose) while you are ashore.

A great advantage to the anchored approach is, if the wind is still contrary when you want to get away, you can haul the boat up to the anchor, raising sail as you go, and get under way without danger of bumping against the dock face.

Prepare docking lines. Only the tyro skipper waits until he is alongside the dock to think about how he is going to tie up; you'll not make that mistake. You will have ready at least two, and preferably four, lines for securing the boat properly, together with several fenders. Each fender will have a line attached to it for making it fast to a cleat or elsewhere *on the boat* to hold it in place. Avoid tying fenders to a dock; they're too easy to forget when you sail away!

You'll save yourself a number of headaches around docks and floats by keeping your boat equipped with four sturdy dock lines. Each should be slightly longer than your boat and made up with a spliced eye not less than two feet long in one end. This is the end you send ashore to be made fast, while you keep the other end on board for trimming the boat in. A loop of this size, you will find, fits comfortably around most dockside cleats, bollards, and pilings.

The line used for your dock lines should be strong enough to hold your boat without breaking, even if the full weight of the hull should pull on it—not less than ½-inch manila, preferably ⅝-inch. Here—as with sheets, halyards, and permanent mooring line —is no place to practice economy. Go as light as you please on fancy sailing clothes, but spend enough to buy *reliability* for any line or piece of gear that must take a strain.

If your docking lines are not made up with spliced eyes, you can quickly make a suitable eye of any size by tying in a bowline, to get a loop that will not slip. Tie such bowlines as you approach the dock, and make up each line for getting it ashore. This means have it coiled neatly, starting from the free end and laid up in a continuous series of even-sized, clockwise loops, finished with the spliced eye or bowline.

Make the approach. As when picking up a mooring, plan an arc of approach suitable to the available sea room. Here, however, since you may have to make a second approach if your boat has too much headway when you arrive alongside the dock, do not strike the jib. But ease the jibsheet as you start your approach, to help cut down your speed. The same command of preparation, "Stand by to round up!" can be used to alert your crew to lower the centerboard all the way, and to prepare the bow line for going ashore. Also to clear the jib and main halyards.

Shoot for the dock. With "Helm's alee!" as a command of execution, point the boat into the wind or as close to it as the approach permits, letting the mainsheet run as you do. To kill excess headway, if you are going too fast, work the rudder rapidly from side to side. Try to come to a stop alongside the dock within easy reaching distance so that you can get a line made fast ashore and back to the bow cleat. Don't be nervous if your first approach is short and there's no one on shore to whom you can pass or heave a line (page 101). Before your headway is completely gone, steer the boat off, trim jib and

mainsheet, sail away, and try again. On the other hand, if you overestimate the distance and are moving too fast as you approach the side of the dock, don't try to stop; sail past and make a fresh approach.

Make fast the bow. The first line to get ashore and make fast should be the bow line. This will keep the boat's nose into the wind until you can get sail down and will prevent the boat from sailing while you make fast the other dock lines.

If you have heaved a line to someone on shore while making your approach, have them secure their end; then you can trim the line in and keep control of the boat's speed as you pull it toward the dock. *Never let anyone pull you in to a dock or float— always ask them to make fast the shore end of the line (the eye), so that you keep control.*

When you've trimmed in the bow line to bring the boat alongside, secure it on the bow cleat with a round turn, two cross turns, and a locking round turn.

Douse all sail. With bow line fast, quickly

Coil dock lines clockwise for easy heaving, with bowline or spliced eye in end that's going ashore

lower jib and mainsail. Set the boom in its crutch and take a few quick turns with the mainsheet around the mainsail, and with the jibsheets around the jib to hold the sails while you make fast the other dock lines.

Secure all dock lines. After the bow line —which should lead to a spot on the dock ahead of the bow—set out the stern line, which should lead from the after cleat to a spot on the dock farther astern. Drop the eye over a cleat or post on shore, and trim in from the boat. Secure two or three fenders between boat and dock at points where chafe seems most likely to occur. Many docks have chafing gear of fire hose or rubber to protect the topsides of boats moored alongside, but nails sometimes work through, so it's good to have the additional protection of your own fenders. Generally they should be placed to bear on the widest part of the boat, and allowance made for some movement fore and aft. Make fender lines fast to cleats with a round turn, two cross turns, and a locking round turn, or to other parts of the boat with two half-hitches.

Bow and stern lines are usually enough to hold a boat securely for temporary mooring at a dock. But if a strong current is running, or a heavy sea, or if there is lots of traffic to make the boat surge back and forth, *spring lines* should also be used. These are docking lines rigged to prevent a boat moving backward and forward at her berth or away from the dock. A *quarter spring* runs from a point on the boat near the stern to a point on the dock opposite her bow. A *bow spring* leads from the bow to a point on the dock opposite the stern.

If there is evident movement of the boat along the dock face in one direction, first rig the spring line that will hold her against this movement; then rig the other.

From this point on, preparations for going ashore are identical with going ashore from a mooring, depending on whether you intend

to leave the boat at the dock overnight or for only a few hours, with one important exception—providing for any rise and fall of *tide* if you are in tidal waters.

Allow for the tide. Tide—the vertical movement of water—is no factor when your boat is on her permanent mooring, because the slack in the mooring line lets her go up and down as the tide comes in and goes out. So, too, there is no problem if she is moored to a float that rises and falls with the tide, provided there is ample depth of water for her alongside the float at *low water* (low tide).

Not so, however, with a dock, which sits immovable while the tide climbs around it every few hours, then subsides. If your boat is tied up at low water, the dock lines must be at full length, to provide for the difference in level between the dock and the water. But as the tide rises along the face of the dock and the boat floats up with it, slack comes into all the lines. Then, unless they are trimmed in to remove the slack, the boat is free to move back and forth along the dock face, and may bang herself up or collide with other boats.

Conversely, if you have tied up at *high water* (high tide), and there is any substantial difference between high and low water, unless extra slack is given to your dock lines as the tide goes out, your boat will be *"hung up"*—suspended by her dock lines—with the possibility either that they will part or that the cleats they are secured to will pull out. If she is hung up any length of time before lines part or cleats pull out, she may drop a number of feet, taking severe structural damage. In any event, when something does let go, the boat may go adrift, adding the problem of a sea hunt to the worries of the unhappy skipper.

This little discussion of tidal effects makes a good case for the practice of leaving someone on board to tend dock lines when you tie up for any length of time at a dock subject to a wide tidal range. Or at least have a friendly dock attendant or harbormaster keep an eye on your lines to slacken off or trim them in until you get back.

Getting away from a dock

With the wind ahead. There's no problem in getting away when you're moored alongside a dock with the wind coming from ahead or off the dock from forward of the beam. Take in your spring lines, coil them down and stow them, then proceed to make sail as though you were getting under way from your mooring after a temporary absence. Here, however, instead of having a

choice of tacks, your tack is dictated by the direction in which you are free to sail.

Hoist mainsail and jib, with plenty of slack in their sheets, and boom crutch out, so that both sails can swing freely. Let go the shore end of the bow line, and take it in; this will free your bow to swing out. Now, back the jib to force the bow farther out, and as the bow swings away from the dock, cast off the shore end of your stern line and pull it in. Trim sheets and start sailing.

If no one is available on shore to let go your dock lines, and you have no crew who can do the job (and also give the bow an extra push out before stepping back aboard), double up the lines so that *both* ends are on the boat, with only a bight over the cleat or post ashore. Then when you're ready to go,

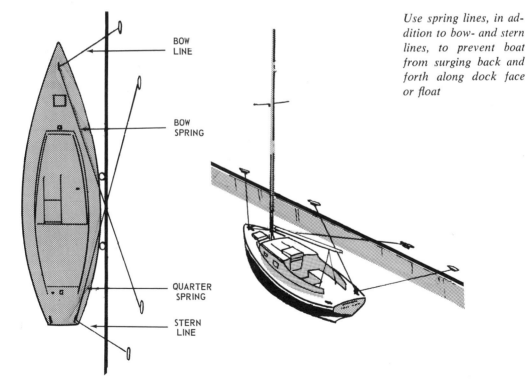

Use spring lines, in addition to bow- and stern lines, to prevent boat from surging back and forth along dock face or float

BOW LINE

BOW SPRING

QUARTER SPRING

STERN LINE

release one end and pull it free of the shore with the other. Make up and stow bow and stern lines as you start sailing.

With a contrary wind. When the wind is blowing directly contrary, forcing your boat against the dock face, you have no problem if you have an anchor out to windward—simply haul the boat up to the anchor, where she will head into the wind, and get sail on as usual. If you are moored alongside the dock, when you have taken in your spring lines, your only care must be to let go your stern line before your bow line, and keep a good strain on the anchor line so that the stern doesn't bump against the dock as the boat comes head to wind. It's a good precaution to remove the rudder for this maneuver, if it was not removed when docking. With the boat headed into the wind, haul her out to her anchor, replacing the rudder and making sail as you go.

If you do not have an anchor out, and would prefer to get under way in the clear, perhaps you can borrow a dinghy and row out well to windward and set an anchor for hauling the boat out. Should you do this, be sure the anchor is securely caught *before* you cast off from the dock. It should be set with a *scope* (length of line) of at least seven times the depth of the water. Follow the procedure detailed above for casting off from the dock.

Sometimes, with a contrary wind, if the docking area is clear between your boat and a side of the dock that faces upwind, you may be able to "walk" your boat around to that side, turn her bow toward the wind, and make sail under the normal conditions of having the wind ahead. To "walk" a boat properly requires one person on shore to tend the docking lines and one on the boat to fend her off from the dock face while she moves toward the desired side of the dock.

Have the man on shore cast off all lines but the one closest to the side where you

want to go, and take them aboard. Then have him release the last line and start pulling the boat toward the new berth, while you, on board, push along the dock face, holding the boat off. Pivot the stern around the corner of the dock and move it downwind at the new berth until the bow is far enough from the corner to resecure the bow line. Get the stern line ashore and resecured, and make sail.

A final method for getting away against a contrary wind, is to have someone stand on the dock and push the bow around toward the wind by using the end of the main boom as a pushing pole. Take in the spring lines, coil them down and stow them. Take the boom out of the crutch *before* hoisting the mainsail, and give the mainsheet plenty of slack to let the boom swing out over the dock and spill wind as you hoist the sail. Raise the mainsail, secure and coil down the halyard. Give the jibsheets plenty of slack, hoist the jib and secure and coil down its halyard.

Ask the man on shore to cast off the stern line, then the bow line, and to start pushing the bow out from the dock toward the wind in a long, curving arc. This will keep the stern from swinging in too close to the dock as the bow swings out. It is always surprising how far upwind a healthy push on the main boom can send a boat. As soon as the bow is into the wind, back the jib and steer the boat toward the desired course. Trim sheets and sail away.

With the wind astern. This is the only situation in leaving a dock or float when the jib should be hoisted before the mainsail. The reason is, of course, to avoid the chance of an accidental jibe while still in the process of getting under way. Use this procedure to eliminate anxiety from your departure whenever the wind is blowing off the dock from abaft your beam.

Take in the spring lines first, coil them down, and stow them. The wind will now hold the boat somewhat off the dock face. Give a little extra slack to the stern line, however, to insure that when you let the bow line go, the boat will be able to pivot downwind away from the dock face without the stern touching. Complete all preparations for making sail: lower the centerboard, clear sheets and halyards, remove sail stops, unfurl the jib, and stow any loose gear. Leave the boom in its crutch, though, since you will not hoist the mainsail until you are well away from the dock.

Next, cast off and take in the bow line, and hoist and secure the jib. Now trim on whichever jibsheet will help the jib fill, to swing the bow away from the dock and get the boat sailing. As soon as the jib begins to *draw* (fill) and give the boat some headway, cast off the stern line and steer away from the dock in a long, curving arc, gathering speed. Get the boat moving as fast as possible, cast off the boom downhaul and prepare to hoist the mainsail. When you have good headway and ample sea room to windward for rounding up, turn into the wind and let fly the jib, hoisting and securing the mainsail as quickly as possible. Remove the boom crutch, take a fresh strain on the downhaul and secure it, back the jib to send the bow off toward the desired tack, trim jibsheet and mainsheet, and steer away on your intended course.

How to heave a line

No chapter on tying up to a dock would be complete without some instruction in the sailorly art of heaving a line, a most useful accomplishment. I recall vividly an amazing demonstration when I was in the merchant marine. Our ship, a deepwater freighter, had run aground in Islais Creek, San Francisco, on a falling tide. It was imperative to get a hawser out quickly to a nearby tugboat to haul our bow off before we were stuck

fast. Yet the tugboat could not get closer to us than 50 yards for fear of grounding, too.

Our Finnish *boatswain* (deck foreman, pronounced "bos'n") took one of the ship's heaving lines and with a magnificent cast heaved it across the stern of the tug, threw a bowline in the other end through the eye of the bow hawser, shouted to the tug's crew to haul in, and in less than a minute the eye was over the tug's towing bitts, made fast to our forward windlass, and the tug was putting a strain on the hawser to pull us off the bank.

Few things mark the sailor more publicly than this ability to heave a line so that it spirals through the air, without snarls or fouling, far and accurately to its target. And while small-boat sailors seldom have occasion to heave a line more than 25 feet, it is often urgent that the cast be successful the first time. Now, as a mail order advertisement might say, *"You, too, can heave a line (any line!) successfully"*—by using this simple method, of which the essence is: Have the line coiled *correctly* in the first place.

A "correct" coil, as we mentioned in discussing dock lines, is one made up of neat, clockwise loops of a uniform size. If the line has an eye in one end, let that be in the last loop of the coil, on the outside, so that it will be first in the air when you heave. When making up the line, tie a bowline in the end that is to stay aboard, making it small enough to fit easily but snugly over the wrist of your non-heaving arm. This will insure you against the beginner's dilemma of having both ends of the line leave the boat with his cast, a never-failing source of amusement to bystanders.

Push the bowline over your left wrist, and with your right hand stretch out the standing part the length of your arm. Bring the standing part back into your left hand to form a bight, with the line leading up and across the left palm, away from your body. Now

Heaving a line, STEP 1—*Tie a bowline loosely over left wrist, coil heaving line in even, clockwise coils in left hand . . .*

STEP 2—*Split coils in half, being sure there are no twists, with right-hand coils ready to heave and left hand held open to feed out rest of coils . . .*

Right: *Heave line high so that it uncoils like a flat spring unwinding, and be sure to keep left hand open.*

Below: *This girl is practicing heaving a line at a cushion to develop accuracy. But she should have the small bowline around her left wrist instead of in her hand.*

slide your right hand along the line the length of your arm again and form a second loop clockwise, passing it into and across your left palm, away from your body. If the line tends to twist and make a foul loop, remove the twist by rolling the line between your right thumb and forefinger. Make loop Nos. 3, 4, 5, and so on, this same way, until all the line is coiled in the left hand. Be sure no loops are twisted.

If your arms are of average length, you'll find that a 35-foot line made up this way gives you about eight loops for heaving. To heave, split the coil in half, holding loops Nos. 1 to 4 in your left hand and loops Nos. 5 to 8 in your right. Be sure each loop feeds

102

to the next in order, with no twists or crossed loops. When within certain range of your target, hold your left hand open toward it, with the four coils free to feed off as needed. Swing the four coils in your right hand in a flat, horizontally rising arc and let them go just before your right arm is pointed at the target. When properly heaved, the coil will stretch out in a long, curving arc like a flat spring unwinding, and you'll be able to make it travel a long distance, even upwind.

Be sure, however, to keep your left hand open so the balance of the coil can feed out freely. There seems to be a natural tendency to close the left hand when the right hand heaves; resist it, or your line will not stretch out to its full length. A good way to overcome this tendency, and to perfect your heaving accuracy, is to practice on shore by heaving a 35-foot length of line at a cushion, life jacket, or other suitable target, placed about 25 feet away.

If you want to make a game of it, place the target in the middle of a circle five feet in diameter, and score yourself on the basis of 10 points for each direct hit on the target, 5 points for each cast that misses the target but lands within the five-foot circle, and 0 points for any cast that fails to hit either. Keep a record of your total score for a series of ten casts, then try another ten, and so forth, until you have begun to score 75 points or more fairly regularly for each ten casts. You'll be delighted to find how rapidly your accuracy develops. It's the cheapest sport you'll find in a day's sailing, and will pay large dividends in satisfaction on the water. You can use it competitively to develop the same skill in your crew.

When you have accuracy under control, you might want to test your skill at heaving against time—put a stop watch on how long it takes to complete ten casts and take your score for the series, then run a competition with yourself to *decrease* your time and *in-*

crease your score. To give you an idea of what to strive for, a fourteen-year-old boy in a Junior Sailing Class completed a series of ten casts of 40 feet each, coiling a 50-foot heaving line after each cast, in a total elapsed time of 3 minutes 15 seconds, with a score of 80 points for the series. A woman student in a Ladies Sailing Class completed a series of ten casts of 25 feet each, coiling a 35-foot heaving line after each cast, in 2 minutes 40 seconds, with a total score of 90 points for the series. *YOU, TOO, CAN HEAVE A LINE* (ANY LINE!) SUCCESSFULLY!

Summary

1. The chief difference between the approach to a mooring and the approach to a dock or float: Go *long* of a mooring and *short* of dock or float, if it must be approached head-on.
2. Before attempting to dock, the approach should be studied for a side that faces upwind (or up current, if that is stronger).
3. If an upwind approach is not feasible, second choice is a leeward face of the dock.
4. A windward dock face is a last resort, and should never be used if a heavy wind and big sea are running.
5. One approach to a windward face is to drop sail while some distance off and let the wind carry the boat down to the dock.
6. Another approach is to anchor upwind and veer scope until the boat's stern is close enough to get a line ashore. The rudder should be removed.
7. When the approach has been decided, docking lines should be made ready.
8. "Stand by to round up!" is the command of preparation for the crew.
9. "Helm's alee!" is the command of execution for pointing the boat into or as close as possible to the wind.
10. If the approach is either short or the boat is going so fast that she cannot be easily stopped, it is best to sail off and make a fresh approach.

11. The bow line is the first to be made fast ashore.

12. The shore end of any dock line should always be made fast first, and trimming in done from the boat.

13. When the bow line is fast, all sail is doused.

14. On the dock, the bow line leads ahead of the boat, and the stern line leads astern of the boat. The bow spring leads to a point opposite the stern, and the quarter spring to a point on the dock opposite the bow. Fenders are hung *from the boat* at the principle chafe points.

15. When docking in tidal waters, provision must be made to slacken dock lines when the tide goes out and to trim them in when the tide rises.

16. In getting away from a dock with the wind ahead, sail is made as though leaving a mooring after a short absence.

17. If no one is on shore to help cast off, bring both ends of each dock line aboard, leaving a bight over a cleat or post ashore, and cast off by releasing one end and pulling it free with the other.

18. To get away from a dock with a contrary wind, a good method is to set an anchor well out to windward, and haul the boat off. Remove the rudder first.

19. Another method is to "walk" the boat around the dock to a side facing upwind.

20. A final method is to have someone on the dock force the bow around into the wind by pushing on the end of the main boom, after sails have been hoisted with well-eased sheets.

21. When leaving a dock with the wind abaft the beam, an accidental jibe is avoided by hoisting only the jib until the boat is well clear and can be turned toward the wind to hoist the mainsail.

22. To heave a line successfully, it must first be coiled in neat, clockwise coils of uniform size, with half the coils in one hand and half in the other, with no twisted or crossed coils.

23. Checklist of nautical terms:

VERBS

drag—To pull loose, as an anchor failing to hold a boat in position.

draw—To fill with wind.

veer—To pay out slack; also, wind shifting in a clockwise direction.

GENERAL

berth—A boat's location at anchor, or at a dock or float.

boatswain (pronounced "bos'n")—Deck foreman in the merchant marine.

bollard—A vertical post on dock or float for securing dock lines.

bow line—A docking line used to control the boat's bow.

bow spring—A docking line to prevent the boat surging ahead.

fenders—Any device to protect a boat's topsides from chafe.

high water—The normal highest point of the tide.

hung up—A boat suspended by her dock lines on a falling tide.

low water—The normal lowest point of the tide.

quarter spring—A dock line rigged to prevent the boat surging astern.

scope—The length of anchor line between the anchor and the boat.

seaman's eye—The ability to judge a boat's carrying and shooting qualities under varying conditions of wind and sea.

spring line—A line used to keep a boat from surging back and forth.

stern line—A docking line to control the stern of the boat.

tide—The alternate rising and falling of the ocean and ocean-connected waters, usually twice daily, caused by the attraction of the sun and moon.

12

Anchoring and Weighing Anchor

Like a pickax, an anchor holds best when pull on it is horizontal

AN ANCHOR IS LIKE a pickax driven into the ground—the more horizontal the pull on it, the greater its holding power and the harder it is to dislodge. Conversely, the more vertical the pull on it, the less holding power it has and the easier it is to *break out* (dislodge).

As a matter of scientific fact, an anchor begins to lose its grip on the bottom long before the pull on it becomes vertical. Tests have confirmed the centuries-old experience of sailors—that when the angle of pull begins to exceed about 20° from the horizontal, the anchor may start to drag.

Whether the anchor is shaped like a pickax, a mushroom, or a plow seems to make no difference—its ability to stay and hold in position the boat attached to it depends not so much on its design or weight, but on keeping the angle of pull below 20°. This is not to say that design or weight are unimportant, but, other things being equal, scope is the most important factor in keeping a boat securely moored by an anchor.

A vertical pull breaks out a pickax—or an anchor

Obviously a 300-pound mushroom anchor would hold a 75-pound dinghy without dragging, even if the scope were no longer than the depth of the water—an angle of pull of 90°, straight up and down. But the same 300-pound mushroom attached to a 10-ton boat would not hold her in place on a scope only equal to the depth of water, except in a flat calm. The boat would start to drag at the first sign of a breeze or any sea motion.

There is a basic relationship between the size of a boat and the ultimate holding power of her *ground tackle* (anchoring equipment). Even with a mile of scope, a 10-pound anchor would not hold an aircraft carrier from dragging. In choosing either a permanent mooring anchor or an anchor to carry on board, this basic relationship must be recognized, and adequate scope then provided in the anchor line for the depth of water where the boat will be moored, to keep the angle of pull below the critical 20°. For the moment we'll consider only the ground tackle carried on board, and discuss permanent moorings in a later chapter.

Choosing an anchor

The process of anchoring begins in equipping the boat with an anchor of suitable size and holding power to keep her securely attached to the bottom of her local waters under the worst weather and sea conditions she might normally encounter. You don't expect to sail in a hurricane, of course, but every sailing area is hit by occasional unpredicted local storms. Your ground tackle should be adequate for you to ride them out in safety, without worry.

Time was, when the rule of thumb of "one pound of anchor per overall foot length of boat" was used as a formula for a boat's everyday anchor. But that was before the development of modern lightweight anchors, like the Northill and Danforth, with their radically increased holding power as the result of scientific experimentation and design. Today, for example, an 8-pound Danforth should provide ample basic holding power for the average sailboat up to 25 feet LOA.

Choosing the rode

The proper length of rode. Rode is the term used for a boat's anchor line, as op-

When angle of pull on anchor exceeds about 20° from horizontal, anchor may begin to drag

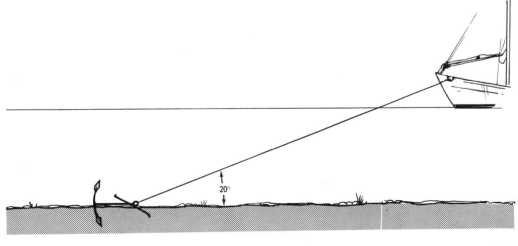

Above: *Northill utility anchor provides great holding power with light weight; especially good in rocks or heavy kelp (Danforth)*

Left: *This Danforth Hi-Tensile anchor has thin, sharp flukes for maximum penetration of bottom under storm loads (Danforth)*

posed to scope, which is the length of anchor line between the anchor and the boat at any one time. As noted above, how much rode you should carry depends on the depth of your local waters—the average amount it takes to reach bottom—plus enough scope for the angle of the rode between anchor and boat to be less than 20°, *with a generous extra allowance for wave and sea motion and storm conditions.*

The geometry of the first part of the problem is simple—an anchor dropped in 10 feet of water in a flat calm would need about 30 feet of scope to keep the angle of pull on it below 20°—*but this is not enough for anything but a flat calm.* Good seamanship dictates that the ratio for scope be not less than *seven times the depth of water.* In

10 feet of water, for example, you would use at least 70 feet of scope. Thus, if the waters where you might normally anchor have an average depth of 15 feet, you should equip your anchor with a rode of not less than 105 feet. Chances are, you will seldom have to use all that scope, but when you do need it, you'll be very happy to have it aboard; a dragging anchor is a worrisome shipmate!

The nylon rode. Nylon is the best material for a small sailboat's anchor rode, for several reasons. Most important, perhaps, is its high elasticity under strain, which contributes a desirable "give" to the rode, relieving the anchor of sudden shocks that might tend to disturb its hold on the bottom. Nylon is stronger, size for size, than dacron, polyethylene, manila, or sisal. It can be stowed wet, will not rot or mildew, is easy on the hands (no splinters), and, if protected from chafe, will last indefinitely. Its cost, in terms of strength, is not greater than manila, yet it will outlast manila by many seasons.

For example, an average small sailboat under 20 feet LOA might carry an anchor rode of ½-inch new manila, with a breaking strain of 2650 pounds and a recommended safe working load of 530 pounds. Yet though a rode of ½-inch nylon would cost more, apart from its other advantages, it would give superior protection, with a breaking strain of 6200 pounds. For docking lines, where chafe is always apt to be a problem, manila is recommended, but for an anchor rode, invest your money in nylon.

Marking the rode. Since it is essential in anchoring to know how much scope you have out, the anchor rode should be marked at 20-foot intervals so that the length can be identified by sight or touch. A simple method is to sew one turn of marline around the line at 20 feet, two turns at 40 feet, three turns at 60 feet, and so on. By running a finger across the mark, you can identify it easily, even on the blackest night.

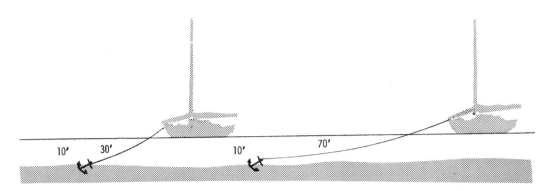

A minimum scope of 30 feet would be needed in water 10 feet deep to keep angle of pull below 20° in a flat calm

A scope of 7 to 1—or 70 feet for 10-foot deep water—allows a comfortable margin of safety to keep angle of pull on anchor below 20°

Securing rode to anchor. Before we take our boat out to practice anchoring, the rode must be properly secured to the anchor so that it will not work loose under strain. First choice for this important connection is an eye in the rode, spliced (page 171) over a *thimble* (a heart-shaped, grooved piece of metal) to protect the rode from chafe where it connects with the *shank* (shaft) of the anchor. It's a good rule, incidentally, to protect line this way whenever there is a line-to-metal contact under conditions where chafe might cause the line to part.

Pass a ½-inch galvanized iron shackle through the eye of the rode and through the hole or ring in the shank of the anchor. Smear the threads of the shackle pin with waterproof grease, and screw it tight. Then pass a couple of turns of galvanized *seizing* (lashing) wire through the eye of the shackle pin, around the shank of the shackle and twist them home, to secure the pin from coming unscrewed accidentally. On anchor rodes used in salt water it is essential that the shackle (also the thimble and seizing wire) be made of galvanized iron, not of brass. Otherwise the iron of the anchor will set up a battery action in the salt water with the zinc in the yellow metal and rapidly corrode the shackle. Neglect of this precaution can cause

LARRY KEAN

Above: *Splice a thimble into end of anchor rode to protect it from chafe where it joins anchor*

Right: *Seize anchor shackle pin with galvanized wire to prevent it from coming unscrewed*

109

a boat to go adrift when its mooring shackle parts.

You may not wish to keep your anchor line permanently attached to the anchor with eye and thimble, but might want, instead, to keep both ends free for possible use as a towing line. In that case, use a bowline to secure the rode to the anchor, as follows: Pass one end of the rode through the hole or ring in the anchor's shank, take a round turn, and tie a bowline in the standing part. The two thicknesses of line on the ring will reduce the possibility of chafe-through. If you leave your rode made up this way, however, be sure to check the round turn occasionally for chafe.

Securing rode's bitter end to mast. If it's embarrassing to have both ends of a heaving line leave the boat because one end was not secured on board, it's doubly embarrassing to have the *bitter end* (the last part) of an anchor rode go over the side; it usually involves an unpremeditated swim to retrieve it. Yet it's an accident easy to avoid by the simple stratagem of keeping the rode secured around the mast belowdeck with a round turn and a bowline, leaving the neatly coiled anchor rode and anchor always ready for instant use without having to remember each time to make fast the bitter end.

Above: *Use a bowline with round turn through shank hole or ring of anchor to secure rode for temporary use*

Right: *Use a round turn and bowline to secure bitter end of anchor rode to mast, and keep coiled and lashed rode on top of anchor, ready for instant use*

Anchoring

1. Make ready the anchor. Usually on a small sailboat the anchor is stowed beneath

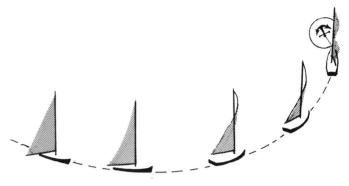

Round up into wind, lose all headway, and let boat start to go astern before you lower anchor

its rode, under the foredeck, alongside the mast, to keep its weight as close to the centerline as possible. The rode should be stowed with two or three lashings of light line to keep its coil intact when not in use. Lift out rode and anchor into the cockpit, on the same side of the boat as the bow chock, since the rode must lead out through it. Remove the lashings and, if the bitter end is not already made fast, secure it around the mast with a round turn and bowline. Place the coil on the cockpit floorboards with loops in order, upward from the bitter end toward the anchor, and no loop fouled or crossed. Check the shackle or bowline connecting rode and anchor.

2. Pick the spot. With anchor ready, choose a spot that lies upwind (or up current, if it is stronger), where you know there will be ample depth of water for your boat, even at low tide if you are in tidal waters. When in doubt, check the local chart. Estimate how much scope you will need to be securely anchored for the existing weather conditions, up to seven times the depth of water. Then try to pick a location that will have ample swinging room, without fouling other boats when you are anchored, and that does not lie directly to leeward of another boat.

3. Douse the jib. Let the jib down by the run, and give it a quick furl with a sail stop or by a round turn with a jibsheet. Secure the halyard and jibsheets.

4. Prepare to lower the mainsail. Clear the halyard, get out the boom crutch and sail stops.

5. "Stand by to anchor!" This command of preparation for your crew tells them to lead the anchor rode forward and into the bow chock, and to pass the anchor forward and *outside the shrouds,* back into the cockpit, so that it can be let go from there, without going up on the foredeck.

6. Shoot for your spot. As in shooting to pick up a mooring, your final sailing angle should be close-hauled before shooting to fetch the location you have chosen. Only, whereas you plan to have a trace of headway when you arrive at a pick-up buoy, now you should plan to have your boat dead in the water, and beginning to make sternway, before you lower the anchor.

7. Lower the anchor. Notice the word "lower." An anchor should *never* be flung, tossed, thrown, heaved, or catapulted over the side; it should be lowered deliberately and carefully, keeping a strain on it with the rode, and letting its weight pull the rode out evenly until the anchor reaches bottom. To let go an anchor any other way is to invite trouble. An anchor tossed overboard drops so quickly it may catch an arm or foot in a loop of the rode. This is an uncomfortable experience at best, on a small boat, with a light anchor. But on a large boat, with a heavy anchor, it could be fatal; men have been drowned by being carried over the side in a bight of the anchor rode.

There is also the possibility that a rode

Always lower *anchor—don't toss or heave it—and avoid possibility of having rode foul it on way to bottom*

feeding out rapidly, without control, may get fouled on a cleat or other part of the boat and be hard to release quickly. Another, more serious danger—because it prevents the anchor getting a proper hold—is having a loop of the rode get hooked around an arm of the anchor itself. If this should happen, even though the other arm of the anchor might bury itself in the bottom momentarily, the pull of the rode would be against the fouled loop instead of against the end of the shank, and the anchor would not hold.

8. Let the anchor take scope. When the anchor reaches bottom, do not immediately pay out all the scope you plan to use; it may settle on top of the anchor and foul it from setting and holding properly. Rather, while

the boat's head falls off before the wind, and the mainsail swings out with mainsheet completely free, let the anchor *take scope from you* as the boat gathers sternway. Keep a light strain on the rode until you have paid out about three times the depth of water, then take a turn around the foredeck cleat and *snub* (check) the line. This should set the anchor.

If it's caught securely, the boat will start heading into the wind again and her sternway will diminish. Keep an unyielding strain on the rode until you are sure the anchor is really caught. Then release the rode from the cleat, ease the strain to let the boat drift astern again, and pay out the balance of your planned scope as the anchor takes it. Secure the rode around the foredeck cleat with a round turn, two cross turns, and a locking round turn. When the boat has rounded up into the wind again, before lowering the mainsail, look around and make a final check of your position against any prominent landmark on shore to be sure you are holding.

9. Check for proper hold. If the boat does not round into the wind when you first snub the rode, after having paid out scope equal to three times the depth of water, it means the anchor has not yet taken proper hold of the bottom. At once, release the rode from the cleat and let the anchor take additional scope equal to twice the depth of water, then snub it again. Should the boat fail to round up this time, make no further effort to set the anchor without hauling it up and taking a look at it. It may have fouled something on the bottom—an oyster shell, kelp, a loop of old line, a baby carriage, any of the thousands of pieces of debris that clutter the bottoms of popular harbors. Trim in your mainsheet to start the boat sailing on the tack where her bow is pointing, haul the anchor in and bring it aboard. Remove any impediment. If there is no impediment, sail the boat to make a new approach to the mooring spot, and try lowering again.

10. Lower the mainsail. With anchor set and all scope out, lower the mainsail. Secure it and the jib as though you were going to leave the boat for a short time (page 89). Leave the centerboard down, however, and rudder and tiller in place.

Weighing anchor

1. Make sail. The process of getting under way from an anchored position is called *weighing anchor.* To weigh anchor, simply reverse the procedure by which you anchored. Start with unfurling the jib and main-

Let anchor take scope as boat gathers sternway, keeping light strain on rode

BOB GRIESER

sail, and raise the mainsail with plenty of slack in its sheet, to let it swing freely, after you remove the boom crutch. Leave the jib unhoisted on the foredeck, with a couple of turns of a jibsheet around it to keep it from blowing about, until you have the anchor up and are sailing again. If you lashed the tiller when you anchored, release it now.

2. *Haul in the rode.* Cast off the anchor rode from the foredeck cleat and start hauling it in, coiling down the slack in uniform, clockwise loops on the sole of the cockpit. Keep hauling until either the anchor breaks out and the slack comes in very easily, or until the rode is straight up and down, directly over the anchor.

3. *Break out the anchor.* Usually the anchor breaks out while you are hauling the boat up to it (after the angle of pull on it exceeds 20°). But if it is still fast when the rode is straight up and down, take a round turn on the foredeck cleat to secure the rode,

then take hold of the rode with both hands between cleat and bow chock, and pull on the anchor with a series of strong pulls, slackening the rode between each pull. If this does not break it out at once, go aft for a few minutes, leaving the rode secured with maximum strain on the anchor, straight up and down. Then try again to break it out, with another series of long, vertical pulls. It should come this time; if not, see procedure for *Fouled Anchor* (page 134). As soon as the anchor is free, haul it in with all speed, cleaning any mud off while it is still in the water, and taking care not to gouge the bow with its *flukes* (sharp ends) as it comes aboard.

4. *Hoist the jib.* The jib can go up as soon as the anchor is free of the bottom. Back it, if need be, to get the boat headed toward the tack you want to sail. Trim the mainsheet, then the jibsheet, and sail your course.

5. *Stow the anchor.* If the rode was coiled

When anchoring in rocky or fouled bottom, bend trip line and buoy to crown of anchor before lowering

down as it was hauled in, it is in a neat coil on the cockpit floorboards, with the last few feet of uncoiled line leading to the anchor. Coil these down in turn. Then tie several lashings around the coil at different places to keep it intact when stowed. Place the anchor alongside the mast, under the foredeck, *capsize* (turn over) the coiled rode and stow it on top of the anchor.

How to rig an anchor trip line. You may sometime have to anchor where the bottom is rocky, or where there are known obstructions that might foul your anchor and make it impossible to break out by usual methods. In such waters, make it a practice to rig your anchor with a *trip line* and buoy before you lower it. A trip line is a light line attached to the *crown* (head) of the anchor, at the opposite end of the shank from where the rode is made fast. A pull on the trip line *trips* (upsets) the anchor—disengages the flukes from the bottom and frees them if they have been caught in an obstruction.

To rig a trip line, use a piece of ¼-inch manila slightly longer than the depth of the water. Tie one end of the line to a ring in the crown of the anchor (or around the crown, if the anchor has no crown ring), using a bowline. Lash the other end of the line around a buoyant cushion or a block of wood, with a clove hitch secured by an extra half-hitch. The buoy will float clear and mark where the anchor is set.

When lowering an anchor with trip line attached, take care to pay out the trip line at the same speed as the anchor rode, *no faster,* to avoid having a loop of it foul the anchor on the way down. When the anchor is on the bottom, however, the rest of the trip line and its buoy can be dropped over the side.

Summary

1. The holding action of an anchor is like that of a pickax driven into the ground.
2. An anchor loses its holding power as the angle of pull leaves the horizontal, and cannot be relied on to hold after the angle of pull exceeds about 20°.
3. Other things being equal, scope is more important than an anchor's design or weight in keeping a boat securely moored.
4. Because modern, lightweight anchors, like the Northill and Danforth, give greater holding power with less weight than older types, they are better suited to small-boat use.
5. The length of an anchor rode should be at least seven times the depth of water where she will usually anchor.
6. The rode should be marked at 20-foot intervals for easy identification by day or night.
7. Nylon is the best material for a small sailboat's anchor rode.
8. A ⅜-inch nylon anchor rode should be adequate for the average small sailboat.
9. The eye of the anchor rode should enclose a galvanized iron thimble where the rode joins the anchor. Instead of an eye, a bowline with an extra round turn, may be used.
10. A ¼-inch galvanized iron shackle can be used to join the rode to the shank of the anchor. Shackle pin threads should be greased, and the pin itself seized to the shackle shank with galvanized wire.
11. In salt water, it is important that no brass or bronze be used in any part of the mooring assembly.
12. An anchor rode's bitter end should be secured around the mast belowdeck with a round turn and a bowline.
13. *The 10 steps of anchoring are:*
    a. Make ready the anchor.
    b. Pick the spot.
    c. Douse the jib.
    d. Prepare to lower the mainsail.
    e. "Stand by to anchor!"
    f. Shoot for your spot.

g. Lower the anchor.

h. Let the anchor take scope, then snub.

i. Check for proper hold—More scope, equal to twice the depth, should be given the anchor, and the rode snubbed again. Should the boat fail to round up this time, the anchor should be hauled in and a fresh approach made.

j. Lower the mainsail.

14. *The five steps in weighing anchor are:*

a. Make sail. Hoist mainsail, make ready jib.

b. Haul in the rode.

c. Break out the anchor.

d. Hoist the jib.

e. Stow the anchor.

15. When anchoring in rocky or obstructed waters, a trip line and buoy should be used. One end of a length of ¼-inch manila, slightly longer than the depth of water, should be secured to the anchor's crown, and the other end secured to a buoyant cushion or float.

16. Checklist of nautical terms:

VERBS

capsize—To upset, or turn over.

seize—To fasten together or bind with a lashing.

snub—To check a line suddenly from running out.

trip—To upset an anchor from the bottom.

weigh—To raise an anchor off the bottom.

GENERAL

bitter end—The last part of a line, especially an anchor rode.

break out—To come free of the ground; also, to unstow.

crown—The point where the arms join the shank of an anchor.

ground tackle—A boat's anchoring gear, including anchors, rode, etc.

rode—The anchor line.

seizing—A lashing made of small line or wire.

shank—The vertical shaft of an anchor.

thimble—A metal ring, grooved on the outside to take a line or wire.

trip line—A light line rigged to the crown of an anchor to permit capsizing it in case of fouling.

weigh anchor—To raise the anchor off the bottom.

13

Shortening Down and Reefing

WHEN THE WIND increases beyond the point where your boat can handle it safely under her normal *working canvas* (everyday sails), you may still be able to sail, either by setting fewer sails or by reducing the area of those you carry. The aim is to lighten the burden on the boat yet maintain enough steerageway to parry sudden puffs. For there is more danger in not having enough sail up than in carrying a little too much.

If you are *overcanvased*—carrying too much sail for the strength of the wind—you can usually deal with increased wind pressure, for a time at least, by *starting sheets* (that is, easing them), or by heading higher into the wind. But there is no defense against insufficient headway—you are at the mercy of the wind because you cannot parry its sudden puffs. This principle should be your guide in deciding whether to *shorten down* (reduce sail) by taking sail off or by reefing.

A quick way to lessen the wind's pressure on the boat is to strike the jib. Although, as we have noted, this throws the boat out of balance by increasing her weather helm, it has the advantage of speed in meeting a sudden overall increase in the force of the breeze. By itself, however, it may not be enough; you may still have so much sail up you are in danger of being overpowered.

You have the alternative, of course, of dousing the mainsail and leaving the jib set. But this gives the boat a lee helm, and makes it impossible to go windward. It is, however, a useful tactic if you are upwind of your mooring and wish only to sail home. But a more desirable way to reduce sail, because it keeps the boat in better balance, with some weather helm, is to reef the mainsail—provided your boat is equipped with reefing gear or your mainsail has reef points.

Reefing with reef points

Even skippers whose sails are fitted for reefing often delay to reef because it involves a certain amount of effort, and they would rather keep on sailing, though uncomfortably, hoping the breeze will moderate. The chances are it will not. When whitecaps start to appear, or when the interval between strong puffs gets shorter, you may be sure the breeze will continue to build. Delay in shortening down will only make it harder later on.

*Reef points let you re-
duce area of sail to keep
from being overbur-
dened*

If your mainsail is equipped with reef points and you do not delay, you will probably be able to lower sail, tie in the reef, and get under way again in less than 15 minutes. Later, when the boat is jumping around, it may take twice as long.

Unless you are sailing single-handed, you do not have to anchor or lower all sail in order to reef, but can reef while sailing under jib alone. Get out your bag of reefing gear, or suitable line for making the necessary lashings. Lower the mainsail and rest the boom in the boom crutch. Reefing is essentially a repetition of bending sail, except that the head and luff are already secured. But a new tack and clew must be secured, and a new foot made fast.

To secure the new tack—search up the luff from the gooseneck until you find the reefing cringle. Open the slide track gate and release from the track enough slides to bring this cringle down to the boom. Then close the gate. With a piece of lashing line, make the cringle fast to the boom with several round turns at the gooseneck, passing the line around the boom and through the cringle each time, and finish with a square knot.

To secure the new clew—work up the leech from the outhaul until you locate the clew reef cringle. *Reeve* (pass) a lashing line as an outhaul through this and through any handy fitting at the end of the boom, pull the line hand-tight, and make it fast. Resist the temptation to put a heavy strain on this reefing outhaul; it will overstretch the sail and may destroy its shape permanently.

To secure the new foot—roll into a tight furl the sail between the boom and the line of reef points and, starting at the luff and working aft, tie each of the reef points to itself to hold the furl in place. Pass one end of the reef point under the furled sail (*not* under the boom), bring it up on the side of the furl, and tie it as snugly as possible to the other end with a reef knot. Since one hand is hidden under the sail during this process, you might accidentally tie two different points together. To avoid this possibility, as you prepare to tie the two ends of the reef point, pull on one end to feel

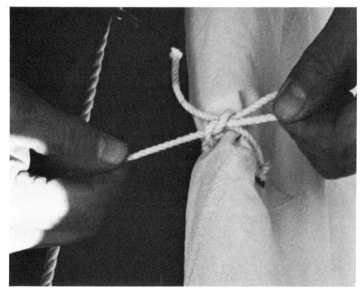

Reef points are passed between furled sail and boom, not under boom, and are made fast with reef knot. Here a loop is left in each reef knot for quick untying.

whether or not the pull is transmitted to the other. If it isn't, search around under the sail with the hidden hand until you find the right end for the reef point in your other hand. If two people are available to reef, let one start at the luff and work aft, while the other starts at the leech and works forward.

When all the points have been tied in, take several turns with an additional lashing through the clew reef cringle and around the boom to make a holddown. Secure this holddown with a reef knot. This should be a different line than the outhaul, because when the time comes to shake out the reef, the outhaul must be let go before the holddown.

Shaking out a reef with reef points

Whereas there's a general tendency to delay putting a reef in because of the effort involved, for the same reason there's an equal and opposite inertia to shaking it out. The skipper hesitates to take the lightening of the breeze as a sure sign that the blow has passed for fear that if he shakes out his reef too soon, he may have to tie it in again should the breeze return. So he hobbles along under less canvas than he needs for sailing his boat effectively until finally it becomes quite clear that the danger is gone. In the meantime he has lost time and distance he might have gained had he only known that a reef can be shaken out as soon as the interval between puffs becomes longer than the duration of the puffs.

A reef may be shaken out easily under way, without lowering the sail. But the boat should be headed toward the wind, and the sheet eased so there is no strain on the sail. Each element of the reef should be cast off in the same order followed when tying in the

reef, beginning with the reef points. Untie the middle reef point first, then work forward and aft until all the points have been cast off. Next, cast off the luff holddown. Then, as quickly as possible, cast off the leech outhaul and the leech holddown; *be sure to follow this order.*

If you let go the holddown before the outhaul, the boom will drop and the weight will be concentrated in a pulling strain at the clew reef cringle that may be enough to split the sail. In fact, it is good practice to *cut* both the leech outhaul and holddown to free them quickly and avoid the chance of a tear. Take up the slack on the main halyard, feeding luff slides back on the track, and secure.

Reefing with roller reefing gear

Many small sailboats have adopted a form of roller reefing gear, which makes it possible to reduce sail area by rolling the mainsail around the boom, like a giant window shade. One of the two essential elements for such a device is a geared fitting at the forward end of the boom to let it be rotated inside a sleeve that attaches to the gooseneck. The other requirement is a cap on the after end of the boom that rotates with the boom, inside an encircling ring to which the mainsheet is secured. Reefing with such a gear is fast and efficient because the sail is kept hoisted during the entire process, and the reef fits better if some strain is kept on the sail while it is being rolled down.

It is, however, an operation that is best performed by at least two people: (1) someone on the main halyard to open the slide track gate on the mast, and to slack off on the halyard a few inches at a time, feeding the sail to (2) someone who cranks the handle of the gooseneck gear that rotates the boom. He must also guide the bolt rope of the luff as it winds around the boom, to prevent it bunching on top of itself.

If a third hand is available, he can stretch the leech aft as the sail comes down and, if it is to be a deep reef, remove any battens that might otherwise be rolled up with the sail. On tapered booms, or booms of square section, special long bolsters may be rolled in with the sail to make it lie more smoothly along the boom.

Because there are no holddowns, outhauls, or reef points to be secured, a reef can be rolled in to whatever depth is desired, in a fraction of the time of ordinary reefing, with less danger of distorting the sail's shape.

Rolling out a reef with roller reefing gear

Besides reducing the tendency to delay reefing, roller reefing gear's ease of operation encourages a skipper to roll out a reef at the first sign of the breeze moderating; so much less exertion is at stake in rereefing if he has been premature. When the reef is rolled out, unless the boat is fitted with a halyard winch, the mainsheet should be eased, to take all strain off the sail and permit it to be hoisted *two-blocks* (high as possible) again without undue effort.

With one person to unroll the boom with the gooseneck gear crank, and another to hoist the unrolled sail and feed the luff slides back on the mast track, the operation is swift and painless. If any battens have been removed, they should be reinserted as the pockets unroll.

Summary

1. When shortening sail, it is better to leave slightly too much sail up than too little.

2. Lowering the jib is a quick way to shorten sail.

3. Lowering the mainsail, while leaving the jib up, greatly reduces wind pressure on the boat, but produces lee helm and limits the ability to go to windward.

4. When whitecaps begin to appear or when strong puffs increase in frequency and duration, small sailboats should shorten down promptly.

5. The steps in reefing a sail with reef points are:
   a. Get out reefing gear.
   b. Lower the mainsail.
   c. Lash the luff reef cringle at the gooseneck.
   d. Reeve an outhaul lashing through the leech clew cringle; do not haul too tight.
   e. Furl tightly the sail between the boom and the line of reef points.
   f. Starting at the luff, tie each reef point in turn toward the leech. Reef points pass under the sail, *not* under the boom.
   g. **Lash down the clew reef cringle to the boom with a separate line for holddown.**

6. These are the steps in shaking out a reef with reef points:
   a. Sail the boat close-hauled and ease the mainsheet.
   b. Untie the middle reef point first, then work forward and aft.
   c. Cast off the luff holddown.
   d. *Quickly* cast off (or cut) the leech outhaul.
   e. *Quickly* cast off (or cut) the leech holddown.
   f. Take up the slack on the main halyard.

7. To roll in a reef with roller reefing gear, the steps are:
   a. With the boat on the wind, slack off the main halyard.
   b. Rotate the boom with the gooseneck gear crank.
   c. Lower sail in unison with the rolling of the boom.

d. Pull out the leech; remove any battens as required.

e. Secure the halyard, stow the gooseneck crank, continue sailing.

8. To roll out a reef with roller reefing gear:

a. Close-haul the boat, with all strain off the mainsail.

b. Take a strain on the main halyard.

c. Unroll the reef and raise the sail in unison.

d. Replace any battens as their pockets unroll.

e. Secure the main halyard, stow the gooseneck crank, resume sailing.

9. Checklist of nautical terms:

SAILING TERMS

overcanvased—Carrying too much sail for the weight of the breeze.

shorten down—To reduce sail by taking sail off or by reefing.

start sheets—To slacken off or ease them.

two-blocks—As high, or as tight as possible.

working canvas—A boat's ordinary sails, for everyday use.

VERB

reeve—To pass a line through an opening, as over the sheave of a block.

14

Capsizing

PEOPLE WHO HAVE NEVER BEEN in a capsize are generally more worried and nervous about its dangers than those who have had the experience—a prime example of imagination's efficiency in frightening us with hobgoblins created out of the unknown. The one sure way to lay this particular group of ghosts is to *practice* capsizing and the routine of righting a boat from a capsize, and learn, in the water, how unfounded are most of the fears.

A perfect instance is the experience of one member of a ladies' sailing class, who was always timid about sailing in any breeze much above a flat calm. She was terrified by the thought of capsizing because she *knew* she'd get caught under the sail, and that, to her, meant practically certain death by drowning. Sure enough, when we practiced capsizing, she *was* caught under the sail—only, instead of being in the dark and drowning, as she had imagined, she found that her head pushed the sail up enough to give her plenty of air, and the sail let enough light through to make it quite bright underneath. She had only to tread water and work herself out to the leech of the sail to be free.

Her relief at finding her preconceived notions groundless was matched by a marked increase in confidence in her sailing from that day forward. She was a bright, intelligent woman, and had studied the art of sailing with great application. But the first minute of that practice capsize did more than all her reading to persuade her that a capsize need not be fatal.

One obvious reassurance against the perils of capsizing is to have everyone on board don a life jacket whenever the wind gets strong enough to cause a capsize. Good sailors, incidentally, have no false pride about wearing life jackets—many small-boat racing sailors routinely wear one of the modern, lightweight, vest-type life jackets to be ever ready for a capsize, in foul weather or fair.

How to prevent a capsize

A boat capsizes because the overturning pressure of the wind or the sea, or both, on her sails and topsides is greater than the grip of her bottom and underbody on the water. So it is apparent that to prevent capsizing,

123

either the pressures on the topsides must be reduced, or the boat's grip on the water increased. Shortening sail is, of course, an excellent way to reduce wind pressure, and should be done when the general wind has increased so much that the boat must be luffed constantly, or sheets must be eased frequently, to continue sailing.

Before that stage is reached—as we saw in our discussion of Two Safety Valves (page 29)—the skipper who keeps enough headway on the boat so she can be steered at all times can use steering and easing of sheets effectively to spill wind. There comes a point, though, when these two measures are no longer enough, with the mainsail shaken so violently.it threatens to break the battens and tear itself to ribbons. Then the skipper is well advised to shorten down quickly.

When the wind pipes up, nothing so effectively increases the boat's grip on the water as proper distribution of her movable ballast. Now every ounce of loose water in the boat becomes an active enemy, pushing the boat toward a capsize. Each gallon of salt water weighs about eight pounds; fresh water nearly as much. To sail in a rising wind with ten gallons of water sloshing around to leeward in the boat is like having a good-sized boy hanging on the lee rail trying to turn you over. As a skipper interested in avoiding a capsize, you'll dispense with that kind of help by keeping your boat bailed dry.

At the same time, you will position your crew and movable ballast as far to windward as possible, to counterbalance the wind's heeling pressure. If the wind is gusty, with knockdown puffs of great violence alternating with periods of relative calm, you must be lively in getting your movable ballast inboard when the puff passes, or you may capsize the boat *to windward*. Three grown men, for example, caught well out to weather on the

rail of a small centerboarder by the abrupt passing of a puff might be enough weight to roll her down and capsize her to windward.

The possibility of a capsize is markedly less with a keel boat than with a centerboarder because of the inherent righting factors of the keel boat and its lower center of gravity. It is a mistake, however, to assume that a keel boat cannot be capsized. Given the right combination of wind pressure and sea, she may be heeled down so far that she takes water over her lee rail, into her cockpit, and loses her basic buoyancy. Marcel Bardiaux, French circumnavigator of the world in his 30-foot sailboat, *Les 4 Vents* (*The Four Winds*) was twice rolled completely over in the Straits of Le Maire as he approached Cape Horn. He was saved from sinking by having closed the hatch and watertight door of his cabin, and by his self-bailing cockpit.

But when a small, open, keel sailboat buries her leeward cockpit rail and takes any substantial quantity of water aboard, unless she has flotation tanks, she will probably sink. Wherefore, the skipper of a wooden keel boat should be quite fussy about keeping seams tight to minimize the amount of water his boat makes when laboring in a heavy blow and seaway.

For capsize demonstration purposes, let us assume we are sailing a small centerboarder in squally weather. Through miscalculation of the sea's stopping power, we miss stays in tacking and are caught in irons, without steerageway. Before we can recover, a violent **puff hits us that we cannot parry. The boat is blown over on her side, and we are all thrown into the water. There's little danger** of going under the sail, unless you happen to be sitting to leeward when the boat capsizes. And, as we saw at the outset, it is not the desperate plight so many beginners imagine.

How to deal with a capsize

There are three basic rules of conduct in a capsize: (1) *to stay with the boat,* (2) *to keep calm,* and (3) *to have a panic-proof routine* for handling the situation. The following steps are recommended:

Count noses. The instant the boat is over on her side, locate each member of your crew. If anyone is missing, search under the boat first, then under the sail, and finally under water in the area.

Don life jackets. If you and your crew are not already wearing life jackets, and unless rescue is close at hand, pull life jackets out of the boat and have each person put one on, regardless of how well he swims. Getting into a life jacket in a rough sea is a very hard job; that's why it's better to put them one *before* you capsize. But you may be in the water a long time before rescue arrives; the life jackets will conserve energy. And even good swimmers can get cold and develop cramps.

Put one man on opposite side. Whether you have been thrown into the water on the windward or leeward side of the boat, send one crew member around to the opposite side to prevent the boat rolling its mast under and turning bottom up.

Tie down loose gear. Before cushions, paddle, or floorboards float away, lash them to the boat with whatever lines are handy.

Douse sails. Cast off main and jib halyards to get the sails down. If you can't reach the halyard cleats, don't hesitate to cut the halyards—you can always replace them later. Slide the mainsail down the mast and lash it to the boom in a rough furl with the mainsheet. Slide the jib down the headstay and lash it in a rough furl to the tack with one of the jibsheets.

Right the boat. If there are three in the crew, place two amidships at the side of the cockpit to start heaving the boat upright, while the man on the bottom side of the boat, opposite to the sail, stands on the centerboard to use it as a righting lever. Instruct him to stand close to the trunk, not on the end of the board, or he may snap it off. When the boat swings upright, check her tendency to roll over in the opposite direction. At this point, you have an impressive demonstration of the basic instability of a boat with uncontrolled movable ballast!

Man the centerboard trunk. Have your tiredest crew member climb into the boat and sit astride the centerboard trunk. If there is a big sea running and it seems feasible to bail the boat, stuff the trunk opening with clothing to prevent water flowing through it into the boat.

Place one person on each quarter. With one person on the centerboard trunk, and one on each quarter to help balance the boat, she can be kept upright until a tow arrives. If bailing is feasible, let the man on the trunk bail out carefully as many buckets as he can without undue fatigue. Or if he has been able to reach the pump, let him use that. Bailing by bucket while straddling a centerboard trunk in a swamped boat can be a very exacting exercise in balancing. Change over bailers when the first man slows down.

Secure towline around mast. When help arrives to tow you, lead the towline through the bow chock and around the mast at deck level, placing a life jacket between it and the mast to cushion the shock and prevent chafe, and secure the line with a round turn and a bowline.

Start towing SLOWLY! Instruct the towing skipper to take a *gradual* strain on the towline until the slack is all out of it, and to tow slowly at first, until the boat is moving well. DO NOT ASSUME HE KNOWS HOW TO TOW A SWAMPED BOAT. Unless you tell him exactly how to proceed, he may gun his engine full speed ahead and break your mast. It has happened, even with professional seamen who should have known the enormous inertia of a submerged boat but didn't.

Tow faster and bail. Once the towed boat is moving well, the towing skipper can increase his speed gradually. This will raise the bow of the tow and send the water aft, making it easier to bail and empty the boat. If the boat is equipped with transom drains or self-bailers, open them and let the boat drain herself. Then close the openings.

THE MOST SERIOUS ERROR in a capsize is to abandon the boat and try to swim for shore. Only when a keel boat capsizes that is not equipped with flotation should there be any need to leave the boat. In all other cases, the skipper and every member of the crew should stay with the boat—it is safer, and the chance of a speedy rescue is infinitely greater. A capsized boat is a larger, more visible object, and will attract more attention, from farther off, than anyone swimming.

Summary

1. Fear of a capsize can be overcome by practicing capsizing and the routine of righting a boat from a capsize.
2. Even experienced small-boat sailors do not hesitate to put on life jackets or vests whenever the breeze gets strong enough to cause a capsize.
3. To prevent a capsize, wind pressure on the boat must be reduced, or the boat's grip on the water increased.
4. One way to reduce wind pressure is to shorten sail.
5. A boat's grip on the water is influenced by the distribution of her movable ballast.
6. Movable ballast should be kept as far to windward as possible, but shifted inboard when puffs pass to avoid capsizing to windward.
7. Keel boats capsize less easily than centerboarders, but can capsize.
8. When a boat capsizes, it is of utmost importance (1) *to stay with the boat,* (2) *to keep calm,* and (3) *to follow a panic-proof routine* to control the situation:
   a. Count noses.
   b. Don life jackets.
   c. Put one man on the bottom side of the boat, the rest on the side with the sail.
   d. Tie down loose gear.
   e. Douse sails and secure them.
   f. Right the boat, with one man on the bottom side (opposite from the sail), standing on the centerboard, close to the trunk.
   g. Let the most tired crew member straddle the centerboard trunk.
   h. If three in crew—each of the other two places himself at one quarter. If only two in crew, second man takes place at middle of transom.
   i. When help arrives, secure towline around the mast with a life jacket underneath, with a round turn and bowline.
   j. Start towing *slowly.* Be sure towing skipper understands why.
   k. Tow faster, and bail when the boat is moving well.
9. *The most serious* error in a capsize is to leave the boat and try to swim ashore.

15

Emergencies and How to Handle Them

IN LEARNING TO SAIL, the normal sequence of events is pretty much the same as in other sports that involve a certain amount of physical risk. The first few times out, there is great timidity, with the beginner slow and unsure as he starts to unravel the mysteries of his new craft. Then, since nothing usually happens at this stage to dampen his ardor, the timidity suddenly disappears and in its place blooms a vast confidence that underestimates the potential dangers and overestimates the ease of dealing with them. This state of overconfidence is apt to continue until something unexpected occurs that gives the neophyte fresh insight into the hazards of the sport, and frightens him back into a safer and more permanently useful orientation— the alert and watchful attitude of the skipper who is neither too timid nor too bold.

This careful skipper will thenceforth have fewer emergencies to deal with than someone who has not been through the mill, since one result of his experience will be to make his preparation for sailing more systematic and careful.

But even a prudent sailor cannot avoid getting caught occasionally by a sudden squall or thunderstorm, or having a sail split. He will, however, have an advantage over the casual skipper in knowing beforehand **how to handle the principal emergencies likely to occur in small-boat sailing**.

Man Overboard

This most urgent emergency demands prompt action to avoid the possibility of drowning, especially if the man may be stunned from being hit by the boom when tacking or in an accidental jibe. Against this emergency, the properly-*found* (equipped) sailboat always has a buoyant cushion or life jacket handy to the helmsman. *At once,* toss this cushion or jacket to the man overboard. Then jibe the boat around and sail back slightly to leeward of him, as though about to pick up a mooring. Shoot into the wind so as to bring him alongside the cockpit on the leeward side, when the boat has little or no headway. If he needs help in getting aboard, reach over and pull him over the side by lifting under his shoulders, or throw a bowline in the end of the mainsheet and slip it over his head and under his shoulders to get better leverage.

In approaching a man in the water, keep to windward of him to provide a lee for picking him up. No marine exercise has a higher potential yield of safety than practicing "Man Overboard" drill under a variety of conditions of wind and sea, by tossing a cushion over the side and keeping a record of how long it takes you to retrieve it.

Thunderstorms

If you make it standard practice to get a radio marine weather forecast each time before going out, you'll seldom be caught out in a thunderstorm. Long before they arrive, they fill the air with static that is heard on the radio in crackling bursts. Also, since they are primarily a summer phenomenon, they are more apt to come at the end of a hot, muggy day, and give warning of their approach by a gradual build-up of heavy, dark gray, or black *cumulus* (heaped) clouds. Keep a sharp lookout, especially, for the high-towering *cumulo-nimbus* (thunderhead) formations that reach up thousands of feet and often take the shape of an anvil head. These are a storehouse of powerful downdrafts and winds of ferocious strength.

Generally thunderstorms work their way across or upwind, with the thunder of their approach getting constantly louder. In tidal waters they travel in the direction of the tide, and may come back when the tide turns. Before they strike, the wind usually goes quite flat, as though hushed in waiting—the familiar "calm before the storm." If the calm is long, the wind will be violent. In any event, when it returns, it will be from a different direction than before the calm.

The smart skipper does not defy a thunderstorm; he avoids it, if possible, by putting

his boat on her mooring, securing all gear, and going ashore. If you are not able to beat the storm back to your mooring, try to find a spot to leeward of the storm's direction of travel—as indicated by the movement of its clouds—and anchor with a scope of at least seven times the depth. Lower and furl all sail, secure all loose lines and gear, and snug yourself down to ride out the blow.

Even if you cannot anchor, lower and furl all sail and secure all gear, and prepare to run before the storm under bare poles. To slow down the rate of your drift (unless it will take you back toward your mooring), submerge a bucket and tow it astern on a 25-foot length of line.

After the calm, when the storm breaks, take note of which arrives first—the wind or the rain. When the wind of a thunderstorm comes before the rain, the storm will not last too long, and you should soon be able to get under way again. But if the rain starts to pelt down while it is still calm, and the wind arrives later, be prepared for a long siege.

During the storm stay away from the mast, shrouds, and headstay, since these are the logical conductors for lightning, should it hit the boat. As a matter of assurance, lightning seldom hits small sailboats, and when it does, it leaves the boat above the waterline. There is actually little danger from a thunderstorm if you don't try to sail in it. The principal discomfort is getting soaked with rain, which can be very chilling. However, if you keep a couple of ponchos on board, stowed on a shelf under the foredeck, you'll always be prepared for sitting out a storm in comfort, even though your regular foul weather gear may be at home.

After the storm has passed, it may take the wind with it and leave you bobbling in a flat calm. This is another reason for trying to get back as close as possible to your mooring before the storm. You won't have so far to paddle when it's over.

Broken Tiller

When the tiller breaks on a boat that is properly balanced—with a slight weather helm—she immediately heads into the wind. Unless you have a spare tiller that can be fitted into place at once, get sail off instantly, lowering the jib first, then the mainsail, and secure them. If you can anchor, do so; if not; drift while you make repairs.

With her centerboard fully down, a boat can be steered without her tiller by adjusting the trim of jib and mainsail, but it is a tiresome procedure. It's much better to carry a spare. Even a small boat can profitably carry a spare tiller, either a duplicate of her regular helm, or a suitable length of 1-inch outside diameter galvanized iron pipe, threaded and capped at one end and equipped at the other with a fitting to engage the head of the rudder. If you don't wish to carry a spare, at least have aboard a sharp knife, for when a tiller breaks, it usually lets go at the rudder head, where the turning pressure is concentrated. By a little judicious whittling you may be able to trim the broken tiller shaft to fit the rudder head.

Another useful item in a small boat's *ditty bag* (repair kit) is a pair of 4-inch C-clamps. These can be used to clamp the handle of the boat's paddle to the rudder head to make a good substitute tiller.

When the tiller has been replaced, make sail again, haul in the anchor, and continue sailing.

Broken Rudder

This is more serious than a broken tiller, though the immediate effect is the same—a boat with weather helm heads into the wind. All sail should be lowered at once and secured, and the boat anchored while repair procedures or a *jury rig* (temporary substitute) are worked out. As noted, it is possible to sail a boat without tiller or rudder by the trim of her sails alone. One memorable example was the experience of the 58-foot aluminum yawl, *Dyna,* which lost her rudder while nearly a thousand miles from England in the same transatlantic race and during the same storm that caused *Ondine* to broach to and jibe accidentally (page 78). With superb seamanship, *Dyna's* owner and skipper, Clayton Ewing, continued in the race, steering his boat by her sails alone, and succeeded in taking fourth place overall among fourteen boats in the race.

Unship the broken rudder and stow it out of the way. You will probably be able to use the boat's oar or paddle as a jury rudder. Or if none is on board, a floorboard may do the job. When you make sail again, leave off the jib if you are sailing single-handed, because steering by paddle or floorboard will keep you fully occupied. Also, since the blade of the substitute rudder will be smaller than the boat's regular rudder, sail area should be reduced to lessen the pressure on the steering blade. Reef the mainsail, if possible. One caution: Put a lashing around your emergency rudder and make it fast to an after cleat, to prevent it going adrift if you should accidentally drop it.

Jammed Centerboard

This is a frequent emergency in small-boat sailing, from a variety of causes. It is not so serious if the board is jammed in a lowered position, since the boat can still be sailed and only presents a problem when she must be *beached* (put on shore) or hauled out. But if the centerboard jams when up, and cannot be lowered, it becomes impossible to sail close-hauled or on a close reach with any efficiency.

A metal centerboard is often jammed by running aground with the board down. This bends it so that it cannot be hauled back into the trunk, and is virtually impossible to repair at sea. Either haul the boat out by running a trailer into water that is deeper than her centerboard, or beach the boat. Only, instead of running her bow on to the beach, as in ordinary beaching procedure, lower all sail and float her in broadside. By heeling her toward the beach, float her in close enough to roll her down on her side so that you can can get at the centerboard and straighten it. Be sure to put a couple of cushions or life jackets under the side you roll down, to protect it against scarring by the beach.

One argument against trying to raise a jammed centerboard at sea is, that you may not be able to get it down again when you need it. Unless you can remove the cause of the jamming, it's better to continue sailing with the board down until you can beach the boat and fix it.

A centerboard that has run out to its full depth because the pennant has parted, may be raised again by lowering a bight of line over the bow and sweeping it aft on both sides, with a tension on it, until it engages the centerboard and brings it back up into the trunk. Replace the broken pennant.

This technique may not be successful, however, with a board when the pennant has accidentally gone down the trunk—a mishap that can be prevented by tying a Figure-8 knot in the end of the pennant to keep it from escaping through its block. If the board is fully down and the pennant has gone with it, retrieve the pennant first and lead it into the trunk to prevent it jamming when the board comes up, since most trunks have little clearance between the sides and the centerboard. To retrieve the pennant, if the trunk is capped, unscrew the cap and try to reach the pennant with a boathook if it will fit in the trunk. If not, lower into the trunk a line with a small weight on it and let it hang below the boat. Send your best swimmer over the side and have him tie the line to the centerboard pennant. Haul in on the retrieving line, get the pennant, and this time tie a knot in its end.

A board jammed in its raised position can sometimes be loosened by working the top from side to side, or by hitting it smartly with the bottom of a clenched fist. Sometimes sheer brute force, applied to the end of the board, may free it to go down, although I can recall sweating for twenty minutes one hot afternoon trying unsuccessfully to push down a board at the mooring, before finally giving up and beaching the boat. It was just well—a small length of marsh reed had fitted itself neatly between the side of the trunk and the board; the pushing had only wedged it tighter.

A more frequent cause of a board jammed so that it cannot be lowered comes from beaching on a pebbly shore and getting a stone wedged between board and trunk. This is practically impossible to dislodge at sea. The boat must be beached again and rolled on her side, and the stone dug out with a screwdriver. When you launch her again, put an old piece of canvas on the beach under the centerboard, or clear the area of all loose pebbles that might cause it to jam a second time.

Broken Halyard

The easiest way to repair a broken halyard is to replace it before it lets go! But many sailors exhibit a misplaced thriftiness by continuing to rely on a piece of line for this important duty long after it has reached the age of retirement. A halyard usually parts because the constant working back and forth across its sheave gradually weakens, then breaks, the tiny fibers that make up the line.

Periodically inspect the last foot or so of each halyard where it joins the sail. Open up the strands of the line and examine closely the individual fibers of the strands for signs of breaking. Manila develops a powdery dust between strands when there has been a lot of wear; synthetic lines begin to look furry and fuzzy inside. Both should be discarded when they reach this stage.

If you have any doubts about the soundness of that end of the line, examine the other end and see if it is sound. If it is, you may still get useful life out of the halyard by turning it *end-for-end,* using the end that has hitherto been cleated, to attach to the sail. Before the start of a Vineyard Race on Long Island Sound one year, we were debating the advisability of "end-for-ending" our ½-inch nylon spinnaker halyard, which had seen hard service in that year's Bermuda Race. But it was close to starting time, so we decided to take a chance. Two nights later, tearing along under spinnaker before a strong easterly and wild sea north of Block Island, the spinnaker halyard parted with a noise like a pistol shot. We were lucky to get the sail in without having the boat overrun it, which would have stopped her like hitting a wall, and probably taken the mast out. As it was, we lost valuable distance and time through having to wait until morning to send a man aloft to rig a new halyard. Subsequently, we rigged double spinnaker halyards so as to always have a spare.

Short of sending a man (or boy) aloft, there is no easy way to replace a broken halyard at sea. On a small boat, before anyone goes up the mast, all sail should be off, and the boat anchored, if possible, to reduce her rolling to a minimum. Discretion must also be used in who climbs the mast. A 150-pound man, for example, would probably overturn the average small centerboarder long before he reached the top of her mast; there isn't enough weight in the hull to keep the center of gravity from rising above the capsizing point.

Whoever climbs the mast should secure the new halyard to the *back* of his belt with two half-hitches, and someone on deck should hold the halyard out from mast while he climbs, to keep it from fouling his legs. Have the climber reeve the new halyard over the sheave and bring the end to deck with him in his teeth.

Of course, if a boat is equipped with flotation and can be righted, bailed, and sailed from a capsize, this is another way of replacing a broken halyard at sea, though damp and inconvenient.

Running aground

Few sailors brag about having run aground, but the story of the man who ran aground in a narrow channel Down East is apt. He was tacking back and forth between mudbanks, approaching the dock under the eyes of some onlookers, but finally took the ground short of the dock. When one of the spectators laughed, an old fisherman looked at him reproachfully, took his pipe from his mouth, spat over the side, and said: *"Feller ain't been aground, ain't sailed very fur."* A prudent skipper learns in advance how to handle this situation.

Centerboard boats have one advantage over keel boats in giving warning of *shoal* (shallow) water before the boat is actually aground—if the centerboard is all the way down. As the board hits bottom, you will probably hear and feel it strike and, if the trunk is not capped, will see the board start to rise. At once, raise the board and try to jibe the boat around and sail back the way you came. Do not sail ahead, hoping to sail over the shoal. The water ahead is likely to be even more shoal, and put you hard aground, whereas you may be able to escape grounding by reversing your course. Jibing is preferable to tacking in this situation because it is faster and because it turns your bow away from the known direction of the shoal water.

If your maneuver is unsuccessful, and you take the ground in spite of it, *don't panic.* Thousands of sailors go aground every year, and most of them get free again without losing more than a little time and some of their spare energy. There are so many different ways of going aground, and on so many different types of bottom, it isn't practicable to discuss each in detail. But the following principles apply to all groundings:

a. *Protect your rudder* from damage by lifting it, if you seem certain to ground. You can always rig it again when you get free.

b. *Raise the centerboard* and secure it, if it has not already been pushed up into the trunk by the grounding.

c. *Avoid driving on harder.* If your sails are still pushing you forward, ease sheets to spill the wind and douse sail as quickly as possible. Shift your crew and movable ballast aft to keep the boat's weight toward the deep water behind you, while you work out a plan to get off.

d. *Sound around the boat* with an oar or paddle and find where the deep water lies, so that you know whether or not the only way out is the way you came in.

e. *Get an anchor out* as far as possible into deep water off one quarter, preferably to leeward; it will provide leverage to help turn the bow away from the shoal and get you off. For this, a modern lightweight anchor is handy if the water is warm enough for swimming. Lash it temporarily to a buoyant cushion and have your best swimmer take it as far out into deep water as its full scope will permit, then drop it.

If the water is too cold for swimming, this is the one occasion when it is permissible to heave an anchor, though it is only feasible

with one of the modern lightweight anchors. The farther you heave it, the more good you'll be apt to do yourself. Get the anchor on deck and clear the coil for running out easily, with the bitter end secured to the mast belowdeck. Lead the anchor forward of the mast and outside the shrouds, back to the cockpit. Stand on the leeward quarter and hold the anchor by a length of rode that lets you swing it comfortably in a large vertical circle, without touching the water or hitting anything on the boat. Make two or three giant circles to get momentum, then, from the top of the circle, let the anchor fly toward the deep water.

Take a strain on the anchor rode to dig the anchor in. If it doesn't hold the first time, try it again. When it finally holds, secure the rode to the foredeck cleat with a strain on it.

f. *Hoist the jib,* and sheet it in to heel the boat and pivot the bow to leeward, meanwhile putting an increasing strain on the anchor rode.

g. *Shift your weight from side to side* rhythmically, to rock the boat and loosen the bottom's grip on her. Keep pulling on the rode in long surges. This treatment can free even a stubbornly held boat. When the bow starts to swing toward the anchor, be prepared for a jibe as the wind crosses over your stern. Have the rudder ready to rerig when the boat moves off the shoal and is headed back toward the anchor. Uncleat the rode, place it in the bow chock, and haul in until it is straight up and down, throw a turn around the cleat to put a strain on it, and let the boat sail the anchor out. Haul it aboard and stow it.

All the anchor procedure may be unnecessary if you have grounded in water shallow enough to stand in and push or lift the boat off. Long Island's Great South Bay is crowded with shoals of this kind. So, too, is Barnegat Bay in New Jersey. You will find that if the water is more than waist deep, however, it is almost impossible to exert any really effective pushing or lifting pressure because the boat rides too high above you and your own weight is lessened by the water.

In water less than waist deep, put your back to the boat and grip the *forefoot* (bottom of the bow) in both hands, with arms straight and knees bent, and rock the boat up and down by alternately straightening and bending your knees. The wave motion you create will help break the ground's hold. Then place your back against the bow and push *with your legs* to free the boat.

If you sail regularly in shoal waters where running aground is a common hazard, equip your boat with a long, stout "shoving pole" of at least 2-inch diameter for pushing against the bottom. Sandpaper it well to remove splinters. When using it, to get maximum leverage, face away from the end resting on the bottom, grip the upper end in both hands with arms extended, and pull down against the pole with the full weight of your body. It is vital to have a strong, rigid pole that will not break under this strain, and possibly send you overboard or impale you. While you are pushing, have your crew shift their weight side to side to rock the boat and accelerate the freeing action.

Easier than any of the foregoing measures is to have someone tow you off the shoal—if you are lucky enough to have a Good Samaritan nearby, as I was in one memorable grounding with my first boat, an old Star, during a smoky sou'wester. The Star wore an 865-pound solid iron, fin bulb keel that extended more than three feet below the surface and gave her great stability for sailing in rough weather. We had been driving across Manhasset Bay, hard on the wind, with the boom sheeted well in, and a sharp angle of heel that blocked the view to leeward. It was lively and exciting sailing until I bent down to look under the boom and

saw we were within a hundred feet of hitting the opposite shore. With a shout to the crew (my wife) to prepare for an abrupt tack, I pushed the tiller hard alee. The boat straightened up as she came into the wind, and we were promptly aground!

Our angle of heel had been so great, we had sailed into water shoaler than the depth of our keel, without striking until we straightened up. The boat's keel was flat on the bottom of the bulb, and about eight inches wide, so we were firmly fast. I sprang forward, lowered all sail, and looked around to size up the situation, particularly to see whether the tide was on its way in or out (something I should have checked before sailing!). A short distance away a small power cruiser was moving up; she had seen us take the ground and was coming to our assistance.

Hastily I freed our anchor rode from the mast below deck and made up about 30 feet into a coil for heaving. Our rescuer nosed carefully toward our stern in the strong breeze until he was close enough to catch our line. This he made fast to a *bitt* (towing post) on his stern while I paid out slack. When his end was fast, I took a round turn around the mast at deck level with my end of the anchor rode, tied in a bowline, and signaled him to take up the slack *slowly*. Gently, he put a strain on the line, and we began to slide astern. Soon we were free.

Wherever a nylon towrope is used, make it fast, if possible, to bitts or to some other part of the boat that cannot pull loose. Nylon has such great elasticity that if a cleat should pull out, it becomes a lethal projectile which can take out an eye or smash a skull. But if only cleats are available, make a bridle of the towline over two cleats to distribute the strain.

There are three lessons in this incident, none more important than one discussed under "Capsizing": Instruct whoever offers you a tow *not* to put a sudden strain on the towline but to take it up gradually, and be ready to slacken at once if anything seems likely to give way. The second lesson: Make the towline fast around the mast on deck, not below. An improvement in my procedure would have been to put a life jacket around the mast, under the towline, as a shock absorber and chafe guard. Apart from observing that we would never have run aground if I had kept a sharp lookout to leeward, the third lesson: Notice how much a boat's draft can be reduced by heeling her over. This can be useful in avoiding a grounding and in freeing a stranded boat.

A few years after the Star episode, we were sailing a 44-foot schooner across Nantucket Sound in a driving nor'easter with heavy rain and low visibility. Through some bad piloting on my part—principally, not trusting my compass—we found ourselves crossing treacherous Tuckernuck Shoal. As nearly as I could tell, we were in an area peppered with four-foot spots, three feet less than our boat needed to float her in flat calm. While the water got paler as it shoaled, we strapped the boat down until her lee rail was awash, and she was at maximum angle of heel. Then with life jackets on, we drove forward. Gradually the green water darkened as we sailed into greater depth; we were across the shoal. Had we not reduced our draft by heeling the boat, we would have grounded. And the Coast Guard on Nantucket, several miles away, would not have seen us in the heavy rain.

Going aground in tidal waters may be harder or easier than grounding in waters where there is no tide—harder, if you happen to take the ground when the tide is going out; easier, if you ground on a rising tide. In the first case, unless you get off promptly, you will have to wait until the tide runs all the way out, then returns to the same height (or higher) before you have enough water to float off. But if you have the good management to run aground with the tide coming in,

once you've lowered sail and gotten your anchor out with a strain on it, you have only to make yourself comfortable until the *flooding* (incoming) waters lift your boat off.

A centerboard boat, with relatively flat bottom, has no special problems if caught aground by an *ebbing* (outgoing) tide. But a deep keel boat may heel over and lie on her side if she goes aground near the top of the tide and there's a substantial difference in height between high and low water. Before she is completely high and dry, it might be possible to get an anchor out into deep water and take a strain on the anchor rode, secured as high as possible on the mast, to hold her upright. If she lies down in spite of such efforts, the angle of heel may seem alarming. Yet, in all probability, she will right herself without filling, as the tide comes. Any openings on the heeled side of the boat should be closed, however, and if the boat has a self-bailing cockpit, the *scuppers* (drain holes) on that side should be plugged to prevent the cockpit flooding before the boat is waterborne again on the returning tide.

While waiting for the tide to come in, study the local beach or shoreline to find how high a tide to expect, so that you will know when the moment has arrived to begin your efforts to get off. Twice a month—at new moon and full moon—tides of maximum height occur. These are called *spring tides,* and their high water is higher and their low water lower than at other times during the month. In between springs, at the moon's first and third quarters, are the tides of minimum range, called *neap tides.*

Fouled Anchor

A fouled anchor presents no problem if you have rigged it with a trip line and buoy (page 115). But sometimes an anchor will become fouled in waters that are supposedly

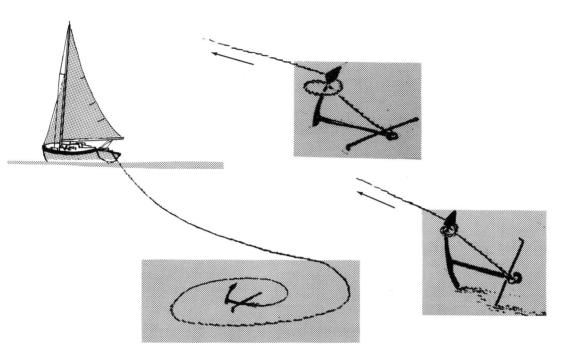

To free fouled anchor, slack off rode and lead it aft, sail boat in tight circle, and head upwind in opposite direction from original setting of anchor

free of underwater obstructions. The simplest and fastest way to free a fouled anchor is to go over the side, swim down the rode to the anchor, and disentangle it. But this is not always feasible if the water is more than 20 feet deep or too cold for swimming. Then the following tactic may work, if you have a modern, lightweight anchor on the bottom: Remove the bitter end of the rode from the mast below deck, lead it out through the bow chock and outside the shrouds, back into the cockpit, and make it fast again to the mast below deck, so that the lead to the anchor is clear from astern. Pay out all possible slack on the rode. Now sail your boat upwind, in a direction opposite to the original setting of the anchor, gathering maximum speed as the boat takes up the slack, until it reaches the end of the rode and puts the full force of

your forward momentum on the anchor. If this does not break it out at once, you may be able to free it presently by keeping the boat sailing on the same heading, with its full strain on the anchor.

An anchor of conventional two-armed design, like the Yachtsman's, may be freed by sailing a loop of the rode around the arm not buried in the bottom, and putting a strain on it in the way a trip line is used. First, remove the rode's bitter end from the mast below deck, lead it forward out of the bow chock and back outside the shrouds into the cockpit again, and make it fast to the mast once more so that it leads directly astern. To catch the loop around the upraised arm, slack off on the rode and sail the boat in a tight circle around the anchor, then another half circle so that the boat is now headed upwind, in the opposite direction from the original setting of the anchor. Sail out the slack in the anchor rode and let the full force of the boat's forward momentum pull on the elevated arm. If the anchor does not come out at once, possibly the loop did not catch. Slack off the the rode again and repeat the procedure. Should you still not be able to free the anchor, haul in the slack until the rode is straight up and down, and pull directly up on it with the maximum force possible.

If all efforts to free the anchor fail and you must abandon it, possibly to retrieve it later, leave enough scope to allow for tide rise, if any, then cut the rode on deck and make it fast to a buoy or wooden float to mark the spot.

Torn Sail

Though a torn sail is dramatic and apt to flap in an alarming way if the wind is blowing hard, it isn't a desperate emergency unless you happen to be on a lee shore and need every ounce of sailpower to keep off. In that case, get your anchor out with all possible speed, and with maximum scope, to avoid going aground while you make repairs.

The principal causes of torn sails are: broken battens, which often poke holes in sails; weak threads that give way along the seams; and worn-out fabric.

By having battens about ¼-inch shorter than their pockets, and inserting and removing them carefully each time you sail, you can minimize breaking. Should a batten break while you're under way, lower the sail at once and remove or replace the broken batten. You aren't likely to damage the sail by finishing your outing with one batten missing.

To prevent tears along seams, examine the stitching of the cloths of each sail occasion-

ally. If you find broken stitches, it indicates the thread has reached the limit of its strength, but if the fabric itself is still strong, the sail can be resewn by a sailmaker. For worn-out fabric there is no real cure but replacement of the entire sail. You may be able to get by briefly with patching, or by replacing one or two cloths, but it is false economy; the money is better invested in a new sail.

Every small sailboat should carry in its ditty bag a supply of sail repair materials, including sail mending tape. A hole poked in a sail can easily be patched before it spreads. If the sail has torn along a seam, it can be sewn at sea and used again. In the Transatlantic Race of 1960 from Bermuda to Sweden, for example, on the 47-foot yawl *Figaro III,* we flew a lightweight spinnaker too long in an increasing breeze, until the sail finally split along the seams for a total of 135 feet. During the next two days and nights every man off watch—including the owner and skipper, Bill Snaith—spent his spare time sewing that sail, with eight stitches to the inch; nearly 13,000 in all. But our labor was not in vain: later on, we were able to fly the sail again, and it was important in helping us win the race and the King's Cup.

When a sail tears, get it off as quickly as possible, before it flogs itself to ribbons. If it's a jib, you can probably sail back to your mooring under mainsail alone, so may want to postpone repairs until you get ashore. Secure the halyard and sheets, and stow the sail below, out of the way.

Should your mainsail split, if you are upwind of your mooring, you may be able to make it back under jib alone. If you do this, however, do not try to pick up your mooring by sailing below it as usual and shooting into the wind—under a headsail alone, you'll have no ability at all to shoot. Instead, as you approach the mooring from upwind, let fly your jib while still a short way off, and pick up the mooring *downwind*. Your momentum and drift can be checked by securing the pick-up buoy's pennant to the foredeck cleat—there is no danger from an accidental jibe, since only your jib is up.

Broken Shroud or Stay

Since the purpose of shrouds is to support the mast laterally, and of stays to give fore-and-aft support, emergency repairs depend on getting a line from the masthead to the deck to replace the broken wire temporarily. Shrouds and stays often let go at their turnbuckles. Sometimes the turnbuckles themselves fail because of defective casting, sometimes the wires of swaged fittings become fatigued and the individual strands fracture where they enter the sleeve of the turnbuckle. Routine annual care should include inspection of all swaged fittings and turnbuckles for hairline cracks or crystallization of the metal.

If a shroud breaks and the mast stands, promptly turn the boat into the wind and put her on the other tack, thereby giving the mast the support of the good shroud, while you make repairs. A broken turnbuckle can be removed from its chainplate, a length of line rove in its place, attached to the shroud with a *genuine carrick bend* (page 175) and a strain put on it, then secured to itself with a *rolling hitch* (page 174). Should the shroud let go so far above deck that you can't reach the end still attached to the mast, lower the jib and use its halyard as a substitute shroud. Remove the turnbuckle from the broken shroud's chain plate and make fast the jib halyard shackle in its place. While the broken shroud is still to leeward, take the maximum possible strain on the jib halyard and secure it

Since a headstay usually breaks when a boat is on the wind, a prompt turning away from the wind and sailing off may save the mast. Recover the jib—which may have gone overboard if it was hanked on to the headstay—take it off and stow it. If the headstay deck fitting has only one hole, remove the turnbuckle and make fast the jib halyard shackle in its place. Take up as taut as possible on the jib halyard and secure it. Secure the jibsheets, if not attached to the sail.

Broken Mast

Unless a mast is stepped on deck, it has the double support of its mast step and of the *partners*—the reinforced section where it goes through the deck. As a result, when it gets a breaking load, a mast is most apt to break off above deck, leaving a stump of some height. Usually it is blowing at the time, so speed is desirable in clearing the wreckage to prevent damage to the hull. Haul the broken section on deck and secure it temporarily. Then take the sails off and stow them out of the way. Strip the mast of all halyards. If no boat is close by to tow you back to port, get your anchor down, with plenty of scope, to steady the boat while you prepare to set up a jury rig, with the boom as a mast and the jib as a jury trysail. Remove the boom from the mast.

Unreeve all lines from the boom, but leave the mainsheet fast to the outhaul end to serve as a headstay. If your jibsheets are not spliced into the jib, they can be used as shrouds. Otherwise the heaving line can be made fast in the middle at the outhaul end of the boom, to serve the same purpose, with a block made fast at the same end to take the jib halyard. If the jibsheets can be used as shrouds, secure them at the outhaul end of the boom, with the jibsheet shackle placed so it will face aft when the boom is in position vertically. Reeve the jib halyard through this shackle for hoisting the jib when the jury mast is rigged.

Now place the boom on deck with the outhaul end facing forward of the mast, remove the mast's turnbuckles from the headstay fitting and chain plates, and reeve each of the three jury supports through its appropriate fitting, pulling ample slack through to keep them from unreeving when the boom is raised.

Lift the boom vertical on the forward side of the mast stump, with the gooseneck end resting on a cushion or lifejacket. As high as possible, lash boom and stump together with one end of the main halyard, using a clove hitch pulled tight and finished with a square knot. Six inches lower on the stump, put a second lashing, and below that as many more as possible, right down to the deck. Now take a strain on the jury headstay, and make it fast to itself with a rolling hitch. Do the same with the jury shrouds.

Get out the jib. If you have used the jibsheets for shrouds, make a jibsheet of the heaving line and secure it to the clew with a bowline. Hoist the head of the jib on the jib halyard to the top of the jury mast, and

secure it. You will have sail to spare, but stretch the luff and secure to the gooseneck the jib hank closest to the deck. With small lines or sail stops, make fast several other hanks to the jury mast. This gives you a loose-footed, emergency trysail under which, after you have hauled in the anchor, you should be able to make port.

Leaking Boat

Even for ordinary bailing, every boat should have a sponge, bucket, and a pump with an intake hose that can reach into the lowest part of the boat on either tack. But though sailing and bailing often go together, especially in rough weather, this isn't quite the same as having to deal with a constant flow of water that threatens the boat's safety. Here crew fatigue becomes a factor, so the emphasis should be on stopping, or at least slowing down the leak, and the first thing is to find it.

Leaks develop in many different places,

A jib made fast to boom, which is lashed to stump of broken mast, makes good jury rig in a pinch

from many different causes: around the centerboard trunk, around the mast step, from dried-out seams on the topsides, from seams below water that lose their *caulking* (antileak stuffing), from lost or sprung fastenings, from split planks, from holes punched in the side or bottom by collision or grounding, and wherever there are pipes or through-hull fittings that can break or corrode.

In hunting for the leak, try changing your tack. If the leak slows down, hold that tack until you can find the source and plug it. The best material for stopping a leak temporarily is something that will absorb water and jam as it swells, to hold itself in place. *Caulking cotton* is ideal. This is long-fibered, soft cotton that is sold by the pound in a continuous, single-stranded rope. It packs easily into a hole or crack, swells as it soaks up moisture, closes the opening tightly, and is not easily dislodged. But any soft cloth will slow down a leak—a piece of cotton rag, a handkerchief, sock, or undershirt. *Sail twine,* which is soft cotton string used for sail repair, can be pulled apart and worked into a leaking seam. *Seam compound*—a kind of marine putty—can be forced into leaks, too, by itself or in combination with caulking cotton.

If the leak is equally bad on both tacks, search for it along the centerline. Should you find it around the mast step, try dousing the jib, or reefing the mainsail to lessen the downward pressure on the mast step, which tends to open up the planking beneath it.

In an extreme case, where the leak is generalized, as along a section of planking, a device could be tried that was used successfully in square-rigger days when a ship was leaking faster than the pumps could free her. A section of heavy canvas, such as an old square sail, was fitted with stout lines at each corner, lowered over the bow, and hauled aft under the ship's bottom until the body of the sail was over the leak. Then all the lines were hauled taut to keep the canvas in place with the ship moving ahead. This would slow down the leak enough so the pumps could keep ahead of it. For small-boat use, a sail bag or a poncho might be similarly rigged with a line at each corner, and juggled into position to cover a large area leak.

Summary

The principal emergencies a skipper should be prepared to handle:

1. **Man Overboard.** Jibe around, and pick up the man to leeward.
2. **Thunderstorms.** Avoid, if possible. If not, anchor, lower sail, and ride out the blow, keeping away from shrouds and headstay.
3. **Broken Tiller.** Carry a spare, or sail by trimming jib and mainsail, with full centerboard.
4. **Broken Rudder.** Use oar, paddle, or floorboard; reduce sail.
5. **Jammed Centerboard.** Beach boat, roll her down, and free board.
6. **Broken Halyard.** Send lightest man aloft to reeve a new one.
7. **Running Aground.** Keep weight aft and attempt jibe around on reverse course. Get anchor out to deep water, take a strain, and try to sail off. Raise centerboard, remove rudder, until free.
8. **Fouled Anchor.** In shallow water, swim down rode and free. Or slack off rode and sail upwind at top speed, opposite to anchor setting, cleat rode and try to twist anchor loose.
9. **Torn Sail.** Lower and sew seam or patch, or mend with sail tape.
10. **Broken Shroud or Stay.** Remove turnbuckle at deck, reeve jury line and secure to shroud with genuine carrick bend. Or rig jib halyard as jury shroud or stay.
11. **Broken Mast.** Rig boom as jury mast, lashed to mast stump. Use mainsheet as headstay, jibsheets or heaving line as shrouds. Run up jib as jury trysail.
12. **Leaking Boat.** Locate leak, stuff with caulk-

ing cotton, rag, or seam compound. For extensive leak, rig sail bag or poncho with four lines and pull taut under bottom over leaking area.

13. Checklist of nautical terms:

PART OF BOAT

forefoot—The base of the bow where it joins the keel.

VERBS

beach—To run a boat ashore deliberately, usually bow-on, for repairs, or as an alternative to anchoring.

caulk—To fill a seam or joint with a material that will render it watertight.

ebb—To flow back to the sea; also (noun), the ebb tide.

flood—To flow in from the sea; also (noun), the flood tide.

heave down—To heel a boat over so as to expose the bottom for repair or inspection.

GENERAL

bitt, bitts—A strong vertical wooden or metal post, or pair of posts, set into the deck and well-secured below, for towing and other heavy duty.

caulking—Material forced into a seam or joint to make it watertight.

caulking cotton—Soft, long-fibered cotton, woven into a continuous, single-stranded rope for forcing into seams and joints to render them watertight.

cumulo-nimbus—Heavy, piled-up cloud mass; thunderheads.

cumulus—Heaped-up cloud formations, with flat bases and rounded outlines.

ditty bag—Formerly, a sailor's personal repair kit, with needles, thread, buttons, etc.; today, a boat's repair kit, with sail-mending materials, small tools, cotter pins, tape, etc.

ebb—The ebb, or falling tide.

end-for-end—Reversing a line to put the greatest strain on the part that has had least wear.

flood—The flood, or rising tide.

found—Equipped, as in a *well-found* boat.

jury rig—A temporary substitute.

neap tides—The tides with minimum range between high and low water, occurring each month at the moon's first and third quarters.

partners—The strengthening structural members or reinforcement of the deck around the mast opening.

sail twine—Light, strong cotton line made of several threads twisted together, used for sail repair, whipping, and other light uses.

scuppers—Holes at deck level to let water drain over the boat's sides or out through pipes leading under water.

seam compound—Any of various plastic or puttylike compounds used in joints and seams to make them watertight.

shoal—A shallow spot in the water; of little depth.

shoving pole—A long, strong, rigid pole for pushing a boat off shoals.

spring tides—The tides with maximum range between high and low waters, occurring each month at the full and new moons.

16

Navigation Rules

NAVIGATION RULES are the marine traffic regulations established by the United States Congress and other governmental authority to prevent collisions on the water. They are divided, principally, into the *International Rules,* which govern traffic on the high seas and coastal waters, and *Inland Rules* for harbors, rivers, and inland waters generally. The U.S. Coast Guard also has rules for Great Lakes traffic and for Western Rivers. In addition, rules by state governments and local authorities may cover waters not under Coast Guard control. But no matter whose rules govern the waters you sail, you may be certain of one thing:

> *Everyone who goes out in command of a boat—even a rowboat—is held responsible for knowing the local navigation rules. Ignorance of the law relieves no one from liability in case of collision.*

It is as vital for you, a small-sailboat skipper, to know your local rules, as for the captain of the largest ocean liner to know the rules for the high seas. If you have any trouble finding what rules govern your local waters, write to the State Boating Law Administrator for your state, at the state capital,

and ask for a copy of the state's navigation rules. He'll either send you one or tell you where to get it.

In the meantime, and until you have exact local knowledge, you'll get a working idea of most of the principles involved from this summary of the U.S. Coast Guard's *Inland Rules.*

Avoid collision. Now is the time in your nautical education when you must be exposed to this venerable four-line epitaph that wraps up an eternal seagoing truth in its hoary lines—

Here lie the bones of Silas McVey,
Who died defending his Right of Way—
He was right, dead right, as he sailed along,
But he's just as dead as if he'd been wrong.

The moral—that it's folly to insist on your right of way if a collision will result—has been built into official law by Congress under a paragraph of the *Inland Rules* called the "General Prudential Rule," Article 27. Unfortunately the rule is stated in the same kind of complex Federal prose that inspired an official sign writer during World War II to have instructions printed "Illumination must be extinguished before the premises are

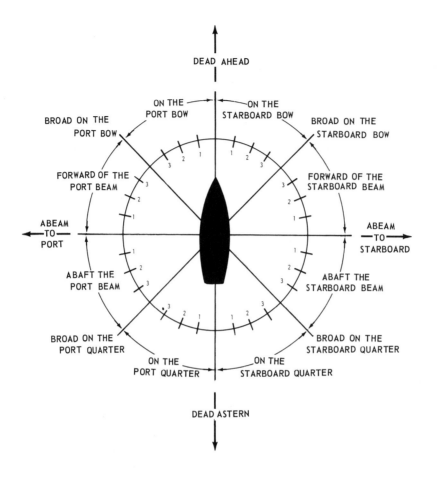

DEAD AHEAD

ON THE
PORT BOW — → —ON THE
STARBOARD BOW

BROAD ON THE
PORT BOW

BROAD ON THE
STARBOARD BOW

FORWARD OF THE
PORT BEAM

FORWARD OF THE
STARBOARD BEAM

ABEAM
—TO—
PORT

ABEAM
—TO—►
STARBOARD

ABAFT THE
PORT BEAM

ABAFT THE
STARBOARD BEAM

BROAD ON THE
PORT QUARTER

BROAD ON THE
STARBOARD QUARTER

ON THE
PORT QUARTER

ON THE
STARBOARD QUARTER

DEAD ASTERN

Circle of bearings is divided into 32 points of 11¼° each for locating objects in relation to boat

vacated" when he meant "Put the lights out when you leave."

Nonetheless, despite its cumbersome wording, Article 27, General Prudential Rule, will repay a moment's study. It says: *In obeying and construing these rules due regard shall be had to all dangers of navigation and collision, and to any special circumstances which may render a departure from the above rules necessary in order to avoid immediate danger.*

In short, "Above all, do what you must to avoid collision," which is a fitting introduction to the whole subject of navigation rules and the right of way between boats for the purpose of preventing collisions. Repeat —"Above all, do what you must to avoid collision"; it's the law.

If your study of the *Rules* were to go no farther, this one rule, followed faithfully, would probably keep you out of trouble. But there's a deal of difference between keeping out of trouble and having fun on the water. As a sailboat skipper, you want to be able to operate your boat for maximum enjoyment at all times, not just execute a continuous series of emergency maneuvers to avoid collision. This means you must know your rights and obligations under the navigation rules for your local waters, and brings us naturally to the subject of *bearings*.

A *bearing* is the direction from the boat to an object. We've already covered some bearings—*dead ahead, broad on the starboard* (or *port*) *bow, abeam to starboard* (or *port*), and *dead astern*. But for locating boats in traffic situations, we need a few more, which are quickly learned if you'll think of the boat as always at the center of a large circle.

The rim of this circle, under the *Navigation Rules*, is considered as being divided into 32 points, equally spaced from each other. Since a circle is composed of 360°, this makes each point 11¼°. Thus, if an object is reported as bearing "one point on the starboard bow," it bears at an angle of 11¼° to starboard, from dead ahead.

Notice how effectively the bearing conveys three important pieces of information: (1) the angle of the object, (2) which side of the boat it is on, and (3) the section of the boat with which it is in line—bow, beam, or quarter.

The points of the bow bearings start at dead ahead and go aft, on both sides, from one point to four points, which is also called "broad on the (starboard, port) bow."

The points of the beam bearings start at abeam, on both sides, and go "forward of the (starboard, port) beam" from one point to four points, which is, again, "broad on the (starboard, port) bow." And the beam bearings also go "abaft the (starboard, port) beam," from one point to four points, which is also called "broad on the (starboard, port) quarter."

The quarter bearings start at dead astern and read forward, on both sides, from one point to four points, or "broad on the (starboard, port) quarter."

It's useful to remember the principal bearings and their values because from them you

can quickly estimate the bearings of intermediate points. *Dead ahead* is 0°, *broad on the bow* is four points (45°), and *abeam* is eight points (90°) from dead ahead. *Broad on the quarter* is four points (45°) from dead astern, and *dead astern* is 16 points (180°) from dead ahead.

Keep clear when overtaking. Under the *Navigation Rules,* ANY vessel or boat approaching another boat from a direction more than two points abaft the beam on either side, is considered to be *overtaking,* and must keep out of the way of the other boat. No change of course by either alters the responsibility of the overtaking boat to keep clear until she is finally past the overtaken vessel. This is one situation where a sailboat never has the right of way over a powerboat, which, under the *Rules,* is considered a *steam vessel* ("any vessel propelled by machinery").

Sailboats have right of way over powerboats—USUALLY! Where there is risk of a collision between a sailboat and a powerboat in any traffic situation except overtaking, the *Rules* (Art. 20) usually require the powerboat to keep out of the sailboat's way, ". . . *the steam vessel shall keep out of the way*

Any boat approaching from direction more than two points abaft beam on either side of other boat is overtaking and must keep out of other boat's way

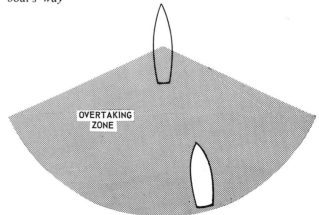

of the sailing vessel." But note carefully this warning to sailboats in Art. 20: "*This rule shall not give to a sailing vessel the right to hamper, in a narrow channel, the safe passage of a steam vessel which can navigate only inside that channel.*"

The logic of this amendment is clear. If a 10-foot sailing dinghy, for example, tried to enforce its right of way over a 600-foot freighter in a narrow channel and was run down as a result, the court might well decide that the dinghy skipper had failed to meet his obligation to take all possible steps to avoid collision, as required by the General Prudential Rule. From a common sense standpoint—what the courts call the viewpoint of the "reasonably prudent person"—the smaller, more maneuverable boat should not be operated in a way to embarrass or endanger the larger craft.

There is another hazard in being overzealous about enforcing your right of way over powerboats—the possibility that the powerboat skipper may not know he must keep out of your way! Of recent years our waterways have been flooded with outboard runabouts by the hundreds of thousands, with an enormous increase in the traffic hazards from uninformed boatmen. So in any crossing situation with a powerboat where there might be danger of collision, do not assume your right of way is known to the

other skipper. Keep watching his bearing; if it does not change noticeably, there is a risk of collision. If you have any doubt about whether or not he is going to give way, prepare at once to take evasive action, before you are too close to him. In avoiding a collision, incidentally, the *Navigation Rules* specify that the boat giving way shall, if possible, avoid crossing ahead of the other.

On the one hand, the *Rules* require the *stand-on* vessel (having the right of way) to "keep her course and speed," so you must not complicate the situation by changing course in a way that would confuse the other skipper if he intended to alter his course. On the other hand, if the *give-way* boat (without right of way) has no intention of changing course—because he doesn't know you have the right of way—you don't want to wait until it is too late to avoid collision. My own practice in such a spot is to take evasive action early, while still far enough away from the other boat, so that even if her skipper knows I have the right of way and intends to let me have it in due course, he cannot possibly misunderstand that I am giving way to him—an unexpected courtesy. And if he does not know I have the right of way, I will have avoided a collision.

I'll never forget one night on the Detroit River, where a friend and I were sailing a Lightning Class sloop in a dying breeze. We had the correct port and starboard *running lights* (navigation lights) showing that we were a sailboat, with a flashlight at hand to shine on our sails, if necessary, for additional emphasis. Suddenly we spotted the running lights of a small outboard runabout a quarter of a mile away, two points on our port bow, coming directly toward us at high speed. At once we shone the flashlight on our sails to advertise that we had the right of way. No change in the outboard's bearing; it bored on, straight for us.

Not waiting to test her skipper's intention

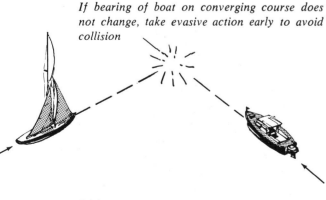

If bearing of boat on converging course does not change, take evasive action early to avoid collision

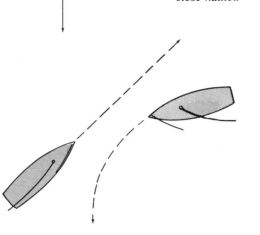

WIND

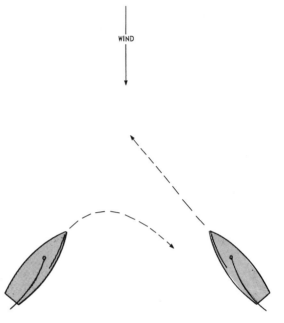

WIND

2ND SAILING RULE—
Close-hauled on port tack must keep out of way of close-hauled on starboard tack

further, I swung the tiller to get out of his path. It was a fortunate decision, for as the boat swept across our bow in a smother of foam at 20 miles an hour, her skipper's voice came floating across the water—apparently in shouted response to a comment of his passenger about the sport of racing over the water at night in an outboard—and these were his exact words: "Yeah, it's just like driving a car, only there are no traffic rules!"

"Running free" must give way to *"close-hauled."* Article 17 of the *Navigation Rules Inland,* covers situations where there might be risk of collision between sailing vessels, and lays down five rules of prevention. First of these is the requirement that a sailboat *running free* keep out of the way of a boat sailing *close-hauled.* A boat is *running free* when she has the wind anywhere from five points (56¼°) aft of her bow to two points (22½°) forward of her stern, which includes close reach, beam reach, and broad reach.

This rule is legal recognition of the fact that it is harder to gain distance to windward than to leeward. Were the close-hauled boat required to give way in this situation, it would be an unfair hardship because, as

we have seen, she would have to sail at least 14 feet to regain every 10 feet of windward distance lost by changing course. The boat running free, however, has no such problem —even though she alters direction to avoid the other boat, she may still sail directly for her mark.

Close-hauled—port tack gives way to starboard tack. Although close-hauled means sailing as close as possible to the wind, it should be noted that this does not mean each boat is necessarily at the same relative angle to the wind; some boats point higher than others. A 12-meter yacht, for example, when close-hauled might sail within three points of the wind, while a square-rigged ship would be considered sharp if she could sail within six points when close-hauled. It is apparent that the rule must be interpreted

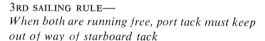

as meaning a boat is close-hauled when sailing as close to the wind as *she* can sail, not as close as *any* boat can sail.

In a situation where both boats are hard on the wind, and are on a collision course, one must give way, even though it will cost him valuable windward distance. To avoid confusion, the rule is: The boat close-hauled on the port tack must keep out of the way of the boat close-hauled on the starboard tack. But if you happen to be the close-hauled boat on the starboard tack, don't assume the other skipper necessarily knows you have the right of way just because you're now dealing with a sailboat rather than a powerboat. Here, as in any marine traffic situation where you may legally have the right of way, be prepared to exercise the General Prudential Rule if there seems to be any doubt about the other boat giving way.

Several years ago, for instance, we were having a glorious late fall sail across Long Island Sound against a fresh sou'wester, in a big 56-foot ketch. We were hard on the wind on the starboard tack, which theoretically gave us the right of way over any boat we might meet coming toward us. About mid-Sound, glancing under the boom to leeward, I noticed a ketch of about 45 feet approaching, close-hauled on the port tack, and waited for her to acknowledge our right of way by falling off and going under our stern. But she held on; her bearing did not change.

When I judged her skipper had had ample opportunity to alter course if he intended to, I decided to change our course instead, giving him the right of way, and let our boat fall off slightly so that we might sail close enough under his stern to hail him. As he tore across our bow at a fine rate of speed we could see only two people on deck—a man at the wheel, and a middle-aged woman, probably his wife, standing aft by the cock-

3RD SAILING RULE—
When both are running free, port tack must keep out of way of starboard tack

pit, facing us as she clung to the leeward rigging. In a gentle but firm roar I shouted my query upwind at her, *"Don't you people know the navigation rules?"* And the answer that came quavering back downwind was, so help me: *"We don't know how to stop it!"*

Our whole ship's company was so overcome with astonishment at this answer, and then with trying to figure how a grown man and woman could let a boat run away with them, that by the time we thought of going to their rescue, they had sailed out of range. To this day I don't know what ever happened to that boat, whether she eventually rammed the State of Connecticut, or kept on sailing to become a Long Island Sound version of *The Flying Dutchman.*

Running free—port tack gives way to starboard tack. This rule is consistent with the preceding rule for the close-hauled situation. When two sailboats are on a collision course while running free, with the wind on different sides, the boat with the wind on her port side must keep out of the way of the boat with the wind to starboard.

The fact that the *Navigation Rules* favor the starboard tack when on the wind, and the

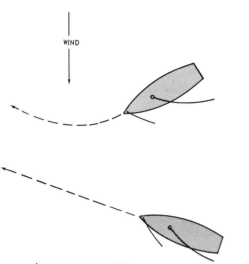

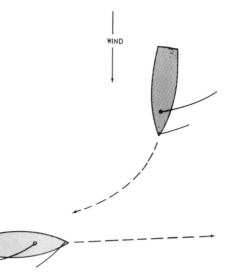

4TH SAILING RULE—
With both running free on same tack, windward boat must keep out of way of leeward boat

5TH SAILING RULE—
Boat with wind aft must keep out of way of other boat

starboard tack with the wind free, helps explain why racing skippers always prefer these two sail trims, since the racing rules, where possible, are patterned on the *Navigation Rules* for situations involving risk of collision.

Running free—windward boat gives way to leeward boat. Danger of collision is unlikely between two close-hauled boats on the same tack, because one is usually more *close-winded* (able to sail higher) and faster than the other. But when they're running free, the *Rules* recognize that two boats might steer different angles that could cause them to converge, with risk of collision, even though they might both be sailing on the same tack. The covering fourth rule is: When both boats are running free, with the wind on the same side, the boat to windward must keep out of the way of the boat to leeward.

This makes obvious sense. The boat to windward gets the wind before the boat to leeward, hence has more control. As a result, it should be easier for her to maneuver and change course to avoid collision than for the leeward boat.

Boat with wind aft gives way. This fifth

rule under Article 17 of the *Inland Rules* is, essentially, a kind of omnibus, or wrap-up rule, intended to establish who has the right of way in all collision situations not covered by one of the four other sailing rules. As we have seen, the first of the five rules gives a close-hauled boat (on either tack) the right of way over one running free (on either tack). But no provision is made in the first four rules specifically for a boat which is neither close-hauled nor running free but which, nevertheless, is on a collision course with one sailing close-hauled or running free. The fifth rule takes care of this situation. The rule is: When two boats are approaching each other on a collision course, the boat having the wind *aft* must keep out of the way of the other boat.

The important word to note here is "aft" which, under the *Rules*, means anywhere from astern to two points (22½°) on either side. The sketch visualizes how this rule helps a skipper resolve instantly a situation where, for example, a boat on a starboard tack, with the wind aft, is on a collision course with a boat sailing a beam reach on the port tack. But the starboard tack boat has the wind aft:

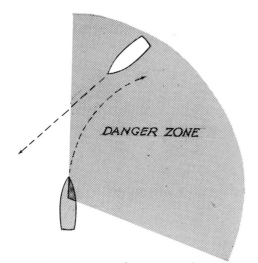

DANGER ZONE—*Any boat approaching powerboat in sector of her horizon from dead ahead to two points abaft starboard beam has right of way*

She must give way to the boat running free on the beam reach, even though on the port tack.

As in the fourth rule, which requires the windward boat to give way to the leeward boat, the logic behind the fifth rule is: The boat with the wind aft gets the wind before the other boat, hence has more control and can more easily maneuver to avoid collision.

The "Danger Zone" for powerboats. You should know about the Danger Zone and the right of way between powerboats for two reasons: 1. As a sailboat skipper, you want to stay as far away as possible from powerboats; to do so, you must know what kind of action to expect when two powerboats are closing on a collision course near you; and 2. You may wish to equip your sailboat with an outboard motor—this would make you a "steam vessel" under the *Navigation Rules* and a "motorboat" under the Federal Motorboat Act every time you turned on the engine, and you would be subject to the rules that apply to all vessels propelled by machinery. Of these, Article 19, which defines the "Danger Zone," is most important; it covers the situation of "Two Steam Vessels Crossing."

The rule is: When two steam vessels are crossing so as to involve risk of collision, the boat being approached on its starboard side must keep out of the way of the other boat.

This makes the "Danger Zone" for a boat under power the 10-point sector of her horizon from *dead ahead* to *two points abaft the starboard beam.* She must keep out of the way of any other powerboat coming toward her in that zone.

This marine traffic rule—giving the boat to starboard the right of way in a crossing situation—has its counterpart on land in the traffic regulation of many states, namely that when two vehicles enter an intersection from different roads at the same time, the vehicle on the right has the right of way. If you like slogans to help your memory, this may serve for the "Danger Zone": *Respect the right of those on the right.*

Fog signals. Under the *Navigation Rules,* during fog and other periods of low visibility, sailboats must signal their location and point of sailing with a foghorn. In normal visibility, a sailboat need not give a signal of any kind, even when there is danger of collision. But *"in fog, mist, falling snow, or heavy rain storms, whether by day or night,"* sailboats under way must blow these signals on a foghorn at least once every minute:

a. When on the starboard tack—*one blast.*
b. When on the port tack—*two blasts.*
c. When sailing with the wind abaft the beam, on either side—*three blasts.*

Apart from these signals, the only other you're apt to hear sounded on a foghorn is the distinctive three blasts of a boat under tow. You can't mistake it—one long blast followed by two short, every minute—and unless you have an appetite for tangling with a towline, you'll give it a wide berth.

Sailing in a fog can be prickly business in crowded waters like Massachusetts Bay, or Long Island Sound, or San Francisco Bay. As a protective measure for these and any waters, it's well to know the signals used by powerboats in a fog:

a. *One long blast* on whistle or siren—a powerboat under way.

b. *One long and two short blasts* on whistle or siren—a powerboat with a tow.

Another fog signal you should know—because you may want to use it yourself sometime—is the rapid ringing of a bell for about five seconds every minute, used by *any* boat at anchor in a fog.

Powerboat signals. During fog and poor visibility, powerboats must give only the whistle or siren signals shown above. But under normal visibility, by day or night, the following signals are used to prevent collision in meeting, passing, and overtaking situations:

a. *One short blast*—"I am directing my course to starboard."

b. *Two short blasts*—"I am directing my course to port."

c. *Three short blasts*—"My engines are going full speed astern."

d. *Four or more short, rapid blasts*—"DANGER! Stop your intention!"

Although whistle signals are specified to be given only between "steam vessels" to prevent collision, occasionally a powerboat skipper may blow at you in a crossing situation—the preceding list equips you to interpret his intention.

Distress signals. On coastal waters and the Great Lakes, as of January 1, 1981, these signals are a Coast Guard *must* for all boats at night and for boats 16′ or longer, by day:

a. *By day*—Hand-held red flares; or hand-held or floating orange smokes; or red aerial or parachute flares; or bright red-orange flag imprinted with black disc and black square.

b. *By night*—Hand-held or aerial or parachute red flares; or automatic S-O-S lantern.

c. *Day and night*—Hand-held or aerial or parachute red flares. CAUTION: Hand-held flares drip sparks. Hold downwind and wear asbestos glove, or bind flare to a boathook.

Additional distress signals, listed in the *Navigation Rules,* include these:

d. *By day* (sound signals)—Continuous sounding of any fog-signal apparatus, or repeated firing of a gun.

By day (visual signal)—A handy distress signal found in the *Pilot Rules* (an adjunct of the *Inland Rules*) is shown below. A white cloth in each hand increases this signal's range. Well-known, unofficial distress signal is the American *ensign* (flag) flown upside

Manual distress signal is made by waving arms as indicated, slowly

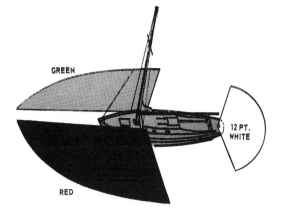

Above: *On non-auxiliary sailboats, Inland Rules call for separate 10-point sidelights and 12-point white stern light*

Below: *Rowing boats, whether under oars or sail, must have a white-light lantern to show temporarily in time to prevent collision*

down. Or a white shirt hoisted to your masthead might get help. You can even use flashes from a mirror to signal distress.

b. *By night* (visual signal). The *Rules'* specification of flames on the boat, *"as from a burning tar barrel, oil barrel, and so forth,"* is not easily arranged on a small sailboat without adding the problem of a fire at sea to the existing distress situation. But a good flashlight can be used to blink out "S O S" in Morse Code (. . . - - - . . .). If you should ever have to send such a signal, however, you'll find it easier to think of the signal as

sounding like this: "Di-di-dit/dah-dah-dah/ di-di-dit. . . . Di-di-dit/dah-dah-dah/di-di-dit. . . . Di-di-dit/dah-dah-dah/di-di-dit," and so forth, rather than as a repeated series of three dots, three dashes, three dots. The "dit-dah" method of sounding the signal gives it a rhythm that makes it both easier to send and to receive. Say it aloud a few times, and you'll hear how naturally the pattern swings together.

By night (sound signal). Same as the day sound signal—continuous sounding of fog-horn, ringing of anchor bell, or firing of a gun.

Lights. Every boat on the water between sunset and sunrise, in all weathers, is requir-ed to carry running lights of a kind specified for her size and type, to warn other boats of her presence and course.

1. *Non-auxiliary sailboats* must exhibit three lights: (a) A 10-point green side light to shine from dead ahead to two points abaft the starboard beam; (b) A 10-point red side light to show from dead ahead to two points abaft the port beam; and (c) A 12-point white light to cover the arc astern from two points abaft the starboard beam to two points abaft the port beam. These lights must be fixed in place, except that in heavy weather, boats under 10 gross tons may keep the lights unmounted but ready at hand to show an approaching vessel in time to pre-vent collision.

2. *Rowing boats*—whether proceeding under oars or sail—do not carry the lights required of larger vessels. But they must have *"ready at hand"* a lantern that shows a white light, for exhibiting temporarily to any boat meeting, crossing, or overtaking them, early enough to prevent collision. As in all situa-tions where there might be collision, by night or day, a prudent skipper does not wait until the last minute to let the other boat know his intention; he acts promptly to avoid trouble.

3. *Motorboats under 26 feet long.* It will

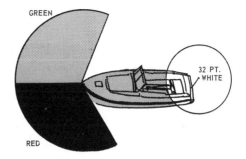

Motorboats under 26 feet long carry combina-tion red-green bow light and 32-point white stern light, placed higher than the combination light

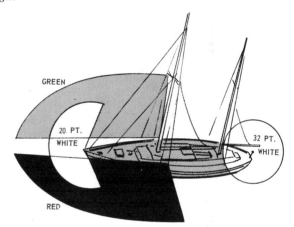

Auxiliary sailboat under sail and power, or un-der power alone, must carry same running lights as motorboat of her size and class

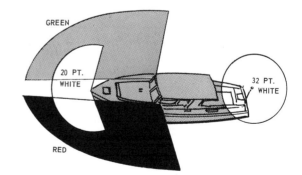

Motorboats 26 to 65 feet long carry separate sidelights, 20-point white bow light, and 32-point white stern light, higher than the bow light

White range lights help determine any change in boat's course or bearing

help you operate your boat more safely at night to know the principal lights most likely to be encountered on your local waters. Under the Federal Motorboat Act, motorboats under 26 feet long need a combination red-and-green light forward—the red showing from dead ahead to two points abaft the port beam; the green from dead ahead to two points abaft the starboard beam. Aft, higher than the combination light, she must have a 32-point white light, showing all around the horizon. An auxiliary sailboat under sail and power or under power alone, is considered a motorboat and must carry the proper running lights for her size and class.

4. *Motorboats from 26 to 65 feet long.* Motorboats between 26 and 65 feet in length wear four lights: (a) forward, as close as possible to the bow, a bright, 20-point white light, to shine from dead ahead to two points abaft the beam on both sides; (b) aft, a bright 32-point white light, showing all around the horizon, and placed higher than the bow light; (c) a green 10-point starboard side light; and (d) a red 10-point port side light.

The two white lights are called *range lights* and are helpful to other boats in avoiding collision, because when the motorboat

wearing them changes course, the relative positions of the two lights also change.

5. *Large ships.* Under the *Inland Rules,* large ships carry the same four lights as motorboats of 26 to 65 feet, but the white range lights are carried more nearly amidships.

6. *Towboats—with tow astern.* To avoid the unpleasant experience of trying to sail between a towboat and her tow at night, be sure to learn what lights they carry in your local waters. Under the *Inland Rules,* a towboat with her tow astern shows the usual 10-point red and green side lights, *plus* a vertical hoist of three white lights. These may be either 20-point or 32-point lights, but they indicate the same thing—a long hawser between the towboat and her tow, and certain disaster if you try to sail between. Barges in tow are supposed to carry 32-point white lights on bow and stern, but these are often very dim or out, so all tows should be given a wide berth.

7. *Towboats—with tow alongside.* In addition to 10-point red and green side lights, a towboat with her tow alongside carries a vertical hoist of two white lights, which may be either 20-point or 32-point lights.

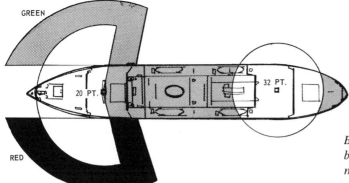

Big ships under Inland Rules basically show same lights as motorboats of 26 to 65 feet, but range lights are more amidships

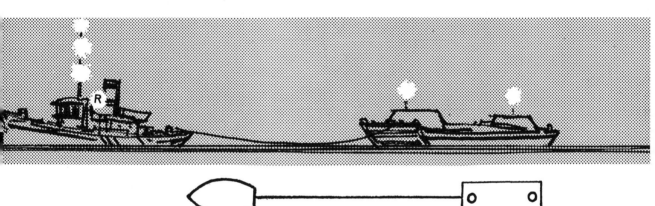

Towboat with tow astern carries vertical hoist of three white lights and usual side lights

Tow alongside, towboat has two white lights vertically, plus red and green sidelights. If pushing ahead, she will also show two amber lights vertically, aft

Summary

1. Marine *Navigation Rules* have been established to prevent collisions on the water. Every skipper is responsible for knowing the local rules.
2. The General Prudential Rule, Article 27, of the U.S. Coast Guard's *Inland Navigation Rules* requires a skipper to do everything possible to avoid collision.
3. Boats in marine traffic are located by their bearing from each other, in number of points *On the Bow, Forward of or Abaft the Beam,* or *On the Quarter,* and whether to Starboard or Port.
4. The horizon around a boat is composed of 32 points, each representing an arc of 11¼°.
5. The major reference bearings are *dead ahead* and *dead astern; broad on the (starboard, port) bow* (four points from dead ahead); *abeam* to *starboard* or *port* (eight points from dead ahead); and *broad on the (starboard, port) quarter* (four points from dead astern).
6. *Any* boat overtaking another must keep out of her way until finally past and clear.
7. Power-driven vessels must give way to sailboats except when the sailboat is overtaking, or when in a narrow channel that limits the power-driven vessel's ability to maneuver.
8. If the bearing of two converging boats remains constant, there is danger of collision.
9. The *give-way boat* must try to avoid crossing ahead of the *stand-on boat.*
10. Article 17 of the *Inland Rules* lists five provisions to prevent collisions between converging sailboats:
    a. A boat running free must give way to one close-hauled.
    b. A boat close-hauled on the port tack must give way to one close-hauled on the starboard tack.
    c. When running free, on opposite tacks, the boat on the port tack must give way to the one on the starboard tack.
    d. When running free, on the same tack, the boat to windward must give way to the leeward boat.
    e. A boat with the wind aft must give way to the other boat.
11. A powerboat's "Danger Zone" is the 10-point sector from dead ahead to two points abaft the starboard beam. Any powerboat approaching in this sector has the right of way.
12. Under the *Inland Rules* sailboats make these fog signals at one-minute intervals, on a foghorn:
    a. Starboard tack—*one blast.*
    b. Port tack—*two blasts.*
    c. Wind abaft the beam—*three blasts.*
13. The *Inland Rules* fog signal for a boat under tow is one long and two short blasts, on a horn.
14. Powerboats and other "steam vessels," under way in fog, must sound one long blast on a whistle or siren at least once a minute.
15. Rapid ringing of a bell is the fog signal for *any* boat at anchor.
16. Normal whistle signals for powerboats are:
    a. *One short blast*—"Steering to starboard."
    b. *Two short blasts*—"Steering to port."
    c. *Three short blasts*—"Engines going full speed astern."
    d. *Four or more short, rapid blasts*—"DANGER! Stop your intention!"
17. **Distress signals required on coastal waters and the Great Lakes:**
    a. *By day:* Hand-held red flares; or hand-held or floating orange smokes; or red aerial or parachute flares; or bright red-orange flag imprinted both sides with a black square and a black disc.
    b. *By night:* Hand-held or pistol-projected or rocket-propelled red aerial or parachute flares; or automatic S-O-S lantern.
    c. *Day and night:* Hand-held or aerial or parachute red flares.
    d. *By day* (sound signals, optional): Continuous sounding of foghorn, whistle, bell, siren, or firing of a gun.
    e. *By day* (visual signals, optional): Stretch arms at shoulder level, wave slowly up and down; or hoist American flag upside down; or wave white shirt; or flash sun's reflection with mirror.

e. *By night* (visual signal): Send S-O-S in Morse Code (. . . - - - . . .) by flashlight, in continuous series.

By night (sound signals). Same as day sound signals.

18. Running lights are required under the *Inland Rules* from sunset to sunrise.

19. Rowing boats, whether under oars or sail, must show a white light to avoid collision.

20. Sailboats without engines must carry 10-point side lights—red to port, green to starboard—and a 12-point white stern light.

21. A motorboat under 26 feet long must carry a combination red-and-green light forward, and, higher aft, a 32-point white light.

22. Motorboats over 26 feet long carry separate 10-point red and green side lights, plus a 20-point white light forward and aft, higher than this light, a 32-point white light. These are *range lights*.

23. Large ships under *Inland Rules* carry lights similar to large motorboats, but the range lights are more centrally located.

24. Towboats with tow astern, carry the usual red and green side lights, plus a vertical hoist of three bright white lights.

25. With tow alongside, a towboat shows the usual red and green side lights, plus a vertical hoist of two bright white lights.

26. Check list of nautical terms:

SAILING TERM

close-winded—Able to sail close to the direction of the wind.

GENERAL

bearing—The direction from the boat to an object.

Danger Zone—For a powerboat, the sector from dead ahead to two points abaft the starboard beam, in which approaching powerboats have the right of way.

ensign—The American flag.

give-way vessel—One not having the right of way.

motorboat—Any boat under 65 feet long propelled by machinery, except tugboats and towboats propelled by steam.

Navigation Rules—Marine traffic rules of the U.S. Coast Guard, covering both Inland and International waters.

overtaking—Approaching from more than two points abaft the beam.

point—An 11¼° arc of the horizon.

range lights—Two white lights carried by "steam vessels"—one forward and low, the other aft and high—to make course changes apparent.

right of way—The right to maintain course and speed in a situation where danger of collision exists.

running lights—Lights carried at night to prevent collision.

side light—A 10-point light fixed to show from dead ahead to two points abaft the beam—red, if to port; green, if to starboard.

stand-on vessel—The one having the right of way.

steam vessel—Under the *Inland Rules,* any vessel propelled by machinery.

17

Buoys, Lights, and Other Aids to Navigation

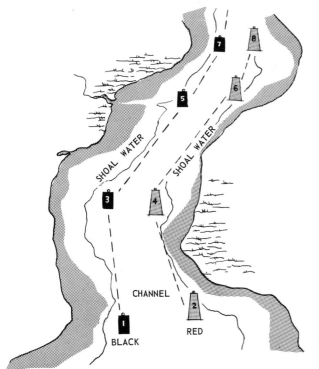

Under lateral system of buoyage, numbers begin at seaward end of channel and get larger on way in, with odd-numbered black can buoys to port and even-numbered red nun buoys to starboard

Buoys

BUOYS ARE THE ROAD SIGNS of the water, indicating where the channels lie, and where the rocks, shoals, and other underwater obstructions are. On navigable waters under the control of the United States Coast Guard, buoys are set out and maintained by the Coast Guard and are marked and numbered according to a method known as the *lateral system*. Individual states may have local markings for lakes and other waters not under Coast Guard control, but the skipper who knows the lateral system of buoyage will have little trouble finding his way on most American waters.

The essence of the system is simple. As a boat approaches harbor from seaward, buoys marking the channel's port side are black and odd-numbered, while those marking the starboard side of channel are red and even-numbered, with the numbers of both black and red buoys getting larger in sequence, starting with Nos. 1 and 2 at the seaward end of the channel. Where no entering-from-seaward course is involved, as in sailing along the coast, the Coast Guard sets

156

out and marks the buoys as though one direction was from seaward.

Color of buoys. Each buoy is painted with a color that shows which side of the channel it marks, or its purpose. The chief colors, as noted, are red, to show the returning skipper the right side of the channel, and black, to show him the left side on entering. *Red—right—returning* is one easy mnemonic device to register the important difference between the two colors. Another is B-P-O-E—*Black, Port, Odd, Entering*—which includes a reminder on the numbering system.

In addition to the red and black, there are buoys of other colors, used for different purposes. This list summarizes the principal colors you're likely to encounter:

Red buoys mark the starboard side of the channel, from seaward toward harbor, and are even-numbered.

Black buoys mark the port side of the channel, from seaward toward harbor, and are odd-numbered.

Red-and-black: Buoys painted with broad horizontal bands of red and black indicate an obstruction in the channel, or a channel junction. Though they may be passed on either side, the preferred channel is shown by the color of the top band and the shape of the buoy (see below). Thus if the top band is red, the buoy should be kept to starboard when entering from seaward. Since buoys sometimes shift their location, it is good practice to give the buoy itself a wide berth in passing.

Black-and-white (vertical stripes): Buoys painted with vertical stripes of black and white mark the middle of the channel, or the *fairway* (open channel), entering from seaward, and may be passed close aboard on either side.

Black-and-white (horizontal bands): Buoys painted with broad horizontal bands of black and white mark the outer limits of fish trap or net areas, and should be given a wide berth.

White buoys indicate anchorage areas.

Yellow buoys mark quarantine anchorage areas.

Buoy numbers. Channel buoys have numbers on them, both as another way of indicating which side of the channel they mark, and to help the mariner locate them on a chart. Coming in from sea, odd numbers are to port and even numbers to starboard. You may occasionally see a buoy with a supplementary letter, as "42-A," for example, where a buoy has been added to a channel after the series for the channel was laid out and numbered.

Many buoys at important locations, or on isolated rocks or reefs, carry both the usual

Black-and-white mid-channel buoys may carry identifying letters; this "NH" buoy marks entrance to New Haven, Conn., harbor

Black can buoys are odd-numbered, mark port side of channel; red nun buoys are even-numbered, mark starboard side of channel

FLASHING—*Not more than 30 flashes a minute*
OCCULTING—*Steady light broken by regular, equal, or shorter periods of darkness*
QUICK FLASHING—*Not less than 60 flashes a minute*

number and the initials of the location. For example, "I BI" marks the port side of the seaward entrance to Block Island Sound, north of Block Island. Sometimes the black-and-white mid-channel buoys and the red-and-black obstruction buoys carry letters, without numbers, to help identify them on a chart.

Buoy shapes. There are many different shapes used for buoys, but only two have any significance. The cone-shaped *nun buoy* is used to mark the channel's starboard side, entering from seaward, and is red. The *can buoy,* painted black, marks the port side of the channel. On red-and-black obstruction or channel junction buoys, the shape has the same significance, and corresponds to the color of the top band. A can-shaped obstruction buoy, with its top band black, for example, would indicate that it should be left to port, entering from seaward. On spar buoys, however, and on lighted buoys and whistle, gong, and bell buoys, the shape has no significance, though the *color* has.

Lights

Color and characteristics of lights. Lighted buoys are used to mark turning points in a channel, hidden underwater dangers, channel junctions, and the middle of the channel or fairway. Each lighted buoy is painted to conform with its function and location, so that it also serves as a day mark, when its light may not be visible. For night use, to make identification more positive, lighted buoys vary one from the other, both by the color and characteristic of their light—

Starboard side, entering from seaward: WHITE or RED.

Port side, entering from seaward: WHITE or GREEN.

These channel lights may be *flashing, occulting,* or *quick flashing.* A flashing light is one that gives not more than 30 regular flashes a minute, with each flash shorter than the period of darkness. An occulting light is a steady light broken regularly by periods of darkness, with each light period equal to or longer than the dark. A quick flashing light shows not less than 60 flashes a minute, and is used to mark a spot requiring special caution, as a wreck, or an important turn.

158

Mid-channel, entering from seaward: WHITE.

Mid-channel buoys carry white lights only, and their characteristic is the Morse Code "A," a *short-long flashing* with a short of about .4 seconds duration, followed by a flash four times as long. It is quite distinctive, not easily mistaken.

Junction and obstruction, entering from seaward: WHITE, RED, or GREEN.

As with mid-channel buoys, junction and obstruction buoys have a quite distinctive characteristic—*interrupted quick flashing.* This is a series of quick flashes for about four seconds, followed by a dark period of the same length. If the light is *white,* it indicates a junction with a channel on both sides. If it is *red,* it should be kept to starboard when entering from seaward; if *green,* to port.

Lights in anchorage, quarantine, fish net, and dredging areas have no significance in the lateral system, and may be of any color *except* red or green, since these colors are limited to channel use. The characteristics of these miscellaneous lights may be flashing or occulting—as described above—or *fixed.* A fixed light is a steady light, one that shines the same color continuously, without interruption.

In addition to the lights of the lateral system, there are hundreds of special lights, such as lighthouses, lightships, Texas Towers, and range lights. You'll quickly learn these major lights for the waters you sail, and their special flashing characteristics, many of which are quite spectacular. With a good understanding of the basic lights discussed above, you should be able to find your way on the water as easily at night as by day.

MID-CHANNEL—*A white light with short-long flash, like Morse Code letter "A" (. —)*

INTERRUPTED QUICK FLASHING—*Series of quick flashes followed by dark period of same length, with flashes colored white, red, or green according to location of buoy*

FIXED—*A steady light, without interruption*

Spars, Bells, Gongs, Whistles, Daybeacons

To round out your knowledge of aids to navigation, you should have some acquaintance with the appearance and use of a group of widely used markers of different types. *Spar buoys* are long, tapered logs or steel tubes used for day marks in less heavily-trafficked channels, and for a variety of other purposes. *Bell buoys* carry a bell that sounds either automatically or by the sea's motion. They are used to mark shoals and channel turning points in areas where fog is a frequent hazard to navigation, and may be lighted or unlighted. *Gong buoys* are used for the same purposes, but carry a single gong or a series of gongs, to sound a different

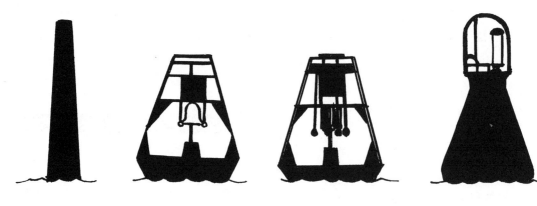

SPAR   BELL   GONG   WHISTLE

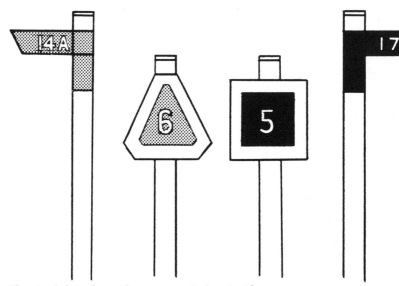

Above: *Shapes of these buoys have no particular significance, but their color and numbering follow lateral system*

Below: *Day beacons are of various shapes and colors; significance must be determined from local chart*

note as a means of distinguishing them in a section where several bell buoys are located. *Whistle buoys* are equipped with a whistle to sound a long "hoo-ing" note that carries a great distance. They are generally used as outer marks along the coast, where the constant motion of the sea can be relied on to compress in the buoy the air that operates the whistle. Whistle buoys may be lighted or unlighted.

Daybeacons are unlighted marks in a variety of shapes and sizes, used to mark obstructions (such as isolated rocks), channel turning points, or harbor entrances. They may be located in the water or on land. Their significance must be determined from the local chart.

CAUTION: In the several *Light Lists* published by the Coast Guard, detailing the location and description of every buoy and light on the navigable waters under its jurisdiction, the following note is inserted to remind mariners that floating marks—which are anchored to the bottom by a weight—may not always be exactly in the position they are supposed to occupy, as shown on the chart; and that lighted aids may not always emit their designated signal: *"It is imprudent for a navigator to rely on floating aids to navigation to always maintain their charted position and to constantly and unerringly display their advertised characteristics. The obstacles to perfect performance are of such magnitude that complete reliability is manifestly impossible to achieve."*

I once lived on an island in Long Island Sound off whose Matinecock Point is located the black, lighted Bell Buoy No. 21. The light gives out a single green flash every four seconds, and helps towboats make the turn with their barges in toward the sand banks of Hempstead Harbor. Three times over a **period of ten years I reported to the Coast** Guard when Bell No. 21 was carried by floating ice anywhere from two to four miles east of its charted position. Had any towboat skipper relied on it exclusively while it was off station, in making his turn into the harbor, he would have run hard aground on the north shore of Long Island.

Summary

1. Buoyage on most navigable waters of the United States is under control of the Coast Guard and follows the lateral system.
2. Under the lateral system, as a boat moves from seaward toward harbor, the channel's starboard side is marked by red buoys bearing even numbers, and the port side by black buoys with odd numbers; with the numbers in sequence from Nos. 1 and 2 at the seaward end.
3. Where no entering-from-seaward situation exists, one direction is designated as though it was seaward, and the buoys are set out and marked accordingly.
4. Red-and-black, horizontally banded buoys mark obstructions or channel junctions, with the top band of color and the buoy's shape indicating the preferred side on which the buoy is to be passed from seaward.
5. Black-and-white, vertically striped buoys mark the middle of a channel or fairway, and may be passed on either side, close to. Buoys with black-and-white horizontal bands mark fish nets or trap areas, and should be given a wide berth.
6. White buoys show anchorages, and yellow buoys mark quarantine areas.
7. When a supplementary letter is used with the number, it means that the buoy has been added since that channel's series of buoys was last numbered. Buoys at important stations or reefs carry a number plus the station's initials. Mid-channel buoys and channel junction buoys sometimes carry letters, without numbers.
8. Only two buoy shapes have significance: the cone-shaped nun buoy, painted red, marking the channel's starboard side, entering from seaward; and the can buoy, painted black, marking the channel's port side. The shape of red-and-black obstruction or channel junction buoys has the same significance, and the color of their top band is painted to conform with the shape.
9. Lighted aids mark turning points, underwater hazards, channel junctions, or mid-channel. Each lighted buoy carries a light distinctive to its function and location.
10. The lights of buoys to be kept to starboard when entering, may be white or red; those to be kept to port may be white or green. The characteristic signal may be flashing, occulting, or quick flashing.
11. Quick-flashing lights mark spots where special caution should be used.
12. Entering from seaward, mid-channel buoys that are lighted show a short-long flashing white light, the Morse Code letter "A."
13. Channel junction or obstruction buoys may carry white, red, or green lights; and they have an interrupted quick flashing charac-

teristic. If the light is red, the buoy should be kept to starboard when entering; if it is green, the buoy should be kept to port.

14. Lights for other areas—anchorage, quarantine, fish trap, and dredging—may be of any color except red or green, and may have a characteristic of fixed, flashing, or occulting.

15. Spar buoys are used to mark lightly trafficked channels and for other purposes. Bell and gong buoys mark shoals and important turning points, where fog is a hazard. Whistle buoys are used chiefly for outer marks. Gong, bell, and whistle buoys may be lighted or unlighted. Daybeacons are of many shapes, and are used to mark important turning points, channel obstructions, and harbor entrances. They may be in the water or on land.

16. CAUTION: The Coast Guard warns mariners not to rely on any floating aid being in its charted position, or to always display its designated light and characteristic.

17. Checklist of nautical terms:

GENERAL

can buoy—A buoy shaped like a can; usually painted black, bearing an odd number and marking the port side of the channel when entering from seaward.

fairway—An open channel.

fixed light—One displaying a constant, unchanging color.

flashing—A light of not more than 30 regular flashes per minute, with each flash shorter than the period of darkness.

interrupted quick flashing—A light showing quick flashes for about four seconds, followed by an eclipse of the same length.

Morse Code "A"—A short-long flashing, showing a short flash of about .4 seconds duration, followed by a flash four times as long.

nun buoy—A cone-shaped buoy; usually painted red, bearing an even number, and marking the starboard side of the channel when entering from seaward.

occulting—A steady light eclipsed at regular intervals, with the periods of light equal to or longer than the eclipse.

quick flashing—Not less than 60 flashes per minute.

spar buoy—A long, tapered wooden log or steel tube used as a channel marker and for other purposes.

18

Marlinespike Seamanship

IF A SHARP KNIFE is a sailor's best friend, a good *marlinespike* is his man Friday, always at hand to perform a variety of useful chores in keeping the boat's lines and rigging shipshape. It is a short, strong, tapered steel rod that is equally useful for freeing the turns of a wet and stubborn knot, for opening up the strands of a line for splicing, or for inserting in the eye of a shackle pin to tighten it. A wooden marlinespike is called a *fid,* and is used for splicing both line and rope.

Starting with knife and marlinespike, and supplemented by a few other tools and aids, marlinespike seamanship is the branch of the sailor's art that deals with the preparation, use, and repair of lines, wire, and rope in all their applications on the water. By extension, it also includes work on sails and canvas.

It is an ancient art, with a vast accumulation of methods and techniques, far beyond the scope of this book. But even a beginning sailor should always carry a knife and marlinespike when sailing, and should know how to tie the knots and hitches discussed in Chapter 5. And the new skipper should know a few more knots, how to take care of his lines, how to make a splice, and the basic

use of a sailor's palm and needle for simple repairs and ropework.

The marlinespike knife

In nearly forty years of sailing, no single piece of equipment has been so useful on so many occasions as my marlinespike knife. The few times I have gone on the water without it I have felt vulnerable and defenseless, it's that important for an emergency. It is called, technically, a "rigger's knife" and is available in several different makes. I prefer one with both blade and spike of stainless steel, so there will be no magnetic influence near a compass. Also, if possible, get one with a marlinespike that locks in its working position. Equip your knife with a $\frac{3}{16}$-inch nylon lanyard, ending in an eye to loop around your belt, and as long as your outstretched arm. This will let you cut a line above your head without removing the knife from your belt.

As a simple safety device, lash a nickel or plastic policeman's whistle to the lanyard a few inches from the knife. It's handy should you ever fall overboard, especially at night,

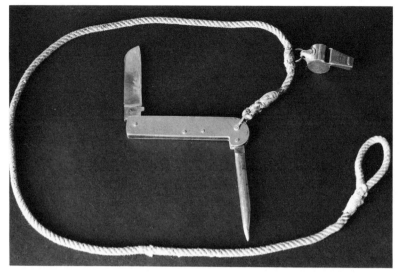

Marlinepike knife, with whistle on lanyard, is a sailor's most useful tool

when the skirl of a whistle will pierce even the howling of a gale and carry hundreds of yards farther than a human voice. It is also useful for getting attention on the water, and as a standby means for signaling distress. Had Ted Sierks, a photographer on the yacht *Apache* in the 1953 Honolulu Race, worn a whistle on his knife when he fell overboard at night, he would have been rescued long before spending thirty terrifying hours in the shark-infested water. Johnny Green, who was helmsman when Sierks went overboard, told me *Apache* stopped about 200 yards short of him when they retraced their course, and could not see the light they had thrown to him, though they would certainly have heard a whistle downwind that distance.

Keeping the knife sharp. Contrary to popular belief, a dull knife is a dangerous instrument. A sharp knife is much safer because it cuts cleanly, with less pressure and danger of slipping. Buy a small whetstone and use it whenever you find the blade is taking too much pressure to do a clean job of cutting. There's only one way to sharpen a blade properly—rub one surface of the cutting edge directly against and across the face of the whetstone, using a little household oil on the stone to preserve the blade's temper; then turn the blade over and rub the other edge. In general it's easier to get a sharp cutting edge on an ordinary steel blade than on one made of stainless steel, and the edge will hold longer. But with a little care a stainless steel blade can be honed to a keen edge, and has the advantages of being rustproof and nonmagnetic.

To sharpen knife, oil whetstone and rub one side of knife's cutting edge directly against and across whetstone, then the other

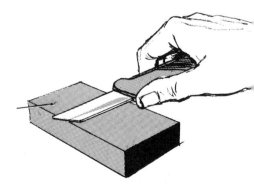

Palm and needle work

Palm, needle, and sail twine. For sewing canvas, certain ropework, and repairs to your sails, your ditty bag should contain a sailor's leather *palm,* several sizes of sail needles, nylon thread for sail repair, and either a ball of cotton sail twine and a lump of beeswax, or a spool of waxed linen thread such as Barbour's No. 8 Cord, for *whipping* (binding) the ends of lines.

The palm is a reinforced needle-pusher of leather that fits over the thumb and fingers of one hand, and has a metal socket to receive the end of the needle. Palms are made in several sizes. Before you buy one, try it on to be sure it fits.

Sail needles differ from ordinary needles in having a tapered triangular section that creates a large enough opening, even in heavy canvas, to let the thread or sail twine enter easily. An assortment of one No. 11, two No. 14, and three No. 17 sail needles will handle most small sailboat sewing jobs. They should be kept wrapped in a piece of oiled canvas, in a plastic tube. Ordinary sail twine must be waxed for sewing, and the beeswax acts as a waterproofer and preservative. Waxed linen, which is widely used by shoe repair shops, is equally effective and much stronger than cotton sail twine. A spool of it lasts a long time.

Plain whipping. Whenever a piece of stranded line is cut, the ends must be bound to keep the strands from unlaying as the line

LARRY KEAN

Leather palm, marline, sail needles, nylon thread, beeswax, sail twine—all essential for sail repair and canvas work

is used. This is easily done with small sizes of nylon line by holding a lighted match or the flame of a lighter under the end until its strands melt and fuse together, which makes a satisfactory temporary binding. For non-synthetic lines, adhesive tape or Scotch tape may be used for a quick binding, but it is neither suitable nor sailorly for extended use. A neater, more serviceable temporary binding is a *plain whipping.*

To make it, first cut a length of waxed sail twine equal to 21 times the circumference of the line you are going to whip (about 26 inches for a ⅜-inch diameter line). Hold the line in your left hand, near the end, with the end facing to the right. Lay the sail twine with its end extending slightly beyond the line's end, and press your thumb on it about an inch back to keep it in place. With your right hand, take six very tight turns with the sail twine, over the top of the line and under, *against the lay,* to bind in the first end of the twine, and clamp the turns with your left forefinger to keep them from un-winding. Pull tight on the free part of the first end to bury it snugly, and bend it back toward the line's standing part, out of the way. Lay alongside it the twine's second end,

and hold it in place with your left thumb. This forms a bight of sail twine extending beyond the end of the line. Now continue the binding turns, taking another six, with each pulled as tight as possible, to bind in the second end of the twine. To make these turns, the bight must be passed over the end of the line each time. Clamp the second set of turns with your left forefinger, and with your right hand pull tight on the twine's second end to bury it snugly. This brings the excess of both ends of the twine to the middle of the whipping. Clip the ends off short. Cut the line off ½-inch from the whipping.

Palm-and-needle whipping. A plain whipping is all right for temporary service, but the only lasting protection to keep the end of a sheet or halyard from *cowtailing* (unlaying), is to sew on a palm-and-needle whipping. This is so easy to do, yet gives such a professional finish to any line, it's a skill every skipper should have. Thread a sail needle with a length of waxed sail twine, and put the palm on your right hand. Hold the line in your left hand, as though to make a plain whipping. About an inch from the end of the line, run the needle between two strands and pull through all but an inch or

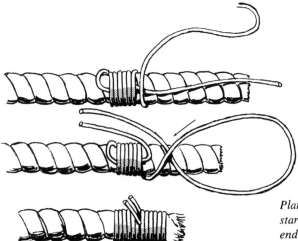

Plain whipping is made against lay of line, starting on standing part and working toward end

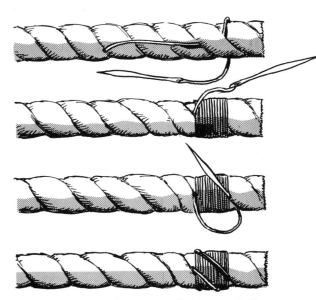

Palm-and-needle whipping is made against lay of line, starting at end and working toward standing part

so of the twine. Bend this end toward the line's standing part and hold in place with your left thumb.

Now take a series of tight turns over the line and under, *against* the lay, working toward the standing part, to bind in the first end. As you complete each turn, pull it as tight as possible, clamping it with your left forefinger to hold the tension. Take enough turns to make a whipping equal to the diameter of the line, but not less than a dozen. Pull taut the final turn and clamp it with your left forefinger. Pass the needle through the line under one strand and pull the twine taut. Now lead the twine back in the *contline* (spiral groove) toward the end of the line, and at the start of the whipping pass the needle under the next strand, against the lay, and bring it out in the next contline and pull the twine taut. This binds the whipping with a first *worming,* or spiral winding.

Lead the twine down the second contline toward the standing part and at the end of the whipping, pass the needle under the next strand, against the lay, bring it out in the third contline and pull the twine taut to complete the second worming. Lead the twine back up the contline to the start of the whipping and shove the needle under the next strand, against the lay, to emerge in the first contline, thus completing the third worming. Repeat the whole process to make each worming double. This brings the needle back to the end of the whipping. Now pass it

under two strands against the lay, pull the twine taut, tie in an overhand knot as far down in the contline as possible, clip it off close, and bury the knot in the contline. Clip off the excess of the first end of the twine, and cut the line off ⅜-inch from the whipping.

Splicing

The eye splice. Like palm-and-needle whipping, splicing is so simple, yet so seamanlike, you'll get great satisfaction from adding it to your repertory of sailorly skills. Essentially, splicing line is a process of braiding six strands together—three of the standing part, and three of the end being woven into the standing part. The principle to grasp at the outset is as follows: The strands of the end are always interlaced with those of the standing part *against the lay,* and as each *tuck* (round of interweavings) is completed, each strand of the standing part is separated from its neighbor by a strand of the end, so that the strands of the standing part alternate with those of the end around the complete circumference of the line.

For practice purposes, equip yourself with a 3-foot length of ⅜-inch, 3-stranded manila or hemp line. If you can get a piece of old line, so much the better; the strands will be easier to open up than on new line, where

Left: *Eye Splice*, STEP 1—*Form eye of desired size, straddle standing part with strands of end . . .*

Above: STEP 2— *With thumb of left hand, push bight of strand No. 1 through opening under strand of standing part closest to neck of eye . . .*

the lay is still tight. Put a plain whipping on one end of the line, the nonworking end. Six inches from the other, or working, end, tie a seizing of sail twine in a tight clove hitch and finish it off with a square knot, clipped short, to keep the end from unlaying beyond that point. Unlay the three strands, and either whip each or bind tightly with Scotch tape to prevent fraying.

Below the seizing, form an eye of the desired size to the right of the standing part, and hold it between your left thumb and forefinger. Straddle the standing part with the three strands, so that one lies on each side of it, and the middle strand lies along the standing part. For convenience in description, we'll name the middle strand No. 1; the strand to its left, on top, No. 2; and the strand to the right of the middle strand, lying under the standing part, No. 3. At this point, be sure the loop is flat and that the line lies naturally, without a twist. If it does

not, roll the end with your right hand to remove the twist, and change the position of each strand to conform, where it meets the standing part. To keep track easily of the strands while splicing, put an ink mark on strand No. 1. You are now ready to take the first tuck.

Bend strand No. 2 down to the left, out of the way, and hold it with your left hand as you squeeze the neck of the eye. With your right hand, twist the standing part away from you to create an opening under the strand of the standing part closest to the neck of the eye. With your left thumb, push a *bight* of strand No. 1 through this opening, and with right thumb and forefinger pull the end of strand No. 1 *backward* through the opening and draw it snug. (You could, of course, push strand No. 1 straight through the opening and draw it snug, but you will find the "thumb-and-bight" system easier and faster. It also makes the strand lie flatter because

Left: STEP 3— *Tuck strand No. 2 of end under strand of standing part to left of strand holding No. 1 . . .*

Below: STEP 4—*Turn eye over and tuck strand No. 3 under third strand of standing part . . .*

FIRST TUCK COMPLETED—*Note how each strand of standing part is separated by a strand of end*

it spreads it slightly.) If you have tucked No. 1 correctly, it now crosses on top of the standing part, under one of its strands. To the left, below No. 1, lies strand No. 2, and to the right, under the standing part, lies No. 3.

To tuck strand No. 2, hold the left side of the eye with your left hand and again twist the standing part away from you to create an opening under the strand of the standing part immediately to the left of the strand holding No. 1. Push through this opening a bight of No. 2, and pull the end of the strand backward through the opening and draw it tight. Strand No. 2 should now lie across the strand of the standing part that holds No. 1, and under the strand to its left.

Beginners most often have trouble with the eye splice because they tuck the third strand of the working end incorrectly. But if you use the following procedure, you should make each eye splice correctly the first time:

To tuck strand No. 3, turn the eye over, so that No. 3 is pointing toward you. With the eye in this position, the top strand of the standing part at the eye's neck is the only one with no strand of the working end under it. To create an opening under this

169

STEP 5—*Start second tuck with strand No. 1, crossing it over one strand of standing part and under next, then doing same with strands No. 2 and No. 3 in turn*

Above: THREE TUCKS COMPLETED—*Note symmetrical appearance of tucks. Three tucks suffice for manila or hemp lines; use at least four for synthetic lines.*

Right: EYE SPLICE COMPLETED—*Before clipping off ends, roll splice under foot several times to settle strands in place.*

strand, hold the right side of the eye in your left hand, again twist the standing part away from you, and with your left thumb push through the opening a bight of No. 3, *against the lay.* Pull the end of No. 3 backward through the opening and draw it snug. Pull each of the strands of the working end down firmly against the neck of the splice and examine this first tuck to be sure it has these two characteristics of the properly made eye splice: (1) strand No. 3 lies *parallel* to the strand of the standing part to the right of the strand under which No. 3 passes, and (2) each standing part strand is separated from the next by a working end strand.

The second tuck is made in the same sequence as the first, starting with strand No. 1. Working against the lay, cross No. 1 over the strand of the standing part to the left, tuck it under the next strand, and pull it snug. Do the same with strand No. 2, then with No. 3. Now pull all three strands back tight toward the neck of the splice to make them lie into the standing part snugly. Check the tuck—each strand of the standing part should be separated from the next by a strand of the working end, and the interweaving should be perfectly symmetrical.

Make the third tuck in the same order as the first two, always starting with strand No. 1, and following the same procedure as for the second tuck. Three tucks are usually enough for manila and hemp lines, but four or five should be taken with synthetic lines, which have more slippery strands. Before

170

Left: EYE SPLICE AROUND THIMBLE, STEP 1—*Seize eye to thimble securely to keep it tight, then proceed as with usual eye splice*

Below: THREE TUCKS COMPLETED—*Note similarity to same stage in usual eye splice*

COMPLETED—*Roll under foot, as with usual eye splice, before cutting ends off strands. Remove seizings from thimble.*

cutting off the excess of the working strands, roll the splice back and forth under your foot several times to settle all the strands into each other. Cut off each working strand about ⅜ inch from the splice. If you cut them shorter, they may work out of the final tuck.

The eye splice around a thimble. First, be sure to use a thimble that fits the line— one with a ⅜-inch groove for ⅜-inch line, etc. Splicing an eye around a thimble is like making an ordinary eye splice, but care must be taken to anchor the standing part tightly to the thimble so that the thimble will be firmly enclosed when the splice is finished. Prepare the working end of the line as for an eye splice, with a seizing 6 inches back, and a whipping or Scotch tape binding on each strand. Lay the standing part in the groove of the thimble, with the seizing of the working end ¼ inch down from the neck of the thimble. Put a seizing of sail twine around the thimble and standing part here to hold the working end securely.

Now, stretch the standing part around the thimble and put a second seizing at the bottom of the thimble to hold the standing part tightly in the groove. Put a third seizing at the neck of the thimble, opposite the first

171

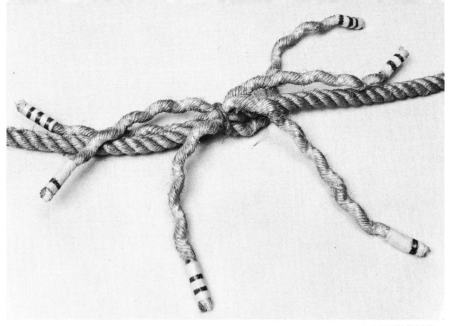

Left: *Short splice,* STEP 1— *Marry strands of two ends together and seize union . . .*

Below: STEP 2—*Tuck strands to right of union first, starting with No. 1, then No. 2 and No. 3 in sequence, using same method as in eye splice, tucking each strand of end over one strand of standing part and under next*

seizing. There should be no slack in the standing part that lies in the groove of the thimble; it should be taut. Otherwise, when the eye splice is completed, the thimble will be loose.

From this point on, proceed as in making a regular eye splice, only at completion of the first tuck pull and work each of the working strands back to make them fit snugly to the neck of the thimble, before taking the second tuck. When all the tucks have been completed (at least three for manila or hemp, four for synthetic lines), roll the splice underfoot to blend it, cut off the working strand ends and the seizings on the thimble.

The short splice. When you have learned the eye splice, you will find it easy to make a short splice, since the tucking follows the same pattern of "over one strand, under the next." For practice, use two 2-foot lengths of ⅜-inch line. Again, if you can get old line, it will be easier to splice. Whip one end of each line, the nonworking end. Unlay each working end about six inches and whip each of the strands, or bind it with Scotch tape.

"Marry" the two working ends by pushing them into each other so that all their strands interlace and alternate. Each strand of one end should lie between two strands of the other working end. Push the strands together

to make their union as snug as possible. Now tie a seizing tightly around both sets of strands at the union to hold them interlocked while you make the splice. For convenience, treat the topmost strand of the working strands on your left as the middle strand (1-L) of that group, and mark it with an ink

Left: FIRST TUCK COMPLETED—*Note that each strand of standing part to right of union is separated by a strand of right end. From this point, complete desired number of tucks.*

Below: STEP 3—*With tucks on right side completed, turn splice around and tuck left-hand strands in sequence, starting with No. 1, until desired number of tucks have been completed*

spot for easy identification. Strand 2-L now lies to the left of 1-L in the direction of the left-hand standing part, and 3-L to the right.

To mark the middle, or strand 1-R, of the right-hand group, put an ink spot on the strand that lies toward you, between strands 1-L and 2-L. This makes strand 2-R lie to the left of 1-R, in the direction of the right-hand standing part, and strand 3-R to the right.

Tuck the right side of the splice first. Hold the left standing part in your left hand, with your thumb at the seizing, and press down firmly on strand 1-R where it starts to cross over strand 1-L. With your right hand twist the right-hand standing part away from you, against the lay, to create an opening under strand 3-L. Push a bight of 1-R through the opening, and with right thumb and forefinger pull the end of 1-R backward through the opening and draw it snug. Now repeat the process with strand 2-R, crossing it over strand 3-L and tucking it under strand 2-L. Then cross strand 3-R over 2-L and tuck it under strand 1-L. This completes the first tuck of the right side of the splice. Each strand of the right standing part should now be separated from the next by a strand of the

working end. The second tuck is made in the same sequence, starting with strand 1-R. When it is completed, take a third tuck to complete the right side of the splice, or four tucks, if splicing synthetic line.

To complete the other side, turn the splice around so the untucked strands of the other working end face to your right. Now start with strand 1-L and tuck it against the lay, over one strand, and under the next. Do the

Above: BOTH SIDES COMPLETED—*Notice symmetry of splice on both sides of union*

Below: COMPLETED—*Roll splice under foot several times to settle strands before cutting them off*

same with strands 2-L and 3-L to complete the tuck. Examine to be sure each strand of the standing part is separated from the next by a working strand, then put in the second and third tucks, always starting with 1-L and tucking 2-L and 3-L in sequence.

When the final tuck has been taken, so that both sides of the splice have the same number of tucks, roll the splice underfoot to blend the strands in evenly, and clip each end off about ⅜ inch from the splice. The completed splice should be perfectly symmetrical. Though the line will now be too big to pass through a small block, it will be almost as strong as the uncut line, and good for further service.

Three special purpose knots

The Rolling Hitch. You will frequently have occasion on the water to make fast a line to a round spar, where the pull will be lengthwise along the spar; or to secure a line to itself while it is under strain so as to maintain the strain; or to put a temporary hold on a larger line to permit shifting it while it is carrying a load. The one knot

that does all these jobs superbly is the *rolling hitch*. It is quickly tied, holds securely, and is easily cast off. The rolling hitch is always tied with the free end leading *away* from the direction of the pull.

To tie: Start as though you were going to make a clove hitch around the spar (or other line)—pass the end of the line around the spar and under the standing part to form a round turn. Cross the end over this round turn and pass it under the standing part again to form a second round turn between the standing part and the first round turn. Cross the end over this second round turn, pass it around the spar and under itself above the first two round turns, and pull the hitch tight. When the hitch is correctly made, any pull in the direction of the first two round turns causes a jamming action by the second round turn on the first, and "locks" the hitch.

The Fisherman's Bend. A useful variation of two half-hitches is the *Fisherman's,* or *Anchor, Bend.* It is a quick way to secure a line to the ring of an anchor when no shackle is available, and provides an extra round turn to distribute the strain and reduce chafe.

To tie: Pass the end of the line around the ring in two round turns and lead the end

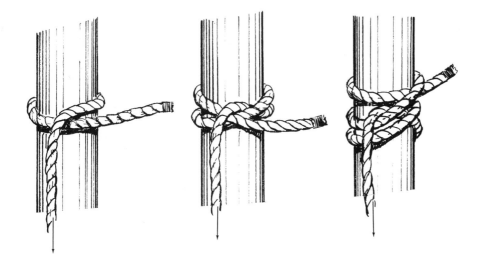

The rolling hitch—Ideal for towing a round spar, and will not slip when direction of pull is away from end of line

The Fisherman's Bend, or Anchor Bend, is two half-hitches with extra round turn to distribute strain. End should be seized to standing part.

across the standing part and under both round turns to make the first half-hitch. Above it, on the standing part, make a second half-hitch, then seize the end to the standing part with a lashing of *marline* (small line, tarred hemp), to prevent it coming adrift.

The Genuine Carrick Bend. Although two bowlines can be used to tie two lines together for heavy duty work, like towing, there is always the possibility of chafe where they cross each other. A better way to secure them is with a *genuine carrick bend,* which interlaces the two lines in a way that distributes

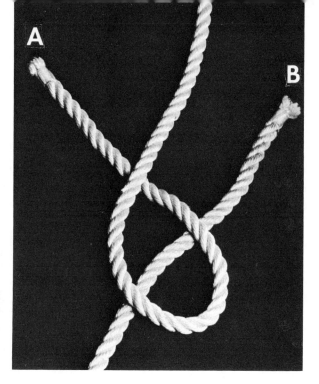

Genuine Carrick Bend, STEP 1—
Pass end B under bight formed by end A with its standing part . . .

Above: STEP 2—*Pass end B across standing part of end A, behind end A, across A's standing part again, under its own standing part, and across bight formed by end A . . .*

Right: COMPLETED—*Pull ends snug and seize each to its standing part*

the strain symmetrically, locks securely, yet is easy to untie even when wet.

To tie: Hold one line in your left hand and form a bight with its end, A, crossing to the left under the standing part. Lay the other line diagonally under this bight, with its end, B, leading from left to right. Pass end B across the standing part of end A, and behind A. Lead end B across A's bight and under its own standing part. Pull the bend snug and sieze the ends to their standing parts.

This bend can be used to tie together two lines of the same diameter or of different diameters. It is superior for emergency use in tying a piece of line to a broken shroud to take a strain on it, and will even hold ⅛-inch stainless steel wire securely when nylon line is used with it. In using a genuine carrick bend for bending line to wire, leave the ends a little longer than when both parts are line, and pull both ends extra tight to snug the turns of the bend together before seizing them and putting a strain on the bend. Because the turns of the genuine carrick bend are gradual, rather than sharp, the wire is not apt to develop kinks.

Sewing

The flat seam. For sewing canvas, equip yourself with a palm, sail needles, sail twine, and beeswax. A *bench hook* to stretch the cloth out, though not absolutely essential, speeds the sewing when there is a lengthy seam to be sewn. Of the three simple stitches that every skipper should know, the *flat seam* is most often used. It is quickly made and is useful for sewing one piece of material on top of another, as in patching a sail.

To sew: Choose your sail needle and gauge of twine according to the weight of the material to be sewn. Wear the palm on your right hand and always sew from right to left. Thread the needle with the twine doubled and run the twine through the beeswax several times to make it slide easier. Start with a length just shorter than your outstretched arm; this will save stopping frequently to rethread the needle. Whenever possible, use the outside edge, or *selvage,* of the canvas for patching, since this is manufactured with a thread sewn into it to prevent raveling.

If the selvage is not available, double the canvas under about ¾ inch and sew each stitch of the flat seam through the doubled material to bury the raw edge. Sew the end of the doubled twine under the stitches of the first 1½ inches of the seam, or if you prefer, tie a knot in the end to secure it. Push the needle through the bottom cloth close to the overlapping edge and bring it up through the doubled material close to the edge each time. Take 4 to 6 stitches to the inch, depending on the weight of the material and the size of the needle. When you have finished a row of stitches, run the needle back under the last 1½ inches of stitches, pull the twine tight and cut it off short. If you are sewing the edges of two pieces of material together with a flat seam, after completing the stitching on one edge, turn the material over and sew the other edge in the same fashion, doubling the material first if it is not a selvage.

The round seam. For speed in joining two edges of canvas together, where it does not matter if there is a welt edge on one surface, the *round seam* is useful. It is not as strong as a flat seam sewn with a double row of stitches, but is suitable for making sea bags and ditty bags, where the raw doubled edge will be hidden from view. In sewing the round seam, the stitching is done on what is to be the inside or back of the finished work.

To sew: Double each edge back on itself about ¾ inch and crease it so that it will stay doubled while being sewn. Put the palm

FLAT SEAM—
Use for quick repairs, with edge doubled under to prevent unraveling

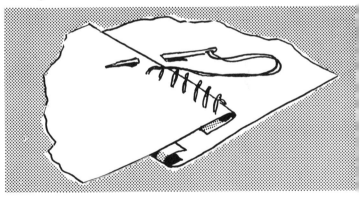

ROUND SEAM—
Use for ditty bags and other work where raw edges will be on inside

on your right hand. Thread a strong needle with a length of doubled twine almost as long as your outstretched arm, and pull it across the beeswax several times. Tie a knot in the end of the twine to anchor it at the first stitch.

Now, with the heel of the needle resting in the socket of the palm, shove the needle through all four thicknesses of the two edges. As the blade of the needle emerges, grasp it with your right thumb and forefinger and pull it through the rest of the way. Pull the first stitch tight. Bring the needle back over the two edges to the side where the first stitch started, and shove it through the four thicknesses a second time, close to the first stitch. This oversews the two edges with the doubled sail twine. Take enough more round stitches, each one close to the next, to join the two edges for their full length. Tie a knot in the twine as close as possible to the final stitch, and cut it off short. When you turn the work over on the other side, the rough

welt is hidden, and the finished appearance is a neat line of close stitches.

Sewing—the herringbone stitch. For sewing the two edges of a rip together, the *herringbone stitch* is used. It has the advantage of pulling and holding the two edges tight as every stitch is taken.

To sew: Double a suitable length of sail twine, wax it, and tie a knot in the end. Bring the two edges of the rip together and, starting where it ends in the fabric, pass the needle *up through* the fabric at the left side of the rip, at the bottom, to bury the knot. Pass the needle *down through* the fabric at the right side of the rip opposite, and bring it up *in the rip,* on the left of the stitch. Pull the twine tight and pass the needle across the stitch and up through the left side of the fabric again to start the second stitch. Sew the stitches as close together as possible for the balance of the rip, but make them of varying lengths to spread the strain over several threads of the material.

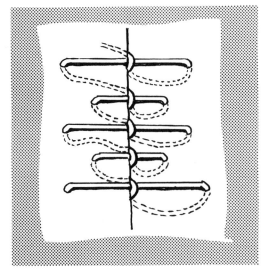

HERRINGBONE STITCH—
Use to join two edges together with no overlap, alternating width of stitches to distribute strain

Summary

1. Marlinespike seamanship deals with the preparation, use, and repair of lines, wire, and rope in marine applications. It also includes work on sails and canvas.

2. Every sailor should carry a "rigger's knife," with a cutting blade and marlinespike, preferably of stainless steel, and on its lanyard a plastic or nickel whistle for emergency use.

3. A knife should be sharpened by repeatedly rubbing first one surface of its cutting edge, than the other, directly against and across the face of the whetstone, with a little oil on the stone.

4. The boat's ditty bag should include a sailor's palm, several sizes of sail needles, nylon thread, and a ball of sail twine and lump of beeswax, or a spool of waxed linen thread.

5. The ends of small nylon line can be fused from raveling, temporarily, by holding a flame to them.

6. Stranded lines can be kept from unlaying temporarily by tying a plain whipping on their ends. The whipping should be as long as the diameter of the line, but at least 12 turns of waxed sail twine.

7. For permanent use, a palm-and-needle whipping should be used.

8. In splicing an eye in 3-stranded line, the middle strand of the working end is tucked first, then the strand to its left, then the strand to its right. All strands are tucked over one strand of the standing part, and under one, against the lay.

9. In a correctly made tuck, each strand of the standing part is separated from the next by a strand of the working end.

10. Three tucks are usually enough for manila and hemp lines; at least four should be used for synthetic lines.

11. In splicing an eye around a thimble, the standing part must be anchored snugly to the thimble with seizings.

12. When making a short splice, the two working ends are "married," and a tight temporary seizing put around all strands at the point of union.

13. In a short splice, the sequence of tucking is the same as in an eye splice, but one side is tucked completely before the other.

14. The **rolling hitch** is used for a nonslipping hold on spars, lines, and ropes. The free end should lead away from the direction of pull.

15. The **fisherman's** or **anchor bend,** is a useful variation of two half-hitches for securing a rode to an anchor ring.

16. The **genuine carrick bend** is an excellent way to join lines or hawsers for towing, and can also be used to join nylon line to wire.

17. In addition to palm, sail needles, and other aids, a bench hook is useful when sewing long seams in canvas.

18. The flat seam is used to sew together an overlap of two or more pieces of material. If selvages are not available, the material should be doubled under and the raw edge buried.

19. A round seam is used to sew two edges of canvas together quickly, where the bulk of a welt seam on one surface does not matter.

20. A rip in canvas can be repaired with a herringbone stitch, which pulls and holds together the two edges with every stitch.

21. Checklist of nautical terms:

    bench hook—A small hook, fitted with a swivel eye at one end for a lanyard, to hold canvas while it is being sewn.

    contline—The spiral groove between two strands of a stranded line.

    cowtailing—The fraying of a line when the strands have become unlaid.

    fid—A round, tapered hardwood spike used to open up strands in line or rope, for splicing.

    flat seam—A stitch used to sew together overlapping pieces of cloth.

    herringbone stitch—A stitch used to sew together the edges of a rip, in which each stitch pulls together the edges and holds them.

marlinespike—A round, tapered metal spike used to open up strands, in splicing line, rope, or wire.

palm—A reinforced leather needle-pusher that fits over thumb and fingers of one hand, and has a metal socket to hold the end of the needle.

palm-and-needle whipping—A permanent sewn binding on the end of a line, finished with worming to hold the turns of the whipping secure.

plain whipping—A temporary binding on the end of a line, in which both ends of the binding twine are buried in the whipping.

rigger's knife—A knife fitted with a cutting blade and a marlinespike.

round seam—A stitch that binds together two edges of cloth, leaving a rough welt on one surface.

selvage—The bound edge of canvas, made with a thread to prevent raveling.

short splice—A splice used to join together two lengths of line of the same diameter by "marrying" their ends and interweaving their strands. It increases the line's diameter.

tuck—In a splice, one round of interweaving of the strands of the working end into the strands of the standing part; also, to interweave.

whipping—A binding, usually of waxed sail twine, put on the ends of line or rope to keep the strands from unlaying.

worming—Small line that fills in the contlines of a stranded line or rope.

19

The Compass and Laying a Course

A SAILOR'S WORLD expands immeasurably when he learns to use a compass. With it and a *chart*—a marine road map—he can sail for ports far beyond his horizon, confident in his ability to hold a course by day or night that will take him to his destination. Until he learns to use a compass, a sailor remains harbor-bound, on the fringes of exploration and adventure.

Yet the marine compass is basically a simple device—a magnetic needle mounted in a round card, floating on a liquid that permits the needle to rotate freely and point toward the earth's Magnetic North Pole. This is the value of the compass to the sailor: day and night, in fog, snow, rain, or fair weather, the magnetic needle never rests from pointing toward a fixed reference point, the magnetic north. By positioning the needle in a fixture that shows outside the compass card the fore-and-aft line of the boat, it is possible to see at any time how the boat is heading in relation to magnetic north. This is the beginning of piloting. For it gives a way to keep your

LARRY KEAN

This sailboat's compass is placed where helmsman can readily see his magnetic heading to steer desired course

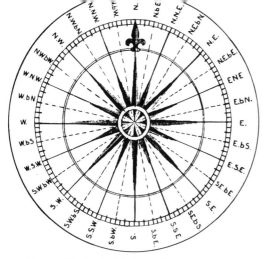

Above: *Typical old-time Mariner's compass card, showing thirty-two named sailing points with quarter points in between*

Right: *The modern Navy compass card shows eight principal points but has 360 steering marks—one for each degree of circle*

Above: *Modern small-boat compass card has steering mark every 5°, numerals every 15°, and shows eight principal points*

boat sailing hour after hour on exactly the same heading in relation to magnetic north; in short, to sail a magnetic course.

Reading the compass

The Compass Card. Before the coming of steam power, which permitted a ship to steer exactly the course she wished to hold rather than an approximate course dependent on the wind's direction, compass cards were marked in large gradations. The usual Mariner's compass card showed 32 points—of 11¼° each—plus 96 quarter points, giving a total of 128 marks to steer by around the full circle. By contrast, today's so-called Navy compass card, which has gradually displaced the Mariner's, has 360 steering marks, one for each degree in the circle, from the 0° North point clockwise around to 360°.

There are still available combination cards —showing 360 individual degree marks on the outer rim, with numbers every 10°, and points and quarter points on an inner rim. The purpose is to give the degree equivalents for the various old-style marks, but it makes a cluttered-looking card. Today, a sailor has little need to know the equivalents for all 32 points, though it is occasionally useful to know these eight—

Compass Point	In Degrees
north (N)	0° or 360°
northeast (NE)	045°
east (E)	090°
southeast (SE)	135°

Compass Point	In Degrees
south (S)	180°
southwest (SW)	225°
west (W)	270°
northwest (NW)	315°

For a small sailboat, I prefer a compass card with fewer gradations and large numbers, so they can be seen easily. And since all piloting is from charts, where courses are determined in degrees, I favor a simple card of the degree type, rather than one with points. One that has a steering mark every 5° and numbers every 15° works fine.

Variation. Since the compass card points constantly toward magnetic north, when the boat rotates, the fore-and-aft line (called the *lubber line*) moves around the outer rim of the card and indicates the heading in relation to magnetic north—the magnetic course the boat is steering. All that remains is to translate this into a *true* course—one that can be plotted on a chart drawn with reference to the Geographical, or True, North Pole, rather than magnetic north. The chart gives the first piece of information needed to make this translation—the local difference, in degrees, between the bearing of magnetic north and of true north from the particular locality. This is the *variation,* and is shown in degrees east or west of true north.

It comes as a surprise to many beginning students of piloting that the Magnetic North Pole and the True North Pole are not identical, and that, except at a very few places on earth, the magnetic compass does not point true north. In reality, the Magnetic North

Pole lies north of Hudson Bay, about 900 miles from the True North Pole, through which all the geographic meridians pass. The size and direction of the angle between the two poles, or variation, varies according to your location. The variation is named *west* when the north-seeking end of the compass is drawn to the left, or west of true north. When it is pulled to the right, east of true north, the variation is *east*.

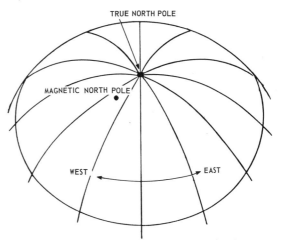

Magnetic North Pole lies about 900 miles from True North Pole, hence magnetic compasses do not point to true north

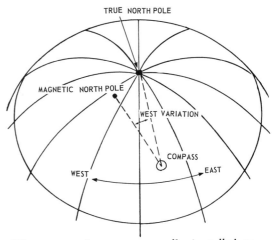

When magnetic compass needle is pulled to left of true north, variation is west

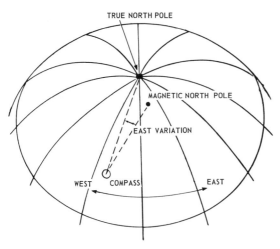

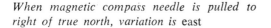

When magnetic compass needle is pulled to right of true north, variation is east

The angle of variation changes slowly from year to year in most places, because the Magnetic North Pole migrates in a small orbit. But the variation and its direction for any locality is shown on the local chart for the year the chart was printed. Also shown is the rate and direction of annual change, usually so small it can be ignored in practical piloting.

The variation is shown geographically on the chart by two *compass roses* (cards), one inside the other, with the *outer rose* representing *true* directions, and the *inner, magnetic*. Each rose is graduated into 360°, with 0° as the north point, and the degrees increasing clockwise around to 360°, which is north again. The magnetic rose is angled in the direction of the variation for the locality, and for the correct number of degrees

as of the year of the chart. On the compass roses shown, for example—from a chart of Eastern Long Island Sound—the variation is 13°15″ *west,* since the compass needle in that area is pulled 13°15″ to the left of true north as it points toward the Magnetic North Pole.

This means that if you were to sail a magnetic course of 013°, it would be the same as sailing a true course of 0°. Or, conversely, if you were to sail a course of 0° true, it would be the same as sailing a course of 013° magnetic. Digest and absorb this rule: *When the variation is west, add it to the true course to get the magnetic course.* This single fact is all you must comprehend to unlock the whole business of translating true courses into magnetic courses, or vice versa. But you must really have a clear picture of what the statement means—a visual remembrance of the relative positions of the numbers on the true compass rose and the magnetic compass rose when there is westerly variation.

Obviously, when the compass card is pulled to the east of true north, the magnetic course will now be smaller than the true course. Such a situation maintains on San Francisco Bay, where the compass roses on the chart display a local easterly variation of 17°15′, with an annual rate of decrease of 1′ as of 1965.

Deviation. Any correction that must be made to a true course to find a compass course, is called an "error." Variation is one kind of compass error, caused by the very earth itself, in that the magnetic north does not coincide with true north. Another kind of compass error is *deviation,* which results when magnetic substances on the boat—an engine, for example—attract the compass needle and prevent it swinging freely toward magnetic north. Deviation changes according to the boat's heading, which shifts the posi-

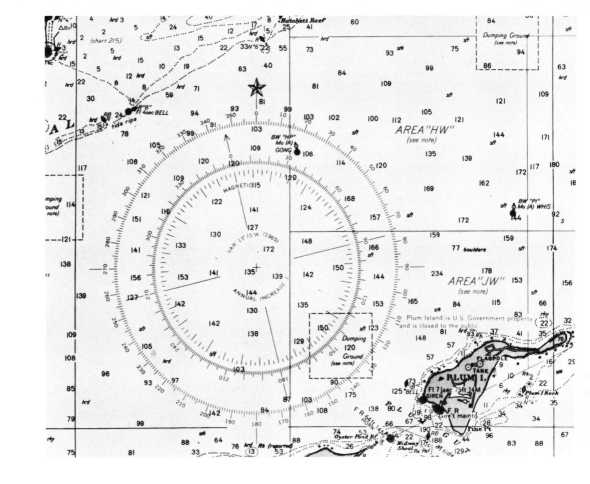

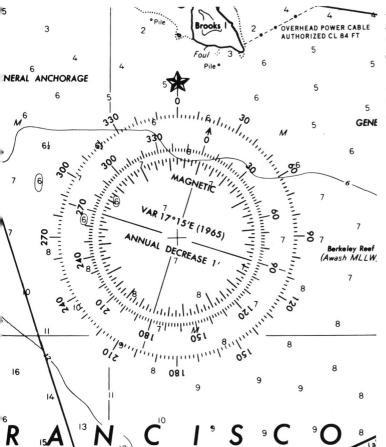

Above: *Inner circle of this compass rose shows local variation is 13° 15' west in 1965, with annual increase of 1'*

Left: *This compass rose shows locality's variation to be 17° 15' east in 1965, with annual decrease of 1'*

tion of the local magnetic mass in relation to the Magnetic Pole.

This error can be eliminated from a compass by positioning small magnets near it to compensate for the local attraction, but the operation calls for professional skill. An easier solution is to make a Deviation Table, showing the error to allow for on different headings. *No magnetic compass can be trusted for piloting unless it has been compensated, or until you know what errors it has, if any, for various headings when in its operating position.*

HOW TO MAKE A DEVIATION TABLE This is simply a record of the boat's compass error on headings at 15° intervals, from 0° clockwise to 360°. Each entry is determined by steering the boat on a known *magnetic* course, as found from the chart, and comparing the compass reading on that heading with the charted course; any difference is *deviation*. Its direction is west if the magnetic course lies to the right of the compass heading.

For example, suppose on Chart #223 for L. I. Sound and East River, you find that the magnetic course between Execution Rocks Light and the square chimney on David's Island, is 290°. You head your boat directly toward the chimney, with Execution dead astern, and read your compass, which shows 294°—or 4° to the right of the charted magnetic course, 290°. Thus, for the magnetic heading of 290°, the deviation is 4° West. Each time you wanted to make good a magnetic course of 290° you would steer 294° by your compass to allow for the 4° west deviation.

In making a Deviation Table, you need actually select only 12 courses, about 15° apart, since each course can be sailed in two directions, to give magnetic courses for a total of 24 headings. Make up the table in card form and keep it handy to the compass. For courses lying between those tabulated,

the deviation can be easily estimated by inspection. A typical Deviation Table might be set up like this—

DEVIATION TABLE
...Sloop LEONORA L
...June, 19—

Magnetic Course	Compass Course	Deviation
0°	006°	6° W
015°	020°	5° W
030°	033°	3° W
045°	046°	1° W
060°	059°	1° E
075°	072°	3° E
090°	085°	5° E
105°	099°	6° E
120°	113°	7° E
135°	128°	7° E
150°	144°	6° E
165°	159°	6° E
180°	175°	5° E

Magnetic Course	Compass Course	Deviation
180°	175°	5° E
195°	191°	4° E
210°	207°	3° E
225°	224°	1° E
240°	239°	1° E
255°	255°	0°
270°	272°	2° W
285°	289°	4° W
300°	306°	6° W
315°	322°	7° W
330°	337°	7° W
345°	352°	7° W
360°	006°	6° W

Deviation can be caused by any article of iron or steel close enough to the compass to exert a magnetic attraction—a pocket knife, portable radio (antenna and speaker magnets), photo light meter (magnet), rigging, anchor, or engine. We were startled one night, while sailing a small boat by compass, to observe that it was obviously reading false. Stars were out and we could determine roughly what our magnetic heading should have been from the position of Polaris, the North Star, which shows fairly accurately where true north lies. Our compass, however, in addition to the expected 12° west variation of the locality, showed an extra 15° of westerly deviation. A hasty inspection uncovered a six-pack of canned soft drink that someone had stowed within a foot of the compass—the steel in the cans had attracted the compass needle away from magnetic north. Had we been sailing in a fog, without benefit of the visual check afforded by the stars, we might not have been so lucky in discovering the error before it did us mischief.

Trust your compass. After this story, it may seem a contradiction to say, in general, *trust your compass;* but it isn't. Once your compass has been checked out for its operating position on the boat, and a careful Deviation Table has been made, do not hesitate to put your faith in what the compass tells you, unless you have *positive* indication that it is reading incorrectly. Especially in fog, resist the temptation to let a hunch about the proper direction to your destination override information given by the compass.

Guard your compass at all times like the sensitive instrument it is, and it will serve you well. Keep all magnetic materials at least six feet away from it. If this is not possible, be sure to check frequently by observation, the headings the compass reports against the magnetic courses you are sailing.

Laying a Compass Course

To *lay* (determine) the course-to-steer between any two points, the first need is to have a chart that shows both points, and the second is to be sure it is feasible to sail a single course between them, without crossing land or foul water. Whereas maps show details of land areas, charts provide information about navigable waters—depths, and type of bottom; location, type, and numbers of buoys and lighted aids; prominent landmarks, like steeples and tanks; harbors; channels, wrecks; reefs; and the variation for the area covered by the chart. For piloting, use the largest-scale chart available.

Some charts cover large areas—these are *small scale charts,* used chiefly for offshore navigation. The chart of the "North Atlantic Ocean, Northern Part," for example, is on a scale of 1:5,870,000, which means every inch on the chart represents more than 92 miles on the earth's surface. For piloting in coastal and inland waters, however, *large scale charts* are used, covering small areas. The largest scale harbor charts, for example, are drawn on a scale of 1:1,200, with one inch on the chart equaling 100 feet on the water. The larger the chart's scale, the more detailed the information it provides for piloting.

When you have established by examination that it is possible to sail a single course between the two desired points without danger, you must deal, in order, with five factors to determine the compass course. For convenience, list them one under the other, like this—

1. True course   ———
2. Variation   ———
3. Magnetic course   ———
4. Deviation   ———
5. Compass course   ———

1. The True course is determined by drawing a straight line on the chart connecting the two points, and finding its direction from the outside, or true, compass rose printed on the chart. This can be done with the edge of a pair of *parallel rulers.* These are two rulers hinged together so that a track

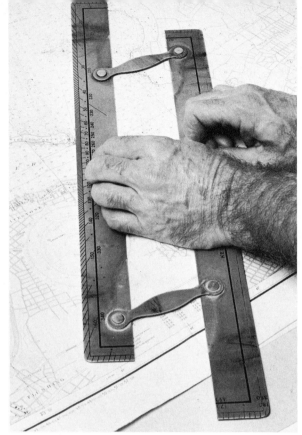

With parallel rulers you can "walk" desired course across chart to nearest compass rose to determine true direction

can be "walked" across a chart by alternately extending one ruler, pressing it down, and bringing the other ruler up to it, then repeating the process. The rulers may be plastic, wood, or metal. To keep them from slipping, a good trick is to glue chamois on the underside of each ruler.

Lay one edge of the parallel rulers along the line connecting the two points which, for convenience, we'll call Point A and Point B. Now walk the line across the chart to the nearest true compass rose, so that the edge of the ruler bisects the small cross at the center of the rose. Where the ruler crosses the outside compass rose *in the direction of Point B,* read off the number of degrees. This is the *true course* from Point A to Point B. Write it down as a three-digit number on the T-V-M-D-C form.

2. Variation. Next, on the magnetic com-

pass rose inside the true rose, note the variation for the area, and fill it in on the form as Item 2.

3. Magnetic course. If the variation is west, *add* it to the true course, or if it is east *subtract* it. In either case, record the result as Item 3 on the form, the Magnetic course. (As a check, this figure should agree with the number of degrees on the *inner* compass rose where the parallel rulers cross it in the direction of Point B.)

4. Deviation. From the Deviation Table for your compass, apply to the magnetic course of Step 3 any required deviation for that heading. If the error is west, *add* it to the magnetic course; if east, subtract it.

5. Compass course, or course-to-steer. This is sometimes abbreviated as psc, meaning "per ship's compass."

The process of converting a true course to a compass course is simple, fast, and accurate when the five elements are arranged as shown. If you wish to keep in front of you a reminder that as you work from true toward compass course, you *add* westerly errors, jot down the letters T, W, A (True—West—Add), alongside the five elements, with an arrow pointing down, like this—

1. True course	——	T
2. Variation	——	
3. Magnetic course	——	W
4. Deviation	——	
5. Compass course	——	A

Two practical problems. 1. You are leaving the eastern exit of Cape Cod Canal, bound across Cape Cod Bay for Boston. To avoid getting lost in the fog that often closes in on the Bay, you decide to sail from buoy to buoy along the Massachusetts coast, rather than risk a long, direct course across the Bay. From Quick Red Flasher #2 at the Canal exit, your first objective is Flashing White Gong Buoy #6A off Manomet Point.

You find the true course is 359°, the local variation is 16° West, and on the resulting magnetic course heading, your compass has a deviation of 3° East. What is the compass course?

Answer: 012°.

2. Sailing out of Mamaroneck Harbor, on Long Island Sound, you want to lay a course from Flashing White Bell Buoy #R 42 to the Flashing White Breakwater light at Glen Cove, on Hempstead Harbor. You determine the true course to be 153°, and the chart shows the variation (to the nearest degree) is 12° west. For the resulting magnetic course, your boat's Deviation Table shows a compass error of 5° west. What compass course should you steer?

Answer: 170°.

Summary

1. Magnetic compasses point toward the Magnetic North Pole. By placing the compass in a fixture that shows the boat's fore-and-aft line outside the compass card, it is possible to see the boat's magnetic heading (magnetic course) at all times.

2. The Mariner's compass card was marked in points and quarter points. Modern, Navy-type cards show degrees, from 0° at the north point clockwise around to 360°, which is north again.

3. For small sailboats, a simple card of the Navy type is preferable, with a steering mark every 5° and numbers every 15°.

4. The angle between the bearing of the Magnetic North Pole and the True North Pole from any location, is called variation, and is expressed in degrees east or west of true north.

5. When the compass needle is pulled to the left, or west of true north, the variation is named *west;* when pulled to the right, east of true north, it is *east* variation.

6. Variation changes slightly from year to year, at a rate shown on the local chart. But the changes are usually so small they can be ignored in piloting.

7. The variation is shown on the local chart by a magnetic compass rose inside a true rose that points to true north, 0°.

8. When the variation is west, it is always *added* to the true course to determine the magnetic course; when it is east, it is subtracted.

9. Deviation is compass error caused by magnetic substances on the boat, close enough to the compass to exert a magnetic attraction. Deviation changes as the heading changes.

10. Deviation can be eliminated by a professional compass adjuster. An alternate solution is to make a Deviation Table, showing the error to allow for on various headings.

11. No magnetic compass can be trusted unless it has been compensated for deviation, or until its errors are known for various headings when in its normal operating location.

12. A Deviation Table is made by steering the boat on a series of known magnetic courses, about 15° apart, from 0° clockwise to 360°, and comparing the compass reading on each heading with the known magnetic course.

13. Deviation is named *west* when the magnetic course is to the *left* of the compass heading, and *east* when the magnetic course lies to the right of the compass heading.

14. Deviation can be caused by pocket knives, portable radios, photo light meters, rigging, anchors, engine, or canned drinks. Magnetic influences should be kept at least six feet away from the compass.

15. When impossible to keep magnetic substances far from the compass, compass readings should be checked frequently against known headings.

16. After a compass has been compensated for its operating position, or a Deviation Table has been made, *it should be trusted,* unless there is positive reason to doubt it.

17. Maps give information about land areas; charts supply details on navigable waters. Small scale charts cover large areas, and are used for offshore navigation. Large scale charts, covering small areas, are used for piloting on coastal and inland waters.

18. To lay a compass course between two points on a chart, first check to be sure a single course will not lead across land or into foul water. Arrange these five factors in a column, then determine each in succession:

    a. True course   ————
    b. Variation   ————
    c. Magnetic course   ————
    d. Deviation   ————
    e. Compass course   ————

19. The true course is found by joining the two points by a straight line and finding its direction from the nearest true compass rose with parallel rulers, or a similar device.

20. Variation is taken from the nearest magnetic compass rose.

21. Westerly variation is *added* to the true course; easterly variation is subtracted from it, to find the magnetic course. This should agree with the course shown by the parallel rulers where they cross the inner (magnetic) compass rose, in the direction of the destination.

22. Deviation for the magnetic course is taken from the boat's Deviation Table, and *added* if it is west, or subtracted, if east. The result is the compass course, or course-to-steer.

23. Checklist of nautical terms:

VERB

lay (a course)—To determine the course-to-steer from one point on a chart to another.

GENERAL

chart—A map of navigable waters, for piloting and navigation.

compass (magnetic)—A device with magnetized needles mounted in a floating compass card that points toward the Magnetic North Pole.

compass card—A round card, graduated either in degrees, from 0° at north clockwise to 360°, or in points of the compass, or both.

compass rose—A compass card printed on a chart, showing degrees.

deviation—Compass error caused by magnetic substances on the boat offsetting the normal pull of the Magnetic North Pole.

easterly deviation—Compass error when magnetic attraction on the boat causes the magnetic course to lie to the right (east) of the compass course.

easterly variation—Compass error resulting from geography, when the bearing of magnetic north is to the right, or east, of true north.

large scale chart—One showing a small area in detail, for piloting.

lubber line—The fore-and-aft line of a boat shown outside a compass card to establish the boat's heading.

magnetic north—The Magnetic North Pole, located north of Hudson Bay, about 900 miles south of the Geographic, or True, North Pole.

Mariner's compass—One with a card marked in points and quarter points; a total of 128 steering marks for the full circle.

Navy compass—One with a card marked in degrees, from 0° at north clockwise to 360°, with a total of 360 steering marks.

parallel rulers—Twin rulers, hinged parallel, for laying off courses.

small scale chart—One showing a large area, for offshore navigation.

true north—The Geographic North Pole, through which all meridians pass.

variation—Compass error resulting from geography, where there is a difference in bearing between magnetic north and true north.

westerly deviation—Compass error when magnetic attraction on the boat causes the magnetic course to lie to the left (west) of the compass course.

westerly variation—Compass error resulting from geography, when the bearing of magnetic north is to the left, or west, of true north.

20

Elementary Piloting

Piloting Aids

PILOTING IS PROBLEM SOLVING for high stakes—the safety of your boat and crew. The basic problem is to get from A to B by the shortest route, without going aground or getting wrecked in the process. To help you solve this problem correctly *each time,* a number of different aids are available. But for a small-sailboat skipper who is interested in venturing far beyond the confines of his local waters, the most important are: plotting equipment; a reliable compass, with a carefully worked out Deviation Table; a *pelorus,* or dumb compass, for taking bearings; an up-to-date chart of the area; a *lead line* for measuring depths; and Tide and Current Tables if you're sailing on tidal waters.

You may not need or use any of these aids when you go out for an afternoon sail. On the other hand, if they are always kept on board, you are prepared to deal with unexpected piloting problems that might arise even during a short sail, like the sudden onset of fog, for example.

Plotting equipment. Since piloting deals both with where you are and where you want to go, you need equipment for plotting on the chart your present position and the course to your next destination. First, a sharp-pointed No. 2 pencil for lightly marking positions and times on the chart. Second, an eraser for cleaning off old plotting marks. Third, a pair of *dividers*—pointed, hinged metal arms—for measuring distances. And fourth, a good pair of parallel rulers for laying out courses; or, possibly, a *protractor* —a single-armed measuring device, equipped at one end with a rotating compass card. Use whichever seems most convenient; I prefer parallel rulers.

A reliable compass. Several excellent, relatively inexpensive small-boat Navy-type compasses are sold, with their cards showing steering marks every 5° and numbers every 15° or 30°. Work out a Deviation Table for every 15° change of magnetic heading, and keep it handy.

A pelorus, or dumb compass. The pelorus is a nonmagnetized, rotating Navy-type compass card mounted on a stand or in a box, with a pair of sighting vanes over it. The card can be rotated until it agrees with the boat's heading, and clamped in position.

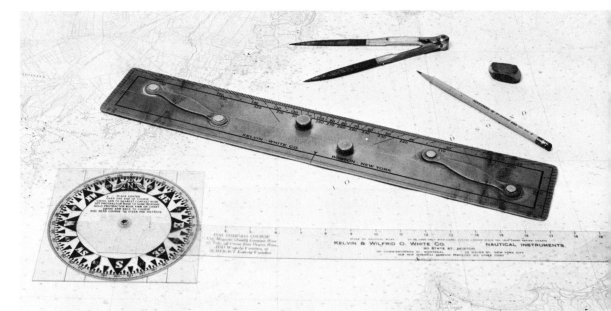

PLOTTING EQUIPMENT—*Protractor, parallel rulers, dividers, pencil, eraser*   LARRY KEAN

Then, when an object is sighted through the two vanes, its compass bearing (psc) can be read directly on the pelorus card. Or the pelorus compass card can be set with its 0° mark pointed toward the bow, on a fore-and-aft line parallel with the boat's centerline, so as to read the *relative* bearing of an object lined up in the sighting vanes. This is a bearing measured from ahead in relation to the boat's fore-and-aft line, expressed in degrees from 0° clockwise to 360°. Both direct and relative bearings are constantly used in piloting.

An up-to-date chart. Next to the practice of continuing to use worn-out lines, using old charts runs a close second as an example of misplaced thrift. It, too, can lead to disaster.

LARRY KEAN

192

Yet it's as easy to tell when a chart should be retired as it is to know when a piece of line is no longer safe. Charts usually carry both the date of their printing and a notation of the date to which they have been corrected. Later corrections can be made from changes reported in the weekly *Notice to Mariners,* issued free to mariners by the Defense Mapping Agency Hydrographic/Topographic Center, Washington, D.C. 20315.

Although it is perhaps too much to expect the casual weekend skipper to keep his charts corrected right up to the latest *Notice to Mariners,* any prudent skipper will at least protect himself by supplying his boat with a fresh copy of the local chart at the start of each season. From season to season depths change, buoys are shifted or discontinued, shoals develop, wrecks and other new hazards to navigation appear. Possibly if charts were not so beautifully made, of such fine, durable paper, skippers would discard them more readily. In the interest of encouraging such discard, I hereby reveal my secret and excellent use for old charts—as wrapping paper for mailing parcels. People who receive packages wrapped this way are delighted, and it's an infinitely safer use for old charts than piloting with them. The investment in a new chart is small, the protection sizable.

A lead line. As the name tells, it's a chunk of *lead* plus a *line.* The lead which is heavy enough to carry the line to the bottom for measuring the depth of water, usually has a small hollow in its lower end. By *arming* the lead—filling this hollow with grease or soap —you can bring up a sample of the bottom: clay, mud, pebbles, sand, whatever. This sample, plus the *sounding* (depth), helps locate your position on the chart, which shows both depths and type of bottom wherever soundings are recorded on it.

The line attached to the upper end of the lead can be marked for every *fathom* (six feet), or in this traditional fashion from sailing ship days—

2 fathoms . . . Two strips of leather.
3 fathoms . . . Three strips of leather.
5 fathoms . . . Piece of white cotton rag.
7 fathoms . . . Piece of red flannel rag.
10 fathoms . . . Piece of leather with a hole in it.

This may seem, at first glance, to be the pickings of a magpie's nest. But a second look will tell you it's a highly practical way of marking a measuring line—each mark is unmistakable from the others both by sight and by feel, for soundings taken at night. This is much better than one modern lead line made up with printed plastic tabs, which cannot be read at night without using a flashlight. In rough weather it's hard enough to take night soundings on a small boat's

You arm the lead with grease or soap to pick up sample of bottom for comparison with chart

LARRY KEAN

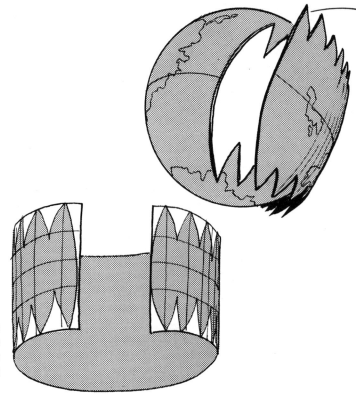

Mercator projection treats earth like a cylinder, with meridians stretched out parallel to each other instead of converging at poles, as they really do

tossing deck without having to fumble with a flashlight to read each cast.

The only modification you might want to make on the traditional lead line markings is to add a single strip of leather for one fathom, or to mark the critical depth for your boat—twice the water it takes to float her. If you make the line of ¼-inch dacron, it will be easy to handle, will not shrink when wet, and will last for years. A 4-lb. lead is a good size to use.

Tide and Current Tables. Many saltwater small-boat sailors will snort at the idea of carrying Tide and Current Tables on board; many, in fact, never even bother to buy them. But this book is written for the skipper who wants to burnish his skill in this great sport, not just get by. Admittedly, a stowage place to keep the Tables dry may be a problem, though every small sailboat should have a well-fitted drawer under the foredeck for such gear. Also, it *is* possible to keep them at home and jot down the tides and current for the day each time you go sailing—if you remember. But if you carry them on board,

you'll always have them at hand when you need them.

Charts for navigation. Charts, like maps, represent a portion of the earth's round surface as a flat sheet. This involves some distortion, of course. To control and minimize the distortion, various methods of projection are used for different purposes. Coastal, inland, and harbor charts, issued by the National Ocean Survey of the Department of Commerce, are drawn on a system known as *Mercator projection.* Charts of the Great Lakes are also issued by the National Ocean Survey, but these are drawn on *polyconic* projection. Each system has its advantages.

Mercator projection treats the earth as though it were a vertical cylinder running north and south, with all the meridians of longitude drawn as straight lines parallel to each other, instead of converging at the True North and South Poles, as they do on a geographic globe. Visualize the earth as an orange, with the segments between the meridians unpeeled and stretched out in width and length to fit them to a cylinder wrapped around it at the equator. At the equator, where the cylinder is tangent to the globe, there is relatively little distortion. But as the distance from the equator increases, everything must be stretched in width and length to open out the meridians and, at the same time, maintain proportions. As a result, areas in the higher latitudes are drawn on a larger scale than those near the equator. This explains the great difference between the relative size of Greenland on the usual geography book flat world map, and its real size, shown on a globe.

But the distortion of Mercator projection serves a purpose—a straight line connecting any two places on the chart represents the true course between them, crossing each of the meridians at the same angle. This is much more convenient for plotting and piloting than using a curved line, which would be needed for a constant true course on another type of projection.

A straight line between two points on a Mercator chart is not, however, the shortest distance between them on the earth's surface, except east and west along the equator, and north and south along the meridians. This is because the shortest distance between two points on a globe is the path traced on the globe's surface by a plane that goes through both points and the globe's center—a *great circle*. The equator is a great circle, since it is the track on the earth's surface of a plane that cuts the globe into two equal halves, north and south. And each of the earth's meridians of longitude is a great circle, slicing through both poles and the center of the earth. Along these great circles on a Mercator chart, a straight line and the shortest distance between two points are identical; everywhere else, the shortest distance is represented by a curve.

For coastal, inland, and harbor navigation, however, the difference between the *rhumb line*—or straight line true course on a Mercator chart—and the shortest distance is so small it can be disregarded in piloting. At a latitude of 40°, for example, the rhumb line between two places 350 miles apart would be about a mile longer than the great circle course.

But when measuring distance on a Mercator chart, the distortion in the projection cannot be disregarded—*distance must be measured only along the meridians,* not along the parallels of latitude. Since each meridian is a great circle, its track around the globe equals the earth's circumference, or 21,600 nautical miles. This figure was established for navigational purposes by considering the circumference as a circle of 360°, with each degree consisting of 60 minutes (60′) of arc —a total of 21,600′. By making the nautical mile equivalent to one minute (1′) of arc, navigators secured a ready means for converting arc to distance, or vice versa, anywhere on the earth's surface. One minute (1′) of arc equals one nautical mile on a great circle; 1° of arc equals 60 nautical miles. Compared with the English statute mile of 5280 feet, the international nautical mile is 6076.1 feet, or approximately one-seventh longer.

In piloting, distances are usually measured in nautical miles, and speeds are expressed in knots, with "one knot"—as noted earlier —meaning a speed of "one nautical mile per hour." This fact is often ignored by the uninformed when they talk of "x knots per hour," which is like saying "x nautical miles per hour per hour."

Many large-scale Mercator charts with little change in latitude from bottom to top, carry separate measurement scales for nautical miles and yardage based on the statute land mile. These can be used safely to measure distance anywhere on the chart. In general, however, the standard practice of navigators is to measure distance on a Mercator chart on the vertical latitude

Right: *On a Mercator chart, always pick distance from meridian latitude scale opposite course*

Below: *Polyconic projection treats earth as a series of cones, each one tangent for a different parallel of latitude*

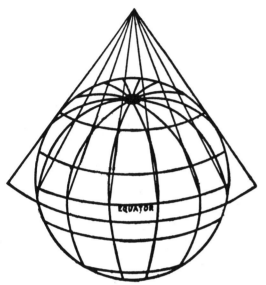

minute scales of the meridians that form the east and west borders of the chart and show the change in latitude between the bottom of the chart and the top. It is usual to refer to a section of the scale at the average latitude of the course being measured. To use a section near the bottom of the chart for measuring a distance near the top would not allow for the change in scale as the latitude increases.

Wherefore, use your dividers to pick off the distance on the minute scale opposite the course, remembering that each minute of arc on the scale represents one nautical mile.

Polyconic projection treats the earth as a series of cones, with each one tangent for a different parallel of latitude, and its vertex centered over the closest geographic pole. The principal advantage of this system is that it enables large areas to be shown with relatively little distortion. Another advantage is

that a straight line between two points on a polyconic chart is very nearly a great circle course, the shortest distance. A further convenience is provided on the Great Lakes charts in showing the true course line and distance *in statute miles* between principal ports.

To measure distance: Each Great Lakes navigation chart is provided with a printed scale of feet, yards, meters, and statute miles for measuring distances. Courses are plotted as on a Mercator chart, from the nearest true compass rose, which also shows the local magnetic variation. But since the distances are given in statute miles on the printed courses, all distance measurements should be taken from the appropriate printed scale, *not* from the latitude scale shown on the meridians at the east and west edges of the chart.

Piloting Procedure

Label the course. When you have determined the course between two points, and the distance to be run, *at once* label the course line with this information. Above the line put a three-digit number for the course, and below, the distance. Place after the course a letter—T, M, or C—to show whether it is a true, magnetic, or compass course. To eliminate confusion, always record on your charts the same type of course. You may wish to use true courses, so that you can then compare your heading with the true bearings of various aids to navigation, read directly from the chart. Or you may prefer to standardize by recording the magnetic course, especially if your compass has little error on the various headings. My own preference is for marking the compass course

(psc), to insure that whoever looks at the chart will know all the errors have been allowed for, and that the course recorded on the course line is the one to be steered.

Record the time at each aid. As you pass each aid to navigation on a course, mark alongside the aid the time of passing, using a four-digit number for the hour and minutes, based on a continuous 24-hour day, instead of the usual A.M. and P.M. For example, 9:15 A.M. would be recorded as 0915; and 3:45 P.M. would be 1545; and 7:30 P.M. would be 1930.

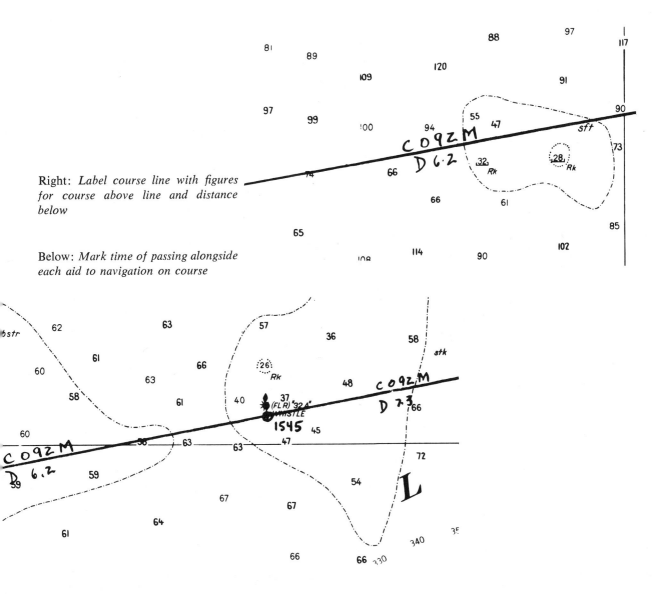

Right: *Label course line with figures for course above line and distance below*

Below: *Mark time of passing alongside each aid to navigation on course*

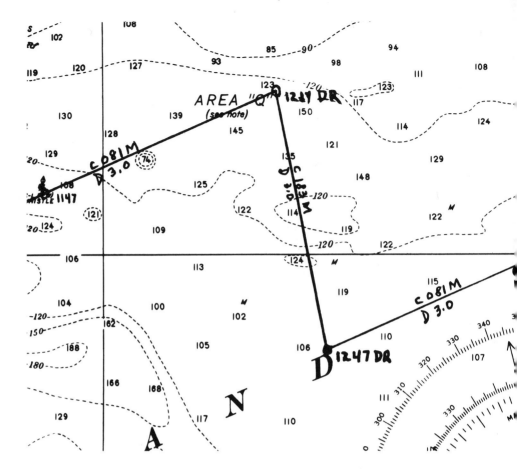

Keep a dead reckoning track. As you sail toward your destination, if it is out of sight, or if intermediate marks are not visible for checking your progress, it is good piloting practice to keep a running record on your chart of each course you steer, for how long, and an estimate of the distance sailed. This is called the *dead reckoning track,* a name handed down from sailing ship days, when it was often necessary to estimate the ship's position by a process of deduction, abbreviated "ded. reckoning," and in time corrupted by sailorly usage to the present spelling. Make an entry on the D.R. track at least once every hour of the course and distance sailed. If you change course or tack before the hour has passed, record each new course and the estimated distance sailed.

Each hour's sailing or each new course should be indicated on the D.R. track with a small circle, and recorded alongside, a four-digit figure for the time, with the letters D.R. New courses sailed can be translated

from compass headings back to true course for plotting on the chart by setting up the five factors and working from the bottom toward the top, remembering to *add* easterly errors and *subtract* westerly, as you convert from compass toward true course:

1. True course   _____
2. Variation   _____
3. Magnetic course   _____
4. Deviation   _____
5. Compass course   _____

From your dead reckoning track, you should always have a reasonably accurate estimate of your position. If a shift of wind forces you away from the original course plotted toward your destination, sail the closest course you can, plot it on your chart and extend the track line to see at what point you should tack over to lay the mark. Allow at least 100° for the difference in heading on the new tack; few small sailboats can tack through less than 100° and keep footing well.

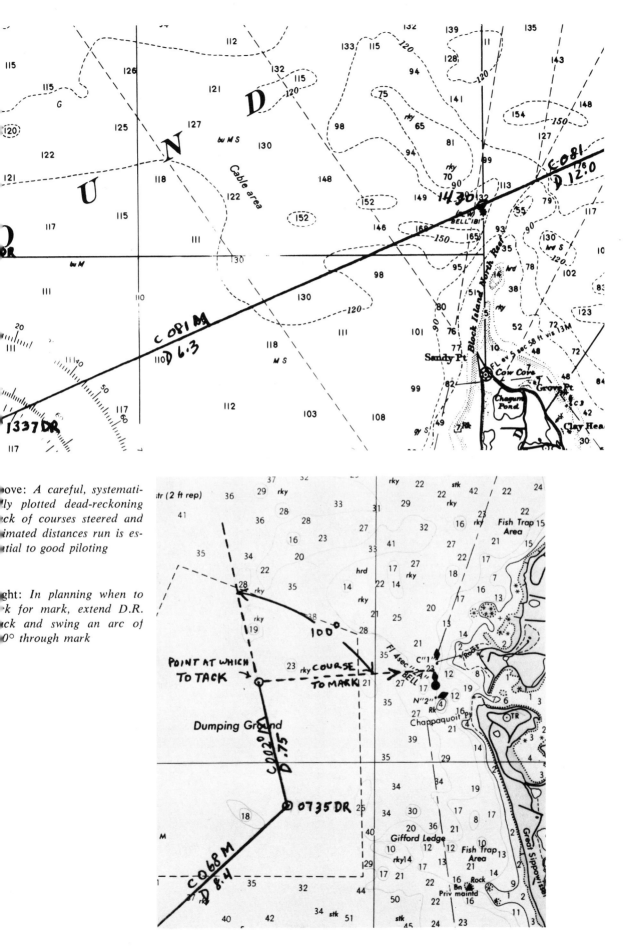

above: A careful, systematically plotted dead-reckoning track of courses steered and estimated distances run is essential to good piloting

right: In planning when to tack for mark, extend D.R. track and swing an arc of ...0° through mark

By plotting lines of position of two charted objects at least 30° apart, accurate fix is obtained where lines cross

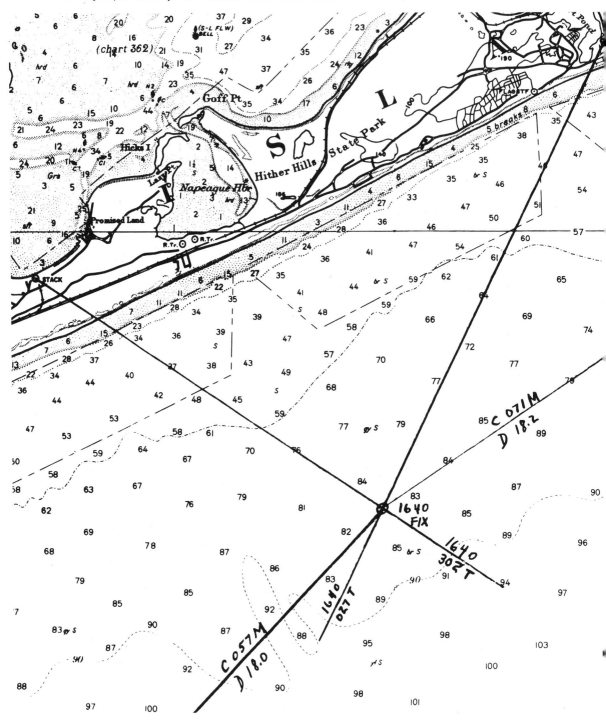

Plotting lines of position and bearings

The line of position. When no buoys or other navigational aids are at hand on the water to tell us our location, it is still possible to get an accurate position, or *fix,* by taking separate bearings on two or more charted landmarks separated by an angle of at least 30°, and plotting them on the chart. These are called *cross bearings*. Each separate bearing is, in fact, a *line of position,* with the boat located somewhere along it. Where two lines of position meet and cross becomes a fix—the boat's actual location.

Taking a bearing. To take a bearing the compass must be equipped with a device for sighting over it, or a pelorus can be used. Place the pelorus so that its 0°—180° axis is parallel with the boat's fore-and-aft line. Rotate the pelorus card until it agrees with the boat's heading, and clamp it in position. Train the sighting vanes on the landmark and note its bearing on the pelorus compass card. Since this is the bearing by ship's compass, it must be converted to a true bearing by the same process as converting a compass course to a true course. Then, to plot it on the chart, the true bearing must be *reversed,* i.e., 180° must be added to permit plotting it from the landmark toward the boat as a line of position. *Sample problem:* In an area where the variation is 12° west, and on a magnetic heading that has a deviation of 3° east, with our compass course 040°, we take the bearing of a charted water tank on shore and find it bears 137° psc. What is our line of position *from the water tank?* Solution: To convert the 137° compass bearing to a

To take bearing with pelorus, line up object in sighting vanes, note its bearing on pelorus card

Line of position is plotted as true bearing from charted object on which bearing is taken

true bearing, we set up the five factors as in working a compass problem, and fill in the numbers from the bottom up:

Known factors			Solution
1. True bearing		Tb	128°
2. Variation	12°W	V	12°W
3. Magnetic bearing		Mb	140°
4. Deviation	3°E	D	3°E
5. Compass bearing	137°	Cb	137°

True bearing of water tank from boat .... 128°

+ 180°

True bearing of boat from water tank .... 308°

(Line of position to be plotted on chart from tank).

Although the line of position is plotted from the water tank toward the boat, it is labeled with its *true* bearing from the boat, and the time at which the bearing was taken. Place the time above the line, and the true bearing below. Incidentally, should the addition of 180° to the true bearing of the object from the boat exceed 360°, subtract 360° from the total to find the bearing to plot from the object.

In crossing two or more lines of position to obtain a fix, it is apparent that the bearings should be taken within a short time of each other—as nearly simultaneous as possible—

or the earlier bearing will no longer be accurate, if the boat is moving with any speed. It should also be noted that cross bearings are most accurate when they are at right angles (90°) to each other. As the angle between two objects becomes less than 90°, the reliability of the fix drops off. Bearings with less than 30° between them should not be used.

Taking a relative bearing. In rough weather a small sailboat jumps around so much it is almost impossible to coincide the moment when an object is lined up in the pelorus sighting vanes with a time when the boat is exactly on course. To avoid taking an incorrect bearing, it is better to clamp the 0° mark of the pelorus card toward the bow on a fore-and-aft line and take a relative bearing.

To take a relative bearing, at the moment when the object is lined up in the sighting vanes, the observer shouts *"Mark!"* and the helmsman notes the compass heading at that instant. Whether or not this happens to be the boat's desired course is immaterial, so long as the observer has secured an accurate pelorus bearing of the object. To convert the relative bearing to a compass bearing, you need only add the two together, subtracting 360° if the total is greater than that. *Sample problem:* While a boat is trying to hold a course of 035° in a lumpy sea, the skipper sets the pelorus 0° mark toward the bow on a fore-and-aft line and sights on a distant lighthouse. When he finally shouts "Mark!" the helmsman's heading is 042°, and the skipper notes that the relative bearing of the lighthouse is 250°. What is its compass bearing? *Solution:* Ignore the fact that the boat's intended course is 035°, and deal only with the 042°—her actual heading when the relative bearing was taken.

Relative bearing of lighthouse	250°
Boat's heading at time of relative bearing	042°
Total	292°
Compass bearing of lighthouse	292°

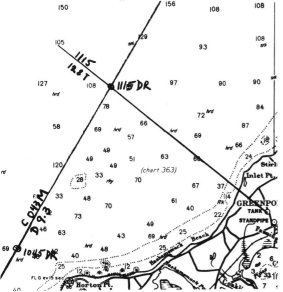

Line of position is labeled with true bearing of object from boat, and time of bearing

To determine compass bearing of charted object, add relative bearing to compass heading at time of bearing, subtracting 360 if total exceeds that amount

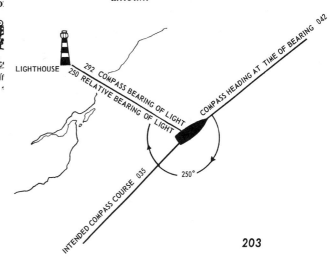

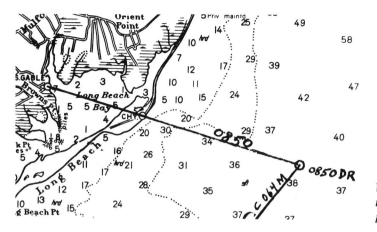

When two charted objects are sighted in line, you have an instant line of position without taking bearing

This compass bearing would be converted as usual to a true bearing, and reversed for plotting.

Finding a line of position from a range. Frequently it is possible to get a line of position from a *range*—two fixed charted objects in line with each other, as a lighthouse and a distant steeple. By drawing a line through the two objects on the chart and extending it seaward, you have an immediate line of position without taking a bearing. As you cross the range, mark the line with a four-digit number for the time. If you can take a bearing at the same time on another charted object lying at more than 30° to the range, you will have a fix.

Making a running fix. Sometimes it is possible to get a single bearing on a fixed charted object, but no other bearing to cross it with at once for a fix, and a substantial interval of time may pass before a suitable cross bearing can be taken on another object. In this situation, it may still be feasible to get what is called a *running fix,* by advancing the earlier line of position along the dead reckoning track and crossing it with the second bearing.

To advance a line of position on the D.R. track that represents the true course sailed since the time of the first bearing, measure

off with dividers and put a pencil dot on the track for the estimated distance sailed. Through this point draw a line parallel to the first line of position. Where this advanced line crosses the line of position of the second bearing, is the running fix. Be sure to label the line that has been advanced with both the original time and the time of the advance. Label the running fix with the later time.

There is no set rule on how far a line of position can be advanced and still give a reasonably accurate position; it will vary with the circumstances and the dead reckoning skill of the skipper. From the variables that can affect the advance, however, it should be evident that the interval must be kept as short as possible, preferably not more than half an hour.

Correcting the D.R. track. Since the D.R. track is a continuous record of a series of estimates of progress made along the route from your departure point to your ultimate destination, whenever you can substitute a fix for a D.R. position, a new D.R. track should be started from that point. The fix may be the result of simultaneous cross bearings, a good running fix, or be established by passing close to a known fixed object like a lighthouse or beacon. By correcting the plotting of the D.R. track in this way,

Advance a line of position by measuring on D.R. track estimated time run since bearing was taken, then drawing new line of position parallel with first and marking both times on it

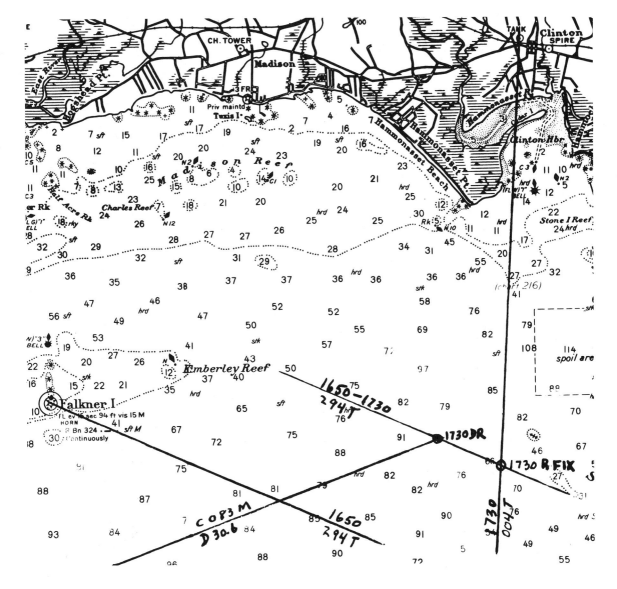

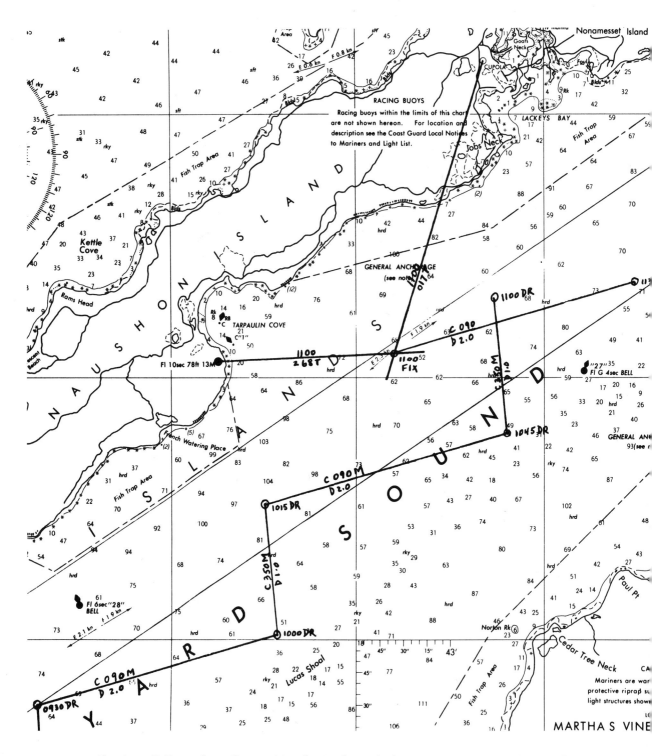

Continue D.R. track until a positive fix is obtained, then start new D.R. track from fix

steering or current errors that might become cumulative are minimized. Equally important, you get a graphic picture of any error pattern that may be developing, and can revise the course to the destination to provide for it.

Piloting in currents and tides

Allowing for current. Current is the horizontal movement of water. It may be caused by the tides flowing in and out along the coast, by wind blowing steadily for a long time over an open stretch of water, or by the constant downstream flow of a river. Regardless of its origin, its effect is the same—to carry a boat along with it, in the direction of the current and at its speed. This means a boat sailing in a known current must allow for the current's *set* (direction) and *drift* (speed in knots) in determining the course-to-steer to reach her destination.

Information about the set and drift of tidal currents is given in *Tidal Current Tables* published by the National Ocean Survey, U.S. Department of Commerce, for U.S. coastal waters. These show the daily times, directions, and velocities for the ebb and flood currents at a vast number of local stations, so that it is usually possible to find a nearby reference point. In addition, sets of Tidal Current Charts are published for Boston Harbor, Narragansett Bay to Nantucket Sound, Narragansett Bay, Block Island Sound and Long Island Sound, New York Harbor, Delaware Bay and River, Upper Chesapeake Bay, Charleston Harbor, S.C., San Francisco Bay, and Puget Sound.

For wind currents, information about the open ocean is provided in quarterly Pilot Charts issued by the Defense Mapping Agency, but none are issued for coastal waters, where they are seldom a problem. River-current information can be obtained from the nearest office of the War Department's Corps of Engineers.

The simplest way to work a current problem is directly on the chart. *Sample problem:* To sail from Point A to Point B your true course to make good is 137°, you are making 4 knots, and are sailing across a constant current setting 212° true, with a drift of 1.5 knots. What true course should you hold to make Point B? *Solution:* Through Point A, at the start of the basic course line connecting Points A and B, draw a line in the direction 212° true, to represent the set of the current. On this line measure 1.5 nautical miles, to Point C, to represent the current's drift. From Point C, with your dividers swing an arc of 4 miles in length, representing your sailing speed, to intersect the basic true course line at Point D. The true direction of the line C—D, 116° true, is the course you must steer *from Point A* to make good the desired course of 137° true to Point B. And the length of the line A—D represents your speed *over the bottom,* which will be 4.2 knots. This is greater than your speed through the water—your

This current diagram shows that when current is abaft the beam, speed over bottom is greater than speed through water

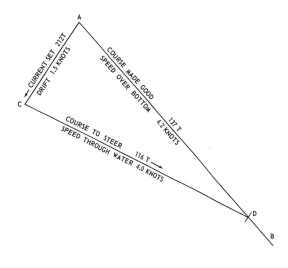

sailing speed—because the current is coming from abaft your beam and is giving the boat some boost, even though its direction forces you to steer 21° to the left of the basic true course to compensate for it.

Knowing how to allow for current in determining the course to steer to a destination is only half the problem. Because sailboats are notoriously at the mercy of the winds and cannot always hold the course they would like to sail, the other half of the current problem is to know how to figure what course you are making good, when sailing in a current of known set and drift. *Sample problem:* Let's assume that the closest you can sail to a desired course of 0°, true north, is a true heading of 047°, and that you estimate your speed through the water as 5 knots. You have checked the local Current Tables and find you are sailing in a current that is setting 155° true, with a drift of 2.0 knots. What true course are you making good? *Solution:* On a meridian, mark Point A for your present estimated position.

From Point A draw a line in the direction of 047° true, to represent your true heading, and lay off on it, to Point B, a distance of 5 nautical miles for your speed through the water. Through Point B draw a line in the direction 155° true, for the current's set, and lay off on it, to Point C, a distance of 2 nautical miles for the drift. Draw line A—C. Its true heading, 070°T., is the course you are making good. And its length, 4.7 miles, is the speed you are making good over the bottom.

This is an instance when both the set and drift of the current are unfavorable—the current is forward of your beam, so that its drift reduces your speed from 5 knots through the water to 4.7 knots over the bottom. And the current's set pushes your course-made-good 23° to the right of your course steered, at a time when the course you prefer lies to the left of the course you are steering.

Don't get the mistaken idea from these two current problems that current is always unfavorable; frequently it is not only favorable but actually helps you sail a shorter course. This is especially true for a sailboat going to windward when she is able to hold a course that brings the current on her lee bow. This has the effect of pushing the boat toward the wind, enabling her to sail a closer, hence shorter, course than she is actually holding. This process is known as *lee bowing the current,* and is a useful tactic to apply whenever possible in sailing to windward on tidal waters.

Often, too, a current's drift will be in the direction you want to go. Then your speed over the bottom becomes the sum of your speed through the water plus the current's drifts, which may be sizable. If, for exam-

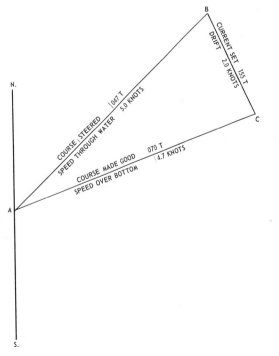

With current forward of the beam, speed over bottom is less than speed through water

A chain of soundings at regular intervals, tracked on tracing paper, can help to locate approximate position on chart

ple, your desired course were 090° true, and the current's set happened to be the same, and your speed through the water averaged 4.5 knots, while the current's drift was 1.5 knots, your speed made good over the bottom would be 6.0 knots.

The effect of current, whether favorable or unfavorable, is apt to become critical when you are piloting your boat in a fog and trying to dead reckon course and time to your destination. For this reason, and to avoid the possibility of developing a large cumulative error that might cause trouble, experienced skippers sailing tidal waters during poor visibility, pilot their way by a series of courses, from buoy to buoy along the route, even though this may mean sailing a longer total distance than a direct course to their goal.

Checking position by soundings. In waters where it is possible to take soundings with relative ease and accuracy, a fairly positive check on your D.R. position may be obtained by taking a series of soundings at regular intervals while sailing a constant compass course, at a constant speed. This can be particularly useful in fog, where you might have no other means for checking your position.

Let's assume that while you are sailing in an area where the depth ranges from 20 to 40 feet, fog rolls in before you have been

able to fix your position, and you want to get an approximate check as quickly as possible. You are able to hold a fairly constant course of 075° true, and *log* (record) a steady 5 knots, or one nautical mile every 12 minutes, .5 mile every 6 minutes. On a piece of tracing paper or thin tissue, draw a straight line long enough to represent the boat's D.R. track for three miles by ½-mile intervals, using the latitude scale opposite your D.R. position to measure the mileage. Now, arm the lead and start taking a series of no fewer than six soundings—one every 6 minutes—of both the depth and type of bottom. Note these data on the tracing paper track at each successive ½-mile interval, starting at a point that represents your D.R. position.

When all six casts have been completed and recorded, place the track on the chart, with the starting point of the series superimposed on your D.R. position and the chain of soundings pointing 075° true, to agree with the course sailed. Compare the record on the tracing paper with the depths and type of bottom recorded on the chart for the same 3-mile course. If they do not agree fairly closely, move the tracing paper around in the same general area, with the chain of soundings always pointing 075° true, until you find a 3-mile section on the chart where your soundings agree substantially with the charted depths and bottom. This will give your approximate position.

In tidal waters, before recording the depths on the tracing paper, they should be corrected for the height of the tide, unless they happen to be taken near Low Water. If this correction is not made, agreement between a chain of actual soundings and charted soundings is likely to be misleading in waters where there is more than a foot or so difference between High and Low Water, since the depths recorded on charts are for *Mean* (average) *Low Water.*

Figuring the height of tide. Listed in the Tide Tables are hundreds of reference and secondary stations by which it is possible to find the daily times of High Water and Low Water at practically any coastal location, together with the day's range of tide. Twice a month the spring tides are higher than Mean High Water and lower than Mean Low Water. At these times extra caution should be used in navigating shoal waters, since the actual Low Water will be below the charted Mean Low Water by an amount shown in the Tide Tables.

"Height of tide," incidentally, should not be confused with "depth of water," which is the distance *downward* from the surface to the bottom. Height of tide is the distance from the theoretical level of the charted depth upward or downward to the actual surface.

To figure the height of tide for any locaiton, at any time, first determine from the Tide Tables the time and the height of the tide preceding and the tide following the desired time. From these, mark down three figures: (1) the duration of rise or fall between the two tides; (2) the range of tide between them; and (3) the time difference between the closest tide and the desired time. With these data, refer to Table 3 in the Tide Tables for the correction to apply to the height of water at the closest time. The result is the height of tide at the desired time.

By arranging all the data in an orderly form, any height-of-tide problem can be worked quickly and accurately, as this example shows.

A. *Times* and heights of tides*
   Location: Glen Cove. N.Y.
   Reference station: Willets Point, N.Y.
   Time Difference: HW — 11 min.   LW — 06 min.
   Height Difference: HW + .2 ft.   LW 0.0 ft.

Time and Date
1515,* July 1, 19—

	Willets Point				Glen Cove	
HW	0350	7.2 ft.		HW	0339	7.4 ft.
LW	1012	0.3 ft.		LW	1006	0.3 ft.
HW	1623	7.3 ft.		HW	1612	7.5 ft.
LW	2240	0.6 ft.		LW	2234	0.6 ft.

   * Eastern Daylight Saving Time

B. *Height of tide at desired time*

Duration of rise (1006 to 1612)	6 h. 06 min.
Time from nearest tide (HW)	0 h. 57 min.
Range of tide (0.3 ft. to 7.5 ft.)	7.2 ft.
Height of nearest tide (HW)	7.5 ft.
Correction from Table 3 (tide rising)	— 0.5 ft.
Height of tide at 1515	7.0 ft.

In localities where daylight saving time is used during part of the year, care must be taken to apply the necessary local correction to the times listed in the Tide Tables (as well as in Tidal Current Tables), since local standard time is used in these publications.

Summary

1. For small-boat piloting, the most useful aids are plotting equipment, compass, pelorus, chart, lead line, and, if in tidal waters, Tide and Current tables.

2. A compass Deviation Table for every 15° change of heading is needed unless the compass has been compensated.

3. The chart should be up to date, no older than the current season.

4. By arming the lead, it is possible to get a sample of the bottom for comparison with soundings recorded on the chart.

5. A standard lead line is marked at 2, 3, 5, 7, and 10 fathoms. These marked fathoms are called "marks"; the unmarked fathoms are "deeps."

6. Mercator charts are drawn on a projection that treats the earth as a north-south cylinder, tangent to the globe at the equator. On a Mercator chart, a straight line between any two places represents the true course between them.

7. Because a Mercator chart stretches out in length and width as the latitude increases, distance must always be measured on the latitude scale opposite the desired course.

8. The shortest distance between any two places on the globe is the track on the globe's surface of a plane going through both places and the center of the globe. But when plotted on a Mercator chart, this track becomes a curve, unless it happens to be the equator or a meridian (these are great circles represented as straight lines running east-west and north-south, respectively).

9. A rhumb line course on a Mercator chart crosses all meridians at the same angle.

The difference in length between a rhumb line and a great circle course is so small for the distances involved in coastal and inland piloting, it can be disregarded.

10. On the meridians of a Mercator chart, and on the equator, each minute (1′) of arc represents one nautical mile. There are 21,600 nautical miles in a great circle's 360°. Each nautical mile is 6076.1 feet, or roughly one-seventh longer than the statute mile of 5280 feet.

11. In piloting, distances are usually measured in nautical miles, and speeds are expressed in knots (nautical miles per hour).

12. Charts for United States coastal, inland, and harbor piloting are drawn on Mercator projection; those for the Great Lakes, on polyconic.

13. A polyconic chart is drawn as though a cone were placed over the earth at the given parallel of latitude, with the vertex above the nearest pole. This makes a straight line between any two points closely approximate a great circle course, the shortest distance.

14. Course lines should be labeled above the line with three figures for the course, and a letter for its name—true, magnetic, or compass—and below the line, with the distance.

15. Time notations on a chart should be recorded as a four-digit figure for the hour and minute of a 24-hour day.

16. The dead reckoning track should show an entry each hour for time and distance sailed, and for each change of course.

17. A boat's position can be established accurately by a fix at the crossing point of two lines of position from simultaneous bearings taken on known, charted objects.

18. Direct compass bearings can be read from a pelorus when its card is set to agree with the boat's heading, on a fore-and-aft line.

19. Relative bearings can be taken with a pelorus by setting its 0° mark toward the bow, with the card's 0°—180° axis on a fore-and-aft line.

20. A relative bearing is converted to a compass bearing by adding to it the observed

compass heading at the time of the bearing and subtracting 360°, if the sum exceeds that amount.

21. Compass bearings are converted to true bearings in the same way compass courses are converted to true courses.

22. To plot the true bearing of a charted object, the bearing is reversed by adding to it 180° (and subtracting 360° if the sum exceeds that amount); this reciprocal bearing line is drawn from the object toward the boat.

23. Relative, rather than direct bearings, should be taken by pelorus whenever rough seas make it hard to hold the boat steady on a course.

24. Ranges frequently provide useful lines of position for piloting.

25. A running fix may be obtained by crossing two lines of position taken at different times, if the earlier one is advanced for the time and distance sailed. In general, however, a line of position should not be advanced more than half an hour because of possible errors.

26. At each fix, or reliable running fix, a new D.R. track is started.

27. To allow for current in determining the course to steer between two points, A and B:
   a. From Point A extend the basic true course line toward Point B.
   b. From Point A draw a line in the direction of the current's set, for a distance equal to its drift, to Point C.
   c. From Point C swing an arc equal in length to the boat's speed through the water, so as to intersect the basic course line, A—B, at Point D.
   d. The true direction of line C—D is the true course to steer to make good the basic true course from Point A to Point B.
   e. The distance A—D represents the boat's speed over the bottom, on the course C—D.

28. To allow for current in determining the course made good:
   a. On a meridian, mark Point A to represent the present D.R. position.

   b. From Point A draw a line to Point B on your true heading, for a distance equal to your speed through the water.
   c. At Point B draw a line in the direction of the current's set, for a distance equal to its drift, to Point C.
   d. The true direction of the line A—C is the course made good, and its length is the speed made good over the bottom.

29. When a sailboat can "lee bow" the current while going to windward, the course made good will be closer to the wind than the course steered, hence shorter.

30. In poor visibility on tidal waters, it is preferred piloting practice to lay courses from buoy to buoy.

31. A chain of soundings, taken at regular intervals while sailing a constant course and speed, when plotted on tracing paper can furnish an approximate position during poor visibility by matching up the sounded depths and types of bottom with those shown on the chart for the area. The soundings should be corrected for height of tide, if in tidal waters.

32. "Height of tide"— which is a distance up or down to the surface from the charted level of Mean Low Water—should not be confused with "depth of water," the distance from the surface to the bottom.

33. To figure the height of tide at any time:
   a. From the Tide Tables find the correction factors, if any, to be applied at the desired location for the time and range of tide at the nearest reference station.
   b. List the day's tides and heights for the reference station, apply correction factors, and list the same data for the location.
   c. Determine the duration of the tide that includes the desired time, and whether rising or falling.
   d. Figure the time interval from the nearest tide.
   e. Figure the range of tide involved.
   f. Determine the height of the nearest tide.
   g. From Table 3 in the Tide Tables, select the correction to apply to the height of the nearest tide.

h. Apply the correction and obtain the height of tide at the desired time.

34. Checklist of nautical terms:

SAILING TERMS

lee bowing the current—To sail with the current on the lee bow, which enables the boat to make good a course closer to the wind than she is actually steering.

GENERAL

arming the lead—To fill the hollow end of a sounding lead with grease or similar substance to pick up a sample of the bottom.

chain of soundings—A series of soundings of the depth and type of bottom, taken at regular intervals on a course of known direction and constant speed, and recorded in a straight line on tracing paper for comparison with soundings recorded on the chart of the area, to determine a boat's approximate position.

course made good—The course actually completed, as opposed to the course steered.

course-to-steer—The course given to the helmsman, which may or may not coincide with the course to make good, depending on factors like current and leeway.

cross bearings—Simultaneous, or nearly simultaneous, bearings taken on fixed, charted objects and plotted on the chart as lines of position to fix the position of the boat where they cross.

dead reckoning—Estimating a boat's position by deduction from the courses and distances sailed.

deep—An unmarked fathom on a lead line.

depth of water—The distance from the surface to the bottom.

dividers—Pointed metal arms, hinged, for measuring distances.

drift—The velocity of a current in knots.

dumb compass—The pelorus, so called because its compass card is not magnetized and does not seek the Magnetic North Pole.

fathom—A measurement unit of six feet.

fix—An accurate determination of position, secured by cross bearings on two or more fixed, charted objects, or by sailing close to a known, fixed navigational aid.

great circle—The track traced on the globe's surface by a plane that goes through its center; the shortest course and distance between any two points on the globe.

height of tide—The distance up or down from the charted level of Mean Low Water, to the surface.

knot—A speed of one nautical mile per hour.

lead—A weight used for sounding depths, usually hollow at one end to permit arming, so as to pick up a sample of the bottom.

line of position—A straight or curved line, on which the boat is somewhere located.

mark—A marked fathom on a lead line; also "Mark!"—a command to note the exact course or time at a given instant.

Mean High Water—The average height of the high tides in an area.

Mean Low Water—The average height of the low tides in an area.

Mercator projection—A system of chart projection that treats the earth as a cylinder running north-south, tangent at the equator, and with all parallels of latitude and meridians shown as parallel straight lines.

meridian—A great circle of the earth that passes through the poles.

nautical mile—A unit of measurement 6076.1 feet long, equal to one minute (1′) of arc on a great circle.

over the bottom—Course or distance measured by actual performance on the chart, as opposed to through the water.

parallel of latitude—A circle traced on the earth's surface by a plane parallel to the equator.

pelorus—A device equipped with a rotating, nonmagnetized compass card and two sighting vanes, for taking bearings; a dumb compass.

polyconic projection—A system of chart projection that treats the earth as a series of cones, each tangent at a different parallel of latitude, with its vertex centered over the nearest pole.

protractor—A plotting device consisting of a single measuring arm, fitted with a rotating Navy-type compass card.

range—Two fixed, charted objects in line with each other.

reciprocal bearing—The bearing of an object, plus 180°; its reverse bearing.

relative bearing—The bearing of an object measured from ahead in relation to the boat's centerline, from 0° clockwise to 360°.

rhumb line—A line on the earth's surface that makes the same angle with all the meridians. On a Mercator chart, the straight line, true course between any two points.

running fix—A fix obtained by crossing two lines of position taken at different times, with the earlier one advanced along the course and for the distance sailed since it was observed.

set—The direction toward which a current flows.

sounding—The depth of water measured by use of a lead line, or other device.

statute mile—A land unit of measurement 5280 feet long.

through the water—The course steered or the speed sailed, as opposed to the course made good or distance covered on the chart.

21

Buying a Boat

You Do Not have to own a boat to learn how to sail, but when you buy your first boat, you'll find both your interest and progress in the art of sailing take a decided jump. Whether the change is due to pride of ownership, or to the feeling of responsibility that descends like a mantle on the shoulders of the "Captain," or because we tend to take more seriously any activity that involves an investment of capital—the cause doesn't matter; it's a change for the better, and one to be encouraged.

Among the many questions that perplex the prospective sailboat owner, perhaps three are most universal: (1) What *kind* of boat should I get? (2) How *large* should it be? (3) Of what *material* should it be made?

1. What kind of boat?

Many beginners have an idea that a small, cat-rigged sailing dinghy should be ideal for learning to sail. They feel that because it's small, they'll be able to handle it easily, and that the limited sail area will not present enough of a target for the wind to cause them much trouble. Both reasons seem plausible, yet both are mistaken.

In actual fact, a sailing dinghy is a very tricky vessel to handle; one much more liable to dunk a beginner than a larger, more stable boat. Its very lack of size makes the placement of ballast critical, with less margin for

The liveliness of a dinghy makes it great sport to sail but tricky for beginner

error, since the sailor may weigh as much or more than the hull. And the sail area, though small, is large enough to hold plenty of wind pressure for a capsize in any breeze strong enough to move the boat. Dinghies are great sport to sail, but they are not the best boat for a beginner. As an indication of exactly how sophisticated they are, even America's Cup skippers race in them to practice tactics and sharpen their racing techniques.

At the other extreme from beginners who want to start in the smallest possible boat, there are those who feel they would learn most rapidly in a large, keel type, cruising sailboat. This, they figure, would be stable enough to forgive any mistakes they might make in handling and wouldn't frighten them out of their skin by capsizing. Again, the argument seems reasonable, but is mistaken. Whereas the dinghy is sensitive to the point of crankiness, and requires a good helmsman to handle it properly, the large cruising boat is relatively insensitive and does not respond quickly enough in ordinary breezes to develop a beginner's helmsmanship. It's like trying to learn riding from a plow horse. And the large sail area of a cruising sailboat presents real problems for a beginner, in sail handling and control.

Somewhere between the two extremes lies the happy medium, what ancient philosophers called the "golden mean"—a boat type that is wholesome and seaworthy, in a size small enough to be responsive, yet large enough to be reasonably stable.

Keel vs. Centerboard. A boat must be suitable for the waters she will sail. Though a centerboard boat can be sailed in deep or shoal waters, a keel boat is best suited to deep water. In shallow areas, like Long

A large cruising boat does not respond quickly enough in ordinary breezes to teach a beginner helmsmanship

Island's Great South Bay and New Jersey's Barnegat Bay, a keel boat's range is much more limited than a centerboarder's by the possibility of running aground. But where the water is deep, and the prevailing winds are fresh, a keel boat has a definite edge over the centerboarder, both in her greater inherent stability and in her ease of handling.

Convenience in launching and hauling by trailer is a factor favoring centerboard boats,

particularly in areas where good mooring space is at a premium. A centerboarder can always be beached or hauled out more easily than a keel boat, and stored on land.

The sloop rig. For beginning sailors the sloop rig has definite advantages over the single sail of a catboat. By dividing the sail area, handling is made easier, and sail can be reduced with better balance in heavy winds. The interplay of jib and mainsail in

This small centerboard sloop is typical of many standard one-design classes suitable for beginning sailor

SAILSTAR BOATS, INC.

sailing to windward is an important aid in developing good helmsmanship. And when sailing off the wind, the jib serves as a warning against an accidental jibe. Another advantage of the sloop is the shorter boom, which lessens the danger of broaching to when running before the wind or on a broad reach.

To sum up, an all-around boat that could be easily trailered back and forth to sail on deep or shallow water would be a centerboard sloop. There are many standard, one-design classes on the market. In deciding among them, you might consider whether or not one class has a local racing group, since you may want to extend your interest to competitive sailing as your skill develops.

2. How large should it be?

The answer—small enough to be responsive, yet large enough to be reasonably stable—deserves some expansion. The lower limit on size would seem to be somewhere around 14 feet overall, to insure a certain degree of comfort in a boat with enough sail area and basic ability to sail safely with at least two adults, in a range of breezes from light to moderate. The upper limit might be set at about 25 feet overall, which would, of course, raise somewhat the strength of the breezes that could be handled without shortening down.

Most prospective owners base their decision on size, at least in part, on how many people they normally expect to sail with them. In this aspect, however, it is well to avoid going overboard, literally. The novice owner-skipper should delay inviting guests who are not good sailors until he is thoroughly competent to sail his boat single-handed in the full range of breezes she is able to handle.

A secondary consideration on size is the relative cost and ease of maintaining and operating a 14-foot boat, as opposed to any larger boat up to 25 feet. Mooring, sails, hauling, storage, and boatyard costs sometimes tilt the decision in favor of the smaller of two choices.

From the standpoint of sailing ability, a larger boat should be able to develop more speed, which is the essential ingredient of maneuverability. There are, to be sure, centerboard craft available that are practically sailing surfboards, with maximum sail area and minimum hull. These go much faster than boats of the same size in conventional designs. And they are exciting to sail, since their speed is hooked up with a tendency to capsize in a flash from a mistake in handling or ballast distribution. But although it is easy to right these boats—because capsizing is a normal occurrence in sailing them—they have the same disadvantage as the dinghy, of being too tender for the proper teaching of beginning sailors. It's like using a racing car to learn automobile driving.

As size increases, a boat's behavior generally becomes less erratic and more controllable. She has larger sail area to keep her moving, even in a light breeze, and more weight to resist shifts of ballast or increase in wind pressure and keep her upright. Her action in a seaway is apt to be easier and less abrupt because her size and speed give her greater momentum to carry through the waves. These are all arguments for buying the largest boat possible, consistent with the other considerations of cost and maintenance.

3. Of what material should it be?

A great many small, wholesome, one-design centerboard and keel sloops are available, built of planked wood, plywood, or fiberglass. As a prospective buyer, you'll be swamped with claims and counterclaims for each material. One way to sift out facts from fancy is to talk with owners—the word of a satisfied owner is better evidence than a bushel of partisan propaganda.

Country-wide, the percentage of small sailboats made of fiberglass has been increasing steadily, and there are many fine sloops available in this material. But wooden boats, whether of plywood or conventional planking, are still widely popular, especially among home builders, and the world's three largest fleets of one-design sailboats (Snipe, Enterprise, Lightning) are built of wood, though fiberglass construction has also been approved for the Snipe and Lightning.

In evaluating the testimony of owners, to arrive at a decision, you may find useful this summary of the relative merits and disadvantages of each type of construction:

Wooden Boats

COST In general, per foot of boat, small wooden sailboats are less costly than those built of fiberglass. A planked wooden boat is apt to be more expensive than one built of marine plywood. But although the plywood is stronger, pound for pound, than planking, its use on hulls is limited to forms largely made up of flat planes. Such forms are excellent for planing hulls, but tend to pound more in a seaway than hulls built up of a series of curves. Molded plywood overcomes this limitation, but its cost is about equal to that of prime planked construction.

MAINTENANCE Wood must be painted or varnished regularly to preserve it. Unpainted wood is subject to dry rot, decay, and marine borers. Wood also dries out and may warp under hot sunshine, especially when painted black. Marine plywood, when not painted periodically, may delaminate. Fungicides, ventilation, and paint can protect wood from dry rot and decay, and preservatives and poisonous bottom paints are available to render it proof against shipworms. Regular maintenance, and avoidance of black paint in hot climates, can minimize drying out and warping. When given a natural, or *bright finish,* wood adds warmth and charm to a boat's interior. A wooden hull gives insulation against the outside water temperature, whether hot or cold.

REPAIRS Wood has a relatively high resistance to damage by impact, and dents and small holes can be repaired with comparative ease without using skilled labor. To replace planking or structural members, however, is an expensive procedure, requiring the services of professional boat carpenters.

DEPRECIATION A wooden boat depreciates physically in direct proportion to the lack of care in maintenance, which means this aspect is almost entirely under the owner's control. There are well-maintained wooden boats more than thirty years old, including famous yachts that are still winning races against modern competitors built of fiberglass and aluminum. Forty or even fifty years is not an uncommon age for a wooden boat that has been properly cared for.

From the standpoint of price depreciation, however, there is no question but that the resale value of wooden boats in general has dropped as the use of fiberglass has expanded. In one-design classes that allow either a wood or fiberglass hull, the resale price of the wooden boats is usually well below that of the fiberglass. A wooden boat with a good racing record might still command a premium over an average fiberglass boat, but this would be the exception rather than the rule.

This price situation creates an important opportunity for the prospective owner, making it possible for an informed buyer to get a lot more boat for his money in a used wooden sloop than in any other material. But the word "informed" should be stressed; the boat should first be surveyed by a competent marine surveyor, or should be bought through a reputable yacht broker who has personally checked it out.

Fiberglass Boats

COST A small, custom-built fiberglass sailboat is likely to cost substantially more than one custom-built of wood. But where the economies of mass-production fiberglass molding have been achieved, as in many of the small one-design classes, the difference in cost between fiberglass and wood is narrowed, though a mass-produced plywood boat of the same design will still probably be cheaper.

MAINTENANCE Ease of maintenance is perhaps the strongest reason for the popularity of fiberglass boats, which are not subject to dry rot or attack by shipworms. Color can be molded into the plastic, though it may fade under sunlight and require painting to maintain its appearance. Sunlight and weathering are also apt to produce surface cracks in fiberglass. These do not apparently weaken the material, but mar its finish and must be filled and painted to hide them. Even when a fiberglass boat does not develop these surface cracks, its finish is apt to become grimy and dull after a while—then the showroom finish must be recaptured by conventional sandpapering and painting.

Though unpainted fiberglass boats are impervious to attack by marine borers, they do accumulate weeds, slime, barnacles, and other marine growths as readily as a wooden boat. This means regular seasonal preparation of the bottom by sanding and painting with an antifouling bottom paint is a necessary part of the upkeep and maintenance of any fiberglass boat moored in waters where these growths exist.

Fiberglass comes into its own, however, in its freedom from the chore of caulking, which is a perennial problem with most planked wooden boats, and even with ordinary plywood centerboarders. *Molded* plywood boats, which are formed as a unit, without seams to supply potential leaking, do not have a caulking problem, either, but their basic costs are comparable with fiberglass. A properly constructed fiberglass boat is molded or laid up as an integral hull, with no seams, and has a theoretical freedom from leakage for the life of the boat.

Perhaps the greatest hidden factor in the maintenance of a fiberglass boat is the skill and care with which the resin and the fiberglass have been united in putting the hull together. If the manufacturer has worked out his engineering carefully, and used the proper proportions of fiberglass and resin, with precision control in his production so that the materials are well bonded, the boat should deliver all the potential advantages of the material. But where there has been skimping on the amount or kind of fiberglass, or where a disproportionate percentage of resin (which is cheaper than fiberglass) has been used, or where the production has been poorly controlled, the boat will not have its designed structural strength and may develop serious cracks or other troubles. The best way over this particular boat-buying shoal is to rely on the reputation of the manufacturer and the testimony of owners about their experience with the class of boat that interests you.

REPAIRS The impact resistance of fiberglass varies according to the weave of the glass fabric and the type of resin used. Heavy-woven glass roving cloth has great resistance to impact, but when it does fail tends to split along the laminations. Felted glass fabric, made of chopped glass fibers in mat form, has lower impact resistance, but holds together better when it fails, without delaminating, and breaks sharply. Because of this, the best construction alternates layers of glass roving and glass mat to secure the advantages of each material. In resins, epoxy is more expensive than polyester, but gives a stronger, harder finish.

Regardless of the original construction of a fiberglass boat, scratches, dents, and small holes are relatively easy to repair with amateur repair kits, using various weights and weaves of fiberglass fabric and either epoxy or polyester resin. In repairing major breaks and holes, not quite the same high degree of professional skill is required as in wooden boat carpentry, since there is no problem of equalizing built-in stresses. Fractures tend to be sharply defined and local, and full continuity of strength can be restored by simple relaminating and bonding methods. This means such repairs can be made by an owner who has good mechanical ability. If done by a boatyard, however, the cost of major repairs is comparable with repairs on a wooden boat.

DEPRECIATION Because of its relative imperviousness to weather, a fiberglass boat has a potential advantage over one of wood, in holding its value with time. But if she is not well maintained and her finish and trim are allowed to deteriorate, while the wooden boat is given care and attention in her upkeep, the advantage is lost. The used fiberglass boat may then sell below the price of her wooden competitor. For the prospective owner who is mechanically handy, this creates the opportunity to buy at a bargain price a fiberglass boat that has been neglected in maintenance but is structurally sound, and thereby get more mileage from his boat-buying dollar by restoring her himself. If there is the slightest reason, however, to suspect that the boat has any structural weakness, it is prudent to make the small investment in a survey by a qualified marine surveyor.

Aluminum Boats

COST Although as this book goes to press, mass production of aluminum sailboats is relatively limited, the value of aluminum as a boat-building material has been so well established for larger sailboats, a discussion of its qualities is in order. At the present time a small, stock sailboat built of aluminum is competitive in cost to a comparable boat of either fiberglass or wood. But when mass-produced aluminum boats become generally available, their prices may well be somewhat lower than those of fiberglass craft.

MAINTENANCE Modern aluminum alloys are corrosion-resistant and, if left unpainted, develop a protective film of oxide that limits corrosion to a shallow pitting of the surface which in no way weakens the metal. This pitting can be prevented by painting, but preparation of the surface is different than for wood or fiberglass. One need is to provide a mechanical hold for the paint on the metal's smooth surface. Another is to cover the aluminum with an insulating barrier to protect it from corrosion by electrolytic action of lead, copper, or other metallic elements in paint, especially in salt water regions. This involves using what is known as a complete *paint system,* in which all elements are compatible, from preparation of the surface and priming to the finish coats. A number of reputable paint manufacturers have developed such paint systems; the important thing is to use one system throughout and not mix elements from different systems.

In practice, a typical system first requires the aluminum to be washed with phosphoric acid. This gets it thoroughly clean of grease and dirt and etches the surface microscopically to receive a priming coat. Immediately on drying, before any oxide film can form, the surface is painted with a *wash coat primer* to seal the pores of the metal and lay the foundation for the insulating barrier.

The primer is followed by one to three coats of an insulating paint, depending on the metallic content and purpose of the finish coats, and the desired thickness of the barrier. Antifouling bottom paints, for example, in salt water, would be applied only after at least two coats of insulating paint had been laid down to furnish an electrolytic barrier of sufficient thickness. When the insulating coats are dry the finish coats are painted on.

A welded aluminum boat, or a hull that has been *stretch-pressed* as an integral piece, gives the same advantage as a fiberglass or molded plywood hull, of freedom from caulking and leakage. On salt water, however, care must be taken to protect the inside of an aluminum hull against accumulations of spray that might come into the boat. Prompt bailing and sponging dry is recommended. Even in a wooden boat an aluminum mast must be protected by an insulating paint barrier, or a waterproot *mast coat,* where it goes through the deck, to avoid corrosion from salt water held in the *mast wedges* (tapered pieces of wood that hold the mast firm at deck level).

Dry rot, however, is not a problem with aluminum, and shipworms have not yet developed an appetite or teeth for the metal. But in waters having marine growth, unpainted aluminum is as subject to fouling as wood or fiberglass, and must be protected with an antifouling paint, applied in a proper paint system, as noted above.

Finally, wherever hull fittings or openings are made and a dissimilar metal is used, like brass or bronze, an insulating barrier gasket or flange must be inserted between the aluminum and the other metal to prevent electrolysis in salt water. Neoprene, micarta, and similar nonabsorbing, nonconducting materials are used for bushings and gaskets to keep the two metals insulated from each other.

REPAIRS Scratches are easily repaired by cleaning to bare metal and repainting the same as the original application. Shallow dents may be removed with a pair of rubber mallets. Using one mallet as a back-up, hammer gradually from the perimeter of the dent in a circular direction toward the center. Refinish the surface as for its original application. Deep dents and gouges can be refinished by cleaning the aluminum surface and filling with an epoxy resin containing chopped up fiberglass. Larger damages and major repairs require a boatyard's professional attention, with costs comparable to the same repairs in wood. Aluminum has a high resistance to damage by impact, however, and is enormously strong when backed up with proper structural supporting members. In this respect, it probably surpasses wood and fiberglass.

DEPRECIATION Physically, a properly maintained aluminum boat shows little depreciation. However, in salt water regions careless maintenance has greater potential for damage than in a fiberglass boat because of the danger of electrolysis and corrosion. This would suggest the wisdom of having a careful survey when buying any used aluminum boat, and certainly when contemplating one that shows signs of indifferent care and upkeep. In buying a new boat of aluminum, the immunity of the metal to deterioration, when properly maintained, might justify a higher initial investment, since it will probably hold its turnover value better than a boat built of any other material.

Summary

1. For learning to sail, the ideal boat is one small enough to be responsive, yet large enough to be reasonably stable.
2. On deep waters where the prevailing winds

are fresh, a good first boat would be a keel sloop of 14 feet to 25 feet overall.

3. For shoal waters, or for deep waters where the boat must be trailered back and forth, a centerboard sloop of 14 feet to 25 feet overall would be a good choice for a beginner.

4. In general, it is advisable to buy the largest sloop, in the 14-foot to 25-foot range, consistent with cost and the problems of maintenance.

5. Small wooden sailboats are apt to cost less initially than comparable fiberglass models, but are more difficult to maintain. Molded plywood hulls are easier to maintain than planked or ordinary plywood hulls. Small repairs are easily made in wooden boats, but major damage needs professional ship carpentry.

6. Wooden boats depreciate physically in direct proportion to the lack of maintenance. In price, they generally depreciate more rapidly than fiberglass boats. When buying a used wooden boat, have it surveyed by a qualified marine surveyor.

7. Small fiberglass sailboats cost somewhat more than comparable wooden models, but have fewer maintenance problems. Small repairs are made easily with amateur repair kits. A skillful amateur can also make major repairs. An important hidden factor in fiberglass construction is the skill and care with which the fiberglass and resin have been united in the hull. This makes it advisable to buy a boat of known quality, and to get owner testimony on boats of any one-design class.

8. Physically, fiberglass boats depreciate only in trim and finish when not maintained. Other things being equal, fiberglass boats have higher relative resale prices than wooden boats. If there is any reason to suspect poor manufacturing or structural weakness, order a survey by a competent marine surveyor before buying a fiberglass boat.

9. Small, stock aluminum sailboats are roughly competitive in price with wooden and fiber-

glass boats. When mass-produced aluminum boats become generally available, their prices may well be lower than those of fiberglass. Aluminum offers the advantage of freedom from many maintenance problems, plus greater strength and resistance to impact than wood or fiberglass. Modern aluminum alloys are corrosion-resistant, but in salt water regions the metal must be painted with an insulating barrier to protect it from electrolytic corrosion. Hull openings and fittings must also be insulated, and the hull must be protected on the inside from accumulations of salt water by prompt bailing and sponging dry.

10. Small repairs in aluminum boats are easily made, but larger repairs call for professional boatyard services.

11. Properly maintained aluminum sailboats depreciate hardly at all, physically. In salt water regions, however, because of the potential hidden damage by electrolysis, in buying a used aluminum boat it is advisable to have a survey made by a qualified marine surveyor.

12. Checklist of nautical terms:

GENERAL

bright finish—A varnished, unpainted surface.

epoxy—A synthetic, liquid resin that can be cured into a hard, tough solid. Used as a binder for fiberglass in boatbuilding and repair, or with various pigments as a paint base, or by itself as an adhesive. Epoxy is stronger than polyester.

fiberglass—Fine, flexible fibers of glass, felted or woven into a variety of fabrics and weights for plastic boatbuilding and repair.

marine plywood—Thin sheets of wood veneer laminated together, usually with the grain of each sheet at right angles to the next, and specially processed to resist the absorption of moisture.

mast coat—A protective, waterproof jacket around the mast where it goes through the deck, to keep water from going below.

mast wedges—Tapered pieces of wood used to

hold the mast securely where it goes through the deck.

molded plywood—Thin sheets of wood veneer laminated together under pressure around a mold, to produce an integral structure of great strength.

paint system—A manufacturer's step-wise procedure for preparing and painting a metal surface, in which each element is chemically compatible with the others, from primer to finish coats.

polyester—A synthetic, liquid resin that can be cured into a hard, tough solid. Widely used as a binder for fiberglass in boatbuilding and repair because of its lower cost than epoxy.

roving—Glass fibers in unstranded rope form, usually woven into a loose, heavy fabric for boat construction.

stretch-pressed—A process for fabricating aluminum by stretching it evenly over a form that is simultaneously being pressed into it, so that there is uniform, minimum distortion over the entire surface.

wash coat primer—The priming coat painted on a dry metal surface immediately after it has been etched clean by a chemical wash.

22

Equipment

IN READING *Robinson Crusoe,* we feel a thrill of satisfaction as he salvages each new piece of equipment from the wreck—axes, guns, powder, shot, saws, rope, and nails—until he finally has enough to live comfortably while he waits for rescue. Yet the process of equipping a small sailboat requires stern disciplining of the very instinct that makes us so enjoy Crusoe's good fortune—there just isn't room in a 14-foot boat to stow all the gear for sailing around the world!

We can control our impulse to load down the boat with attractive but unnecessary gear by approaching the problem with three questions in mind: (1) What is necessary for survival? (2) What is needed for safe operation? (3) What is needed for comfort?

Equipment for survival

Life jackets. A small sailboat must carry one Coast Guard-approved personal flotation device for each person on board. Various types of PFD are approved for different sizes of craft—but every boat, even board boats, must have one for each person. And it must be readily accessible. Where a choice is permitted between a life jacket and a buoyant cushion, I prefer the jacket—it leaves both hands free, and in a real emergency, a buoyant cushion would be a tiring support for any length of time. One or two cushions should be on board, however, as emergency aids for a man overboard.

Bilge pump. A rugged, hand-operated pump of big capacity is a must. It should have a positive, nonclogging action, and an extension hose to reach into the deepest part of the boat, even on an angle of heel.

Bucket. As an auxiliary bailing device, a bucket has no equal, and every boat should carry one. Some of the new plastic buckets combine great capacity with light weight, an important factor when there is a lot of water to be bailed.

Anchor and rode. An anchor of suitable size and holding power, together with a strong rode of adequate scope—at least seven times the average depth of the local waters. The rode should be strong enough to double as a towing hawser, even with the boat partially submerged, as after a capsize.

Foghorn. The *Navigation Rules* require a sailboat to give fog signals on a horn. But the foghorn is also an excellent emergency distress signaler, for sounding a continuous noise.

Paddle or oar. A paddle is easier to stow, but the oar has an advantage in moving a boat by *sculling*—working the blade from side to side over the stern. The oar's longer blade also gives more leverage when used as an emergency rudder.

Heaving line. For a rescue line to a man overboard, or to another boat, a 35 to 50-foot length of ⅜-inch manila should always be at hand, made up in a coil for heaving. A heavy knot shaped like a ball and called a *monkey's fist* can be worked into one end if additional heft is wanted to carry the line, though any sailor worthy of the name should be able to heave 50 feet of line by itself.

Spare tiller. It should be complete, with all fittings, ready to slip over the rudder head for emergency use.

Distress signals. Several hand-held flare/smoke combination signals for day or night use, *plus* an asbestos glove for holding them when burning. Also a yard-square flag of International Orange, imprinted with a black square and black disc.

Flashlight. Preferably waterproof, and equipped with leakproof batteries—essential to have on board for the day sail that, because of a fickle breeze, develops into an unplanned night outing.

First-aid kit. An assortment of plastic first-aid strips, antiseptic ointment, burn lotion, adhesive tape, and a plastic resuscitube for artificial respiration—all packed in a waterproof, rustproof container.

Ditty bag. The shoreside parable, "For want of a nail the shoe was lost . . ." has its equivalent on the water in a dozen situations: a timely few stitches or a bit of sail tape on a rip might save a sail . . . some caulking cotton worked into a leaky seam

could prevent a sinking . . . a spare cotter pin might hold a turnbuckle in place and save the mast. A ditty bag with these contents equips you to deal with the principal emergencies—

Pliers
Screwdriver
6 feet of galvanized wire
2 four-inch C-clamps
2 ¼-inch galvanized shackles
6 brass cotter pins
Small can of penetrating oil
Small can of waterproof grease
Sailor's palm and assorted sail needles
Spool of waxed linen thread
Spool of nylon thread
Roll of sail-mending tape
Ball of Italian marline
1 yard 6-oz. canvas
4 feet of caulking cotton
Spool of electrician's tape

Stow cotter pins, sail needles, nylon thread, and caulking cotton in waterproof plastic containers. The ditty bag itself should be of stout canvas—the typical bank money bag is excellent. Sew a piece of marline at the neck for tying it shut.

Rigger's knife. This is listed separately from the ditty bag because the knife-and-marlinespike combination should be worn by the skipper, ready for instant service without having to dig through the ditty bag. A plastic whistle sewn on the knife's lanyard can serve as an additional emergency signaling device.

Equipment for Safe Operation

Boathook. Handy for picking up moorings, retrieving hats blown overboard, and for fending off at dock or float. Drill a hole an inch from the end and tie in a 6-inch loop of ¼-inch nylon for a handle.

Docking lines. Two lines of ½-inch or ⅝-inch manila, each slightly longer than the boat, and with a 2-foot spliced eye at one end. If you have room, carry four such lines.

Fenders. Three small but tough fenders should be carried, equipped with lanyards and fitted with holes at both ends so they can be hung either vertically or horizontally. Cylindrical rubber and plastic fenders are available for small-boat use; their higher first cost may be justified by their longer life than canvas fenders.

Sail stops. Four 6-foot long sail stops of 1-inch nylon web or canvas should be carried for quick, neat furling of mainsail and jib.

Chart. Every small sailboat should have on board an up-to-date chart of the local waters, corrected at least to the start of the season.

Equipment for comfort

Water. A 1-quart canteen of fresh water should always be aboard; it will be as welcome as a spring in the desert the day the wind fails, or when your mouth is dry after an exciting battle with the elements.

Ponchos. Two rubber ponchos will more than pay their way in comfort for the small space they occupy, the first time you get caught in an unexpected rainstorm.

Sponge. Keep one of the large brick-shaped viscose sponges in the bailing bucket for soaking up the last bit of seat-dampening moisture in the bilges.

Survival biscuit. It's not really that dramatic, since you're not likely to starve to death while sailing a small boat on local waters. But a package of chocolate-flavored survival biscuit, sealed in a waterproof plastic envelope, is a fine and comforting shipmate

to have on board for an appetite that's been sharpened by several extra, unplanned-for hours on the water.

Equipment for piloting

For a boat that's going to stay within the confines of a local harbor or lake, a copy of the latest chart of the area will probably meet all piloting needs. But for the skipper whose eye is set on distant ports for overnight sailing or cruising, these items are recommended to make his piloting accurate and successful—

Charts. Up-to-date charts should be carried for all areas to be visited.

Compass. A small but accurate Navy-type compass should be mounted within easy view of the helmsman and as far as possible from any magnetic influence (remember, incidentally, that most leakproof flashlight batteries are steel-jacketed, and might cause compass error; zinc-jacketed batteries will not). The compass should have a Deviation Table showing the error for each 15° change of heading, from 0° to 360°.

Parallel rulers or protractor. To determine courses and for plotting, either device is satisfactory. Parallel rulers are easier to use when their sliding surfaces are lined with chamois.

Dividers. For measuring distance on the chart's latitude scale.

Pencils, eraser. Sharp No. 2 lead pencil, and gum eraser for plotting.

Pelorus. To take either direct or relative bearings, a pelorus is most useful. Or relative bearing lines can be marked on deck, reading from ahead at 4-point intervals toward the amidships helmsman's position.

Tide and Current Tables. A practical necessity in tidal waters.

Lead line. A 10-fathom line is ample, with a 4-pound lead.

Equipment for night sailing

Running lights. If you have a rowing boat that also sails, you can get by at night with a flashlight to shine upon your sails in time to prevent collision. But a prudent skipper will not be content merely to "get by"; a policy of "getting by" in equipment that affects directly the boat's safety is not good seamanship. If you want to sail at night, equip your boat, whatever her size, with proper running lights—a 10-point green starboard side light, a 10-point red port side light, and a 12-point white stern light—all of a size and intensity to be visible at least two miles, as required by the *Navigation Rules* for Inland Waters. These lights do not have to be kept on board, unless you plan to sail frequently at night, when it might be a nuisance to lug them back and forth.

Kerosene-burning running lights are messy to fill and carry on a small boat, where their stowage becomes a problem. On the other hand, small battery-operated running lights are very subject to corrosion, especially on salt water. They should be protected by sealed plastic bags when not in use, and their contacts brightened occasionally with a file. Use leakproof batteries only.

Spotlight. Although a flashlight should be a regular part of a boat's emergency gear, a long-ray spotlight should be added for night sailing. It gives brighter warning to an overtaking boat when flashed on the sails, helps to spot buoys and their numbers at a distance, and is invaluable for picking up a mooring. This is one piece of equipment you may prefer not to leave on the boat, since it might be useful in making your way out to the boat and back at night.

You may want to expand the gear in any or all of the categories above—there are no distress flares listed, for example, or waterproof matches, or spare sheets and halyards (though the heaving line can serve); no extra battens or turnbuckles, or dozens of other pieces of gear you might feel are desirable to have aboard, including a second anchor. Racing sailors will certainly feel the lists are filled with items they can leave ashore; it's their privilege to omit whatever they feel weighs down the boat too much. They take a calculated risk in the interest of speed. Though the novice skipper may want to add gear, it might be a good idea to sail for a while with only the items listed; perhaps the other things will not seem so important later. In any event, a boat equipped as suggested in the several categories, should be able to handle almost any emergency with despatch and success.

Summary

1. Equipment for a small sailboat can be kept to a basic minimum by choosing it for three categories: (a) For survival, (b) for safe operation, and (c) for comfort.
2. These items are recommended *for survival:*
    a. Life jackets—one for each person on board, plus two buoyant cushions.
    b. Bilge pump—non-clogging type, of big capacity.
    c. Bucket.
    d. Anchor and rode—heavy enough and scope for seven times the average depth of local waters.
    e. Foghorn.
    f. Paddle or oar.
    g. Heaving line—35 to 50 feet of ⅜-inch manila line.
    h. Spare tiller.
    i. Distress signals for day and night.
    j. Flashlight, with leakproof batteries.
    k. First-aid kit, in waterproof, rustproof container.
    l. Ditty bag, with small tools and sail repair materials.
    m. Rigger's knife—cutting blade and marlinespike combination.

3. For *safe operation,* a small sailboat should carry these items:
   a. Boathook.
   b. Docking lines (2).
   c. Fenders (3).
   d. Sail stops (4), 6-feet long.
   e. Up-to-date chart of local waters.
4. For *comfort,* these items are recommended:
   a. Water, in a 1-quart canteen.
   b. Ponchos (2).
   c. Sponge.
   d. Survival biscuit.
5. Equipment for *piloting* includes:
   a. Latest charts of areas to be sailed.
   b. Compass, with Deviation Table.
   c. Parallel rulers or protractor.
   d. Dividers.
   e. Pencil and eraser.

   f. Pelorus.
   g. Tide and Current Tables (in tidal waters).
   h. Lead line of 10 fathoms, with 4-pound lead.
6. For *night sailing* a sailboat should carry:
   a. Running lights (port, starboard side lights; stern light).
   b. Long-ray spotlight.
7. Checklist of nautical terms:

GENERAL

monkey's fist—A fancy, ball-shaped knot, used as a weight in the end of a heaving line to give it greater carry.

sculling—Propelling a boat forward by working and twisting the blade of an oar from side to side over the boat's stern.

23

The Permanent Mooring

AFTER EVERY GREAT STORM during the boating season there is a sudden revival of interest among boat owners in the subject of permanent moorings, an interest of especial intensity among those whose boats have fetched up on the beach because of ground tackle failure. Although variations in the holding qualities of different bottoms and the dragging characteristics of different hulls make it impossible to prescribe the equipment to be used for each permanent mooring situation, the principles discussed in this chapter may provide you with permanent protection against ever joining these unhappy ten o'clock scholars.

There is such a thing, of course, as being fouled by another boat that has torn loose, and having your own mooring fail under the double load. But this is the exception. Most boats drag or go adrift because their total mooring assembly was defective in one or more ways. Perhaps the mooring was of the right type, but the anchor rode was too light and chafed through or parted. Or possibly there wasn't enough scope in the rode for storm conditions. Or a shackle may have failed, or a deck cleat pulled out.

Assembling the Mooring

Against all the above hazards the prudent owner prepares himself, because he realizes that his permanent mooring is second only in importance to the boat itself. He talks with local sailors to find a location that will be sheltered, if possible, from the direction of the worst storms, and learns what types of mooring have proved successful locally. Then, since the mooring must hold the boat securely day and night, under all conditions, he plans each of the following elements to withstand the severest storms of the locality: (1) mooring anchor, (2) rode and scope, (3) mooring buoy, and (4) foredeck cleat.

1. The mooring anchor. "Mooring anchor" does not mean an old engine block or a lump of concrete. It refers to an anchor made specifically for use as a permanent mooring—with a shape and design for burying itself to get a good grip on the bottom, and with no projections to foul the anchor rode as the boat swings around overhead. Old engine blocks, which are sometimes used because of their weight, fail on both counts.

Concrete is poor for a different reason—in water it loses 42 per cent of its weight. This, coupled with its tendency to remain unburied, disqualifies it for mooring use, even though it may be as smooth as a ball.

For soft and muddy bottoms the most widely used permanent mooring is a *mushroom anchor* which, as its name implies, is shaped like an upside-down mushroom. Great weight is concentrated in the wide bell of the mushroom, causing it to work its way down gradually in the ooze until it is completely buried, with its stockless shank vertical and the eye in the top of the shank even with the bottom. The full holding power of a mushroom anchor is not obtained until it is buried like this, which makes it advisable to put the mooring down a week or two before securing a boat to it. When it is lowered to the bottom, a strain should be put on the rode to tip the anchor over on its side, so that the edge of the bell will dig into the mud. Then the rode should be pulled hard in several different directions to work the bell from side to side and start it on the way to burying itself completely.

The weight of mushroom to use varies, naturally, with the size and shape of the boat and the resulting pull. As a general rule the ratio is 10 pounds of mushroom anchor to each foot of overall length. For a 20-foot boat, this would require a 200-pound mushroom. Admittedly, many owners of 20-foot boats use less than this, but in ground tackle, as in every phase of equipment affecting the boat's survival, good seamanship errs on the side of safety. I have never heard of a boat taking damage because her mooring was too heavy, but have seen many boats on the beach after a storm because their moorings were too light.

Holding power, as we have seen, is only partially the result of weight; it is also affected by the anchor's design. Great hold-

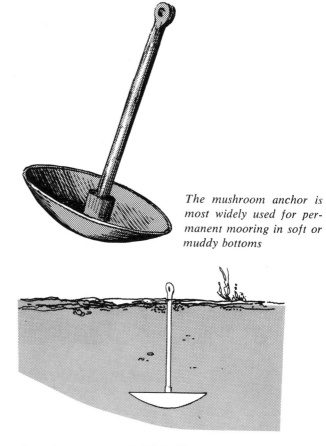

The mushroom anchor is most widely used for permanent mooring in soft or muddy bottoms

A mushroom anchor's full holding power is not developed until it is completely buried

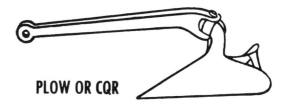

PLOW OR CQR

The Plow or CQR anchor gives greater holding power than a mushroom per pound of weight for permanent mooring

ing power for permanent moorings is embodied in such modern anchors as the Danforth "fixed fluke" mooring anchor and the CQR Plow anchor, both of which are stockless and nonfouling. These two give far superior holding power, pound for pound, than the ordinary mushroom. As an example

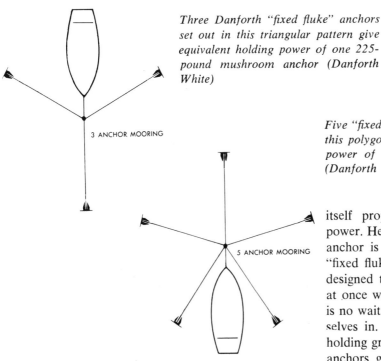

3 ANCHOR MOORING

5 ANCHOR MOORING

—for a boat of 15 feet length overall, three Danforth 5-pound "fixed fluke" anchors, set out in a triangular pattern with the boat riding to a pennant secured at the middle of the triangle, give the equivalent holding power of a single mushroom weighing 225 pounds.

In addition, this triangular mooring pattern cuts a boat's swinging radius nearly in half, a great advantage under the crowded conditions of many harbors today. Danforth, incidentally, recommends that all permanent moorings, regardless of type, be set out in multiple-anchor arrangements of either 3-anchor triangles or 5-anchor polygons, to minimize swinging. The polygon pattern increases holding power still more. For instance, a boat of 20 to 25 feet overall moored with five Danforth 5-pound "fixed fluke" anchors set in a polygon would be secured by a holding power equivalent to a 500-pound mushroom.

In hard or sandy bottoms a mushroom anchor is not suitable because it cannot bury itself properly to obtain its full holding power. Here a sharp-pointed, digging type of anchor is called for, such as the Danforth "fixed fluke" or the CQR Plow. These are designed to cut into the bottom and dig in at once when a strain is put on them; there is no waiting period for them to work themselves in. And because hard sand is better holding ground than soft mud, these modern anchors give still greater performance. The Danforth 5-pound "fixed fluke," for example, increases its holding power from 450 pounds in muddy bottoms to 3000 pounds in hard sand.

2. The rode and scope. For a permanent mooring, keeping the angle of pull below the 20° breaking-out point is even more important than for a temporary anchoring, since no one is likely to be on board to let out more scope during a storm with maximum high water. Yet it is apparent that in most harbors limited swinging room makes it impractical to use a scope of the recommended seven to ten times maximum high water depth to provide protection for storm conditions. Either a multiple-anchor arrangement must be used or, if a single anchor is set, the angle of pull must be kept low by using a combination of heavy chain in the rode near the anchor, plus lighter chain to an anchor buoy, and less scope than if the rode were all line. It may also be advisable to *back the anchor.* This is a method for further reducing the angle of pull by shackling a heavy weight, like an automobile engine flywheel, on the chain about six feet from the anchor. The *backer* must be lifted clear before there can be any direct pull on the anchor.

Besides keeping the angle of pull low, the weight of the rode and backer also contributes spring to the line, to absorb shocks and surges that might tend to work the anchor loose. By leading the light chain to a mooring buoy, and a length of nylon mooring pennant from this to the boat, an additional element is introduced into the rode to keep the angle low. This is the lifting power of the buoy, which acts as a counter force to the pull of the boat on the rode, since the buoy must be dragged completely under before there can be a direct pull on the chain. Still more stretch and elasticity is given to the total rode by the length of nylon pennant.

As to the length of the rode, local conditions are the governing factor, whether riding to a single anchor or to a multiple-anchor pattern. But you will probably not want to use less than three times the maximum storm

depth of water, depending on the holding quality of the bottom. In figuring the depth, be sure to include an allowance for the vertical distance from the water to the bow chock.

A rough rule for the breakdown of the rode into heavy chain, light chain, and nylon pennant is a proportion of 5-4-1. Thus a rode of 100 feet total length, would have 50 feet of heavy chain attached to the mooring anchor, 40 feet of lighter chain leading from the heavy chain to the mooring buoy, and a 10-foot length of nylon from the light chain at the buoy, to the boat. The nylon mooring pennant would be fitted with a light pick-up buoy and pennant for convenience in anchoring.

Though local conditions must finally determine both the scope and size of ground tackle to be used, for an average day sailer up to 25 feet overall, heavy galvanized chain of ⅜-inch diameter should normally be adequate, combined with light chain of $\frac{5}{16}$-inch diameter. Many boat owners use ¼-inch

Scope for permanent mooring line should not be less than three times storm depth of water, plus allowance for vertical distance from surface to boat's bow chock

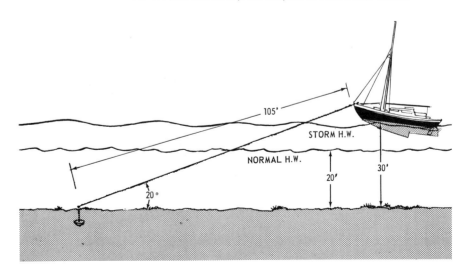

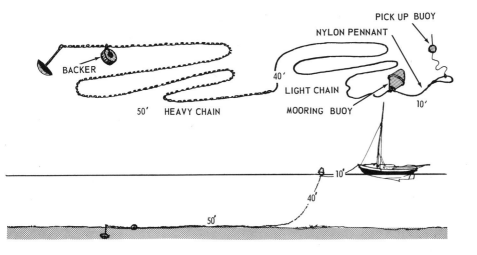

Better-than-average mooring line assembly for small boat

chain for small boats, but the added longevity and safety factor of the $\frac{5}{16}$-inch diameter makes it a good investment, as well as the fact that it may also be usable if you should buy a larger boat later. For the mooring pennant, $\frac{5}{8}$-inch nylon should be suitable, since it has greater strength than 1-inch manila; but it must be protected from chafe by a proper serving of canvas or leather where it goes through the bow chock. A galvanized thimble should be spliced into the end of the pennant that attaches to the light chain, to receive the connecting shackle.

Shackles are also used to attach the heavy chain to the mooring anchor, the backer to the heavy chain, the light chain to the heavy, and the light chain to the mooring buoy. In salt water, as already noted (page 109), it is essential that all metal parts of the mooring assembly be of the same metal, to avoid galvanic corrosion. Use galvanized shackles with galvanized chain. Because of the dragging action on the bottom that might loosen even well-seized shackle screw pins, anchor shackles with round pins should be used for securing the heavy chain to the anchor shank, for attaching the backer to the heavy chain, and for joining the light and heavy chains. Spread the cotter pin well

in each round pin to secure it. Screw pin shackles are all right for securing the light chain to the mooring buoy, and the mooring pennant to the light chain. Smear the threads of each pin with waterproof grease and set the pin up hard, then run a galvanized wire seizing through the pin eye and around the shank of the shackle to keep the pin from backing out.

3. The mooring buoy. Since the chief purpose of the mooring buoy is to support the weight of chain between the bottom and the surface, it must be large enough and buoyant enough to do this even when storm conditions have greatly lengthened the amount of chain

Round-pin shackles are more secure than screw-pin type for use with chain on bottom; be sure to use iron cotter pin

234

to be supported. Although chain loses some of its weight when immersed in water, galvanized chain of $\frac{5}{16}$-inch diameter still weighs about 1 pound per foot, and ⅜-inch chain about 1½ pounds. Using these figures, you can estimate the minimum lifting power required of a mooring buoy for any particular mooring. Test it in shallow water before setting it out.

Galvanized metal balls, with a rod through the middle, have long been used for mooring

Secure both mooring chain and thimble of mooring pennant to bottom ring of mooring buoy, not to opposite ends of rod

Below: Rig a separate preventer around mast and through mooring-line eye to protect boat against foredeck cleat pulling out

buoys. But they have the unfortunate habit of rusting through and sinking, and are also vulnerable to .22 rifle fire by amateur marksmen, who seem to haunt all waterfronts. Much better are buoys made of fiberglass or one of the other modern plastics that combines high buoyancy with a tough skin. Whatever type of float you select, be sure to attach *both* the light chain and the mooring pennant at the underside of the buoy, not to opposite ends of the rod going through it.

4. The foredeck cleat. No fitting on a small sailboat is as strong as the mast for securing the pennant of a permanent mooring. It is, however, usually inconvenient to lash the pennant directly around the mast each time you finish sailing. An alternative method, which I have used for years with complete safety, is to lash the mooring pennant's eye on the foredeck cleat with the pennant of the pick-up buoy, then rig a separate preventer lashing around the mast. This preventer is a piece of mooring line with an eye spliced in one end and the free end whipped. It is secured to the mast by leading the free end around the mast and through the eye, and to the mooring pennant by leading the free end through its eye, taking a light strain and tying in a bowline. Now, even if the deck cleat should pull out, the boat will be held safely.

The foredeck cleat should be backed up by a substantial block of wood on the underside of the deck to distribute the load, and should be through-bolted, *not* screwed, to this block. Since rain water might work its way down the bolts into the back-up block and cause dry rot, paint it generously with a good fungicide, like Cuprinol or Wood Life, and set the bolts in seam compound to prevent leakage.

Marking Your Mooring

When you set out your permanent mooring, if it has been properly made up, the chances are you will be able to leave the anchor and chain on the bottom for at least a couple of seasons before hauling them for inspection. During the winter, if you are in a tidal area, you will probably mark the mooring with a long spar secured to the chain by a pennant just long enough to let the top of the spar show above the surface at low water. Sometimes these spars are cut loose by ice, or their pennants break; then the chain must be recovered by dragging the bottom with a *grapnel*—a small anchor with several claws.

As insurance against this accident, it is wise to take cross bearings when you set your mooring out so that you know its location accurately. One method is to make a permanent visual record by taking two photographs of the shoreline, preferably at right angles to each other, from the spot where you put your mooring overboard. Then should you ever lose it, you have a definite starting point from which to start dragging in ever-widening circles.

To identify your mooring permanently and prevent the possibility of confusion with neighboring moorings, a small cast-iron or lead plate with your initials can be shackled into the heavy chain near the anchor. Use a round-pin shackle.

Use a grapnel to drag for lost moorings and other objects on bottom, and rig trip line to eye in anchor's crown when you do

Summary

1. Before setting out a permanent mooring, talk with local boatmen, and pick a location sheltered from the direction of the worst storms; also learn what moorings are most effective locally.
2. Each of the four elements of the mooring assembly should be planned to hold the boat during the severest storms:
   a. Mooring anchor.
   b. Rode and scope.
   c. Mooring buoy.
   d. Foredeck cleat.
3. The mooring should be an anchor designed for permanent mooring use, not an old engine block or a lump of concrete.
4. One mooring widely used for mud bottoms is the mushroom anchor. It should be set out a week or two before a boat is secured to it.
5. A general rule for the weight of mushroom is 10 pounds of anchor for each overall foot of boat length.
6. Modern anchors like the Danforth "fixed fluke" and the CQR Plow give much greater holding power, pound for pound, than mushroom anchors.
7. Permanent moorings set out in multiple-anchor arrangements of 3-anchor triangles or 5-anchor polygons are recommended for superior holding power and to cut the boat's swinging radius.
8. For permanent mooring on hard or sandy bottoms, a sharp-pointed, digging type anchor should be used. These dig in at once under strain, and have even greater holding power in hard sand than in mud.
9. To keep the angle of pull on a permanent mooring below the 20° breaking-out point, even under storm conditions, the rode can be made up of heavy chain near the anchor, lighter chain to a buoy, and a length of nylon mooring pennant to the boat. As an additional safeguard, a heavy weight can be shackled to the chain near the anchor.
10. Local conditions govern the scope of the rode, but it should probably be not less than 3 times the sum of the maximum storm depth of water plus the distance from the water to the bow chock.
11. A rough rule for composition of the rode is 50 per cent heavy chain, 40 per cent light chain, and 10 per cent nylon pennant.
12. Though local conditions must finally determine both scope and size of ground tackle, for an average day sailer up to 25 feet overall, heavy galvanized chain of $3/8$-inch diameter should normally be adequate, combined with light chain of $5/16$-inch diameter, and a mooring pennant of $5/8$-inch nylon.
13. In salt water, to prevent galvanic corrosion, all metal parts of the mooring assembly should be made of the same metal.
14. Round pin shackles, rather than screw pins, should be used to secure the heavy chain to the anchor, the backer weight to the heavy chain, and the heavy chain to the light. The cotter pin of each round pin must be spread to secure it.
15. Screw pin shackles can be used to secure the light chain to the mooring buoy and the mooring pennant. The pins should be seized with galvanized wire.
16. The mooring buoy must be buoyant enough to support the full weight of the chain at storm depth of water. A buoy of fiberglass or other plastic is better than a metal ball or can. Chain and pennant should be shackled to each other underneath the buoy.
17. When the mooring pennant eye is lashed to the foredeck cleat with the pennant of the pick-up buoy, a preventer lashing around the mast can be used for greater security.
18. The foredeck cleat should be through-bolted, not screwed, to a substantial block of wood on the underside of the deck.
19. When setting out a permanent mooring, take cross bearings of prominent shore points, or two photographs of the shoreline as nearly as possible at right angles to each other, to locate the mooring accurately if you ever have to drag for it.
20. A cast-iron or lead plate with your initials,

and secured by a round-pin shackle to the chain near the anchor, identifies the mooring when it is hauled and prevents confusion.

21. Checklist of nautical terms:

GENERAL

back the anchor—To fasten a heavy weight, or *backer,* on the rode near the anchor so as to reduce the angle of pull.

grapnel—A small anchor with several claws, used for dragging over the bottom to recover lost anchors and other objects.

mushroom anchor—An anchor shaped like an upside-down mushroom, with a heavy, wide bell, used for permanent mooring in muddy bottoms.

24

Haul-out, Storage,
and Maintenance

BOATING IS TODAY a year round sport in many parts of the country, particularly where the weather remains mild. Yet even boats sailed in southern waters must be hauled out periodically for routine inspection and maintenance. As for boats in northern waters, when the frost is on the pumpkin and fingers get numb from handling sheets and halyards, it's a sure sign that the time for the winter haul-out has arrived.

Even enthusiastic sailors find sailing loses some of its allure as the temperature drops and every dash of spray becomes a baptism by ice water. In this respect, we can disregard the expanding cult of "frostbite" dinghy sailors—theirs is specialized sailing to sharpen racing skills, with the added appeal of making a roaring fire feel doubly welcome after the ordeal is over. But the names they give their boats reveal how matters really stand, so far as solid enjoyment is concerned: *Agony, Sang-Froid, Ordeal,* for example.

Whether you live in the North or South, one of the great advantages of owning a small sailboat is ease of storage. With mast unstepped, she can easily be fitted into one side of a two-car garage. Mast and boom can be lashed to the garage beams and suspended overhead. Or the boat can be set up in a cradle and stored outside under a tarpaulin. She can even be left on a trailer, with a tarpaulin over her, in a side yard handy to the house.

If you must haul out for the winter, whether you store the boat inside or out is a matter of personal preference. Inside storage requires no cover, and the boat is always accessible for working on it. Wooden-planked boats, however, are apt to dry out more during inside storage, especially if the space is heated. Outside storage demands more care in covering the boat for protection against the weather, and adds the inertia of removing the cover and replacing it each time you want to work on the boat.

Unless you have access to a garage or yard at home, you'll probably store your boat in a boatyard. If there is a choice of more than one, ask local sailors for a recommendation, particularly if you want to do any part of the maintenance work yourself. Some yards insist on doing all outside work on a boat; others demand everything below the waterline; relatively few let an owner do all his own maintenance.

Before you sign up with any yard, try to learn its reputation for reliability in the work it does as well as in the prices it quotes for work versus the final charges. Find, too, how well the yard keeps its promise on getting a boat overboard on schedule. When you have decided on a yard, visit it and reserve space early in the fall. Adequate storage to house America's boats during the winter in northern waters becomes a greater problem every year; owners who postpone reserving space until they are ready to haul get least consideration from a yard, if any.

The Haul-out

Before hauling, beach the boat and take off the rudder, tiller, and all loose gear—sails, lines, anchor, pump—everything except the paddle, two life jackets, fenders, and dock lines. Unreeve jib and main halyards, jibsheets and mainsheet, coil them and remove them from the boat. Unship the boom and put it on the beach. Now push the boat off and paddle her alongside a dock where the mast can be unstepped. Cast off the turnbuckles on shrouds and headstay, bring the wires in to the mast and hold them in place with a lashing. Lift the mast out of the step and lay it carefully on deck, in a fore-and-aft position, with the butt facing forward. Support the mast forward and aft with a life jacket under it to prevent it rubbing against sprayboards or cockpit coaming while the boat is being hauled. Run a lashing from the foredeck cleat around the mast to secure it from shifting. Tie a second lashing around the mast aft, near the stern. With one of the dock lines as a towline made fast to the foredeck cleat, either tow the boat to the ramp or beach for haul-out, or paddle her in.

Storage

The cradle. If you must haul your boat for the winter the best support for her during storage will be a cradle built to her shape, giving well-distributed support forward and aft, with no long, unsupported overhangs. If you use a trailer as a cradle, eliminate any sharp pressure points where the hull touches the trailer by inserting flat blocks of wood wrapped in canvas, to distribute the load. Brace the cradle strongly and be sure the boat is secure enough in it for you to walk around on and work on safely. Take out the floorboards and open any hatches to secure maximum possible ventilation. Bail and sponge the bilges dry, and remove any drain plugs and leave the drain holes open for the winter.

The scrub down. As soon as possible after hauling, scrub down the topsides and bottom with a stiff brush and fresh water to remove weeds, barnacles, or other marine growth. These come off with relative ease while still alive, but cling with the literal grip of death if allowed to dry out. Follow up the scrubbing with a thorough *sanding* (sandpapering) of the bottom, using No. 1 grit of "Wet-or-Dry" sandpaper, soaking wet, to remove loose bottom paint and smooth the surface for next season's priming coat. By wet sanding, paint dust is eliminated, though the bottom must be hosed or sponged off again after the sanding is completed to remove the loosened paint. This is much better, however, than breathing it. *Important:* When dry sanding fiberglass or any antifouling bottom paint, *always* wear a dust mask. The dust of fiberglass and of metallic paints is highly irritating to the lungs, while paints containing mercury are poisonous.

Winter priming coat. Wooden-planked

VENT

VENT

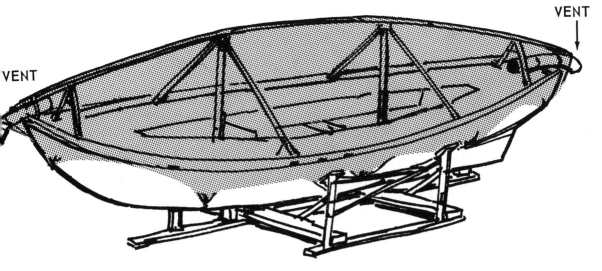

Any cover placed over boat should be well supported by strong framework and have provision for ventilation to avoid dry rot

boats that are to be stored until spring benefit from a winter priming coat applied after the bottom has dried from the wet sanding and hosing down. It serves the dual purpose of preventing excessive shrinkage in the planking during the layup and of laying down a primer for a final coat of antifouling paint before the boat is launched in the spring. A mixture of equal parts of creosote and bottom paint works well for the priming coat.

The winter cover. Although many boats stored outside have custom-sewn winter covers, any stout, waterproof tarpaulin will do the job adequately if it is well supported and provision is made for ventilation under it. The supporting framework should be strong and rigid enough to support the weight of the tarpaulin, even in a strong blow, and should be pitched steeply to shed snow. All sharp corners should be rounded off to prevent chafing through the cover. By extending the framework slightly beyond bow and stern, it is possible to create space for air to circulate under the cover. Ventilation is important, particularly with wooden boats, to prevent condensation of moisture that might cause *dry rot.*

This is a fungus infection of wood that turns it soft and spongy. It thrives, despite its name, on fresh water moisture in dark,

unventilated spaces, especially the ends of the boat—under the foredeck near the stem, and under the afterdeck along the transom. Dry rot can be prevented by painting the wood with a fungicide like Cuprinol or Wood Life, and by good ventilation. Once it gets a start, however, the spores of the fungus spread quickly through the boat like a cancer. Extensive surgery may then be needed to remove the rotted wood, which has no strength.

Use a tarpaulin slightly longer than the overall length of the boat, to enclose the framework completely, and wide enough to reach the waterline on both sides when in place. Grommets should be set into the edges of the tarpaulin every few feet for athwartships lashings to hold it securely. Use new ¼-inch manila for these lashings. Since you will probably keep the tarpaulin for more than one season, you may want to attach one end of each lashing to a grommet with an eye splice, and put a palm-and-needle whipping on the other end to bind it permanently.

Maintenance

A winter work list. If you are hauling for the winter, before you bed the boat down

241

under her winter cover, go over her from stem to stern with an eye of a suspicious buyer. Make a list of maintenance jobs to be done on the hull during the winter so that she will be in new-boat condition, ready to go overboard on time, come spring. Examine each cleat and fitting for signs of looseness or fatigue, especially headstay fitting and chainplates. Check the mast step and centerboard trunk. Make a note of what painting must be done, whether interior, deck, topsides, or bottom; also, varnishing. With a detailed work list, you can plan in advance how to make the most outdoors of each winter warm spell as it arrives. Planning is half the battle.

Indoor work list. Nowhere is the wisdom of the poet's "procrastination is the thief of time" more apparent than in maintaining a boat. For as certainly as you postpone until spring the many details of maintenance that can easily be done when the boat is hauled, just as surely will you find there are not enough hours in the day to get everything done at the last minute. For this, take the word of a reformed sinner—a man who, during his first years as a boat owner, never got his boat overboard until summer was far advanced, because he always waited until spring to start his overhaul. That I kept the boat in the water until snow fell—usually the first week of December—was small excuse. Properly organized outdoor and indoor work lists, and a resolute facing of reality squarely to do the jobs during the winter, would have given me weeks more of sailing. May you profit by my sad example!

CARE OF LINES Fill a washtub with cool, fresh water and soak overnight all sheets, halyards, dock lines, and anchor rode to remove salt or grit. Remove the lines, drain the tub, refill it, and thoroughly soak the lines again. Then remove each line, coil it loosely while still wet, hang it outside to dry (not in the sun), then store it hanging, with

good ventilation all around, in a cool, dry place—*not* over a furnace. For easy identification in spring, tag each line by name.

CARE OF SAILS The best possible care for a suit of sails is to return them to a sailmaker each winter to rinse, scrub, clean, and overhaul for broken stitching or other wear. If this is not feasible, immediately after hauling give your sails a thorough double rinsing in cool fresh water to remove salt or grit. Soak them in a bathtub, if possible, or spread them out on a lawn and souse them repeatedly on both sides with a hose. Light stains may be removed by gently washing the area by hand in warm water with a mild, neutral detergent, or by laying the sail on a flat, smooth surface and scrubbing with a brush. Rinse the sail freely with clear, fresh water. While rinsing the sails, be sure to include the sailbag, which usually accumulates its own quota of salt or grit and grime during a season.

Dry out sails completely before putting them away for the winter. Spread them out flat, or hang them up as they dry, to avoid wrinkles. If you dry them on the lawn, put support underneath to provide air circulation, otherwise moisture from the grass will condense on the underside of the sail. A sail is not ready to be stored until the doubled-over thickness, or *tabling,* at each corner is perfectly dry, as well as any bolt rope that may be sewn into the luff or foot. Before folding the sails and replacing them in the sailbag, inspect all slides, hanks, seams, and batten pockets for broken stitching. Make repairs as needed. If any repairs require professional attention, take the sail to a sailmaker now, not next spring. Not only will he have more time, but you may get a better job and probably a lower price. Equally important, your sails will be ready when you want to go overboard.

CARE OF SPARS AND RIGGING Overhauling of mast and boom is best done inside during the winter months, especially if any varnishing is involved. Few things are more disheartening than to sweat through the labor of careful sanding and preparation of a spar for varnishing outdoors, and then have a dust-filled breeze blow up as you finish putting on the first coat. Avoid the frustration by storing spars inside, where you can eliminate drafts after varnishing or painting.

Remove the masthead fly and store it in a safe place. Examine the mast from truck to butt for *checks* (cracks) or signs of weakness. If it is a wooden mast and needs refinishing, remove all fittings—labeling each —and add the refinishing job to your indoor work list. Aluminum masts are easiest to maintain when *painted* aluminum or some other color, using a complete paint system, as described in Chapter 21. If, however, you prefer to keep a shiny finish, scrub the mast down well with fresh water, sand it lightly to remove any surface corrosion, and give it a good waxing with several coats of high-grade auto body wax. This will make it gleam like a new spar, though the wax finish is not as durable as a painted finish.

Inspect the *tangs* (mast fittings) of the shrouds and headstay for loose screws. Go over every inch of wire for broken strands or splintered wires (called *meathooks* from their effect on human skin), and replace any wire that isn't perfect. Squirt some penetrating oil on the screws of each turnbuckle, remove the cotter pins, and work the turnbuckle body up and down the screws to remove any tendency to bind. Wipe off excess oil and replace the cotter pins. Look critically at the joints of the sail track. If slides have been sticking when you raise and lower sail, align the track on both sides of the offending joint and tighten the screws holding the track to the mast. Should the joint still be out of line, you may need to hammer the high side down to fit, or file away the difference.

If your mast is equipped with *spreaders* (horizontal struts), examine their fittings at the mast for signs of water seepage. Dry rot sometimes gets a start in a wooden mast when rain water collects in the spreader joints and doesn't dry out. It is a good precaution to swab these joints liberally with a fungicide, then seal them with a marine seam compound to prevent water accumulation.

Give the boom the same rigorous inspection as the mast, from outhaul fitting to gooseneck. Check the condition of the outhaul by opening up its strands to see if the line is still sound. If the boom must be refinished, add it to the indoor work list.

CARE OF TILLER, RUDDER, AND FLOORBOARDS. By the end of a full season of sailing, tiller, rudder, and floorboards have all taken a lot of abuse. Repainting is usually indicated for the floorboards, and possibly revarnishing for tiller and rudder. All painting or varnishing should be preceded by a fresh water rinse to remove salt or grime, then a careful sanding to take off as much as possible of the loose old surface. In varnishing, it is recommended to make a final sanding with a grit at least as fine as No. 6 sandpaper, to leave the surface satin-smooth. Varnish should be flowed on, with a full brush, not brushed back and forth as paint is, because brushing develops bubbles that remain and mar the finish. Be sure, always, to use a separate brush for varnish, never one that has been used for painting.

When painting, avoid an overfull brush, and work the paint out evenly by brushing it back and forth. Two thin, well brushed-out coats give better protection than one heavy coat. When painting floorboards (or any surface that will be walked on), add a small quantity of ground walnut shells to the paint to give the surface a nonslip quality. This material is available commercially at marine supply stores. Walnut shells have an advantage over fine pumice or sand used for

243

the same purpose, in remaining better suspended in the paint and not requiring such constant stirring to prevent settling. This assures more uniform distribution of the nonslip material over the painted surface.

ODD JOBS For quiet enjoyment, few winter activities can compare with sitting by a fire of a stormy night, repairing a sailboat's running rigging with palm and needle. The hooting of the wind in the chimney is a stirring reminder that each line must carry its full load without parting in heavy weather, an accent to the importance of the work in hand. So schedule for the fireside all marlinespike seamanship—whipping, splicing, making up new dock lines, sewing straps on cushions, sail repairs, or making a lead line.

Odd jobs for the workshop include refinishing old battens, making new ones, overhauling running lights, making a spare tiller, refinishing the boat's paddle or oar, and stenciling the boat's name on life jackets, bucket, foghorn, ditty bag, and other pieces of the boat's gear.

Your reward for adopting this kind of systematic approach to the boat's maintenance will be many hours of delightful sailing early in the season, when the winds are fair and the waters uncrowded because other owners are ashore busily proving that procrastination is indeed the thief of the best of all time—time on the water, sailing.

Summary

1. If a boat is to be hauled for the winter and not to be stored at home, boatyard space should be reserved early in the fall.
2. Before signing up with a yard, learn its reputation for reliability and charges; also, what work they demand for themselves.
3. Inside storage at a yard is more expensive but leaves the boat open for working. Outside storage is cheaper, but requires a winter cover that must be opened each time for working.
4. Before hauling out, remove all loose gear and the boom. Lay the boat alongside a dock to unstep the mast. Tow the boat to ramp or beach, or paddle her in for haulout.
5. A boat cradle should be built to the hull shape, and strongly braced to permit working on board without danger of collapse. When a trailer is used, pressure points should be blocked with flat pieces of canvas-wrapped wood.
6. Remove floorboards, open hatches, sponge bilges dry, and take out drain plugs for the winter.
7. A fresh water scrubdown of topsides and hull is important immediately on hauling out. Follow it with a wet sanding of the bottom, and hose it off. If the bottom is dry-sanded, wear a dust mask to avoid nhalation of dangerous dusts.
8. A winter bottom-priming coat of equal parts of creosote and bottom paint helps protect wooden-planked boats from excessive shrinkage.
9. A boat's winter cover may be custom-sewn, or a ready-made, strong, waterproof tarpaulin, fitted with grommets for athwartships lashings. The cover's supporting framework should be strong and rigid, steeply pitched, have rounded corners and edges, and extend beyond bow and stern to permit free circulation of air.
10. Poor ventilation encourages dry rot. It can be prevented by good ventilation and by painting wood with a fungicide. Infected wood either should be treated with a dry-rot curative like BoatLife's *Git-Rot* or Calahan's *Calignum,* or should be cut out and replaced to prevent the dry rot from spreading.
11. Before covering the boat, go over her thoroughly and make an outdoor work list of all maintenance and repair jobs to be done during the winter on the deck, interior, topsides, and bottom.
12. An indoor work list, should be made, cov-

ering these items:
a. Care of lines.
b. Care of sails.
c. Care of spars and rigging.
d. Care of tiller, rudder, and floorboards.
e. Odd jobs.
13. Checklist of nautical terms:

SAIL TERM

tabling—The broad hem, or tapered reinforced sections of a sail, to strengthen it and distribute the strain.

STANDING RIGGING

spreaders—Horizontal struts extending out from the mast on both sides to hold out the shrouds and support the mast.

tangs—Tongue-shaped fittings that secure the upper end of shrouds and stays to the mast.

GENERAL

Calignum—A dry-rot curative marketed by H. A. Calahan Co., Mamaroneck, N.Y.

checks—Cracks

dry rot—A fungus that infects wood exposed to fresh water moisture in dark, unventilated spaces. It renders wood soft and spongy.

Git-Rot—A dry-rot curative marketed by Boat-Life Co., Hicksville, N.Y.

meathooks—Slang term for wire splinters.

sanding—The process of rubbing a surface with sandpaper.

Index*

* *Numbers in boldface indicate that an illustration appears on that page.*

Flashlights, 226
Flat seam stitching, 177
Floorboards, care of, 243
Fog, checking position in, 209-210
Fog signals, 148-149
Foghorn, 226
Foot, defined, 2
Fore-and-aft trim, 25-28
Foredeck, defined, 5
Foredeck cleat, 235-236
Forward, defined, 2
Freeboard, defined, 5

"General Prudential Rule" (*Inland Navigation Rules*), 141-142
Genuine carrick bend knot, 175-176
Git-Rot, 241
Give-way vessel, defined, 141, 154-155
Gong buoys, 159-160
Gooseneck, 3
  defined, 2
Granny knot, 42
Grapnel anchors, 236
Great Lakes, Charts of the, 194, 196
Green, Johnny, 164
Grommets, defined, 56
Ground tackle
  defined, 107
  for permanent mooring, 230-238
Gudgeons (rudder), 53
Gunwale, defined, 5

Half-hitch (overhand) knot, 39-40
Halyards
  broken, handling, 130-131
  clearing, 54
  coiling down, 46-47, 58
  defined, 6
  hitch, 38, 46-47
  securing, 88
Harden up, defined, 74
Headboard (mainsail), 55
Headstay, defined, 2
Heaving line, 91
  how to heave, 101-104
Heel, controlling angle of, 22-25
Helm
  correcting a lee, 28-29
  defined, 2

weather, defined, 27-28
Herringbone stitch, 178
High water, 98, 210
Hollyday, H. Robins, 24
Honolulu Race (1953), 164
Hoyt, Norris D., 78
Hull, 4-5, 17-32
  controls for the wind
    on the boat, 21-29
    on the sails, 17-18
  defined, 4
  safety valves, 29-30
  steering, 18-21

In irons
  defined, 68
  getting out of, 69
Inland Rules, 141
International nautical mile, length of, 195
International Orange flag, 149, 154, 226
International Rules, 141

Jakobson, Irving, viii
Jakobson, Shipyard, viii
Jam cleats, 8
  defined, 8
Jibing, 76-83
  accidental, 28, 76-78
  controlled, 79-81
Jibs
  as emergency trysail, 138
  in anchoring, 111
  defined, 2-4
  hoisting, 56-58, 114
  in mooring, 86
  securing, 89
  trimming, 14-15
  winging out, 82
Jibsheets, 54
  defined, 8
  emergency uses of, 138
  making fast, 64
  securing, 88
Junior Sailing Class, 104

Kean, Larry, viii, 39, 102, 103, 165, 168, 169, 170, 172, 173, 174, 188, 192, 193, 196, 201